Gilbert T. Stephenson

Modern Business

A SERIES OF TEXTS PREPARED AS
PART OF THE MODERN BUSINESS
COURSE AND SERVICE OF THE
ALEXANDER HAMILTON
INSTITUTE

ALEXANDER HAMILTON INSTITUTE
NEW YORK

Modern Business

EDITOR-IN-CHIEF
JOSEPH FRENCH JOHNSON
Dean, New York University School of
Commerce, Accounts and Finance

MANAGING EDITOR
ROLAND P. FALKNER

ASSOCIATE EDITORS
LEO GREENDLINGER, CHARLES W. HURD

Volume Titles	Authors
1. BUSINESS AND THE MAN	Joseph French Johnson
2. ECONOMICS OF BUSINESS	The Editors
3. ORGANIZATION AND CONTROL	Charles W. Gerstenberg
4. PLANT MANAGEMENT	Dexter S. Kimball
5. MARKETING AND MERCHANDISING	The Editors
6. ADVERTISING PRINCIPLES	Herbert F. de Bower
7. SALESMANSHIP AND SALES MANAGEMENT	John G. Jones
8. CREDIT AND THE CREDIT MAN	The Editors
9. ACCOUNTING PRINCIPLES	The Editors
10. COST FINDING	Dexter S. Kimball
11. CORPORATION FINANCE	William H. Walker
12. BUSINESS CORRESPONDENCE	Harrison McJohnston
13. ADVERTISING CAMPAIGNS	Mac Martin
14. RAILWAY TRAFFIC	Edwin J. Clapp
15. FOREIGN TRADE AND SHIPPING	J. Anton de Haas
16. BANKING	Major B. Foster
17. DOMESTIC AND FOREIGN EXCHANGE	E. L. Stewart Patterson
18. INSURANCE	The Editors
19. OFFICE MANAGEMENT	The Editors
20. THE EXCHANGES AND SPECULATION	Albert W. Atwood
21. ACCOUNTING PRACTICE AND AUDITING	John T. Madden
22. FINANCIAL AND BUSINESS STATEMENTS	Leo Greendlinger
23. INVESTMENT	Edward D. Jones
24. BUSINESS AND THE GOVERNMENT	Jeremiah W. Jenks

ADVERTISING PRINCIPLES

BY

HERBERT F. de BOWER, LL.B.
Vice President, Alexander Hamilton Institute

MODERN BUSINESS

VOLUME 6

DR. NORMAN A. WIGGINS

ALEXANDER HAMILTON INSTITUTE

NEW YORK

COPYRIGHT, 1918, 1919, BY
ALEXANDER HAMILTON INSTITUTE

COPYRIGHT IN GREAT BRITAIN, 1918, 1919, BY
ALEXANDER HAMILTON INSTITUTE

The title and contents of this volume as well as the business growing out of it, are further protected by laws relating to trade marks and unfair trade. All rights reserved, including translation into Scandinavian.

Registered trade mark, Reg. U. S. Pat. Off., Marca Registrada, M. de F.

MADE IN U. S. A.

PREFACE

Advertising as a means of "public utterance" has been practiced for ages. Only recently, however, has advertising become an important factor in business. Its possibilities first began to be appreciated when increased production demanded more effective and far-reaching methods of distribution. Widening markets, perfection of the printer's art and the reading habit have brought advertising to its present state of high development.

Advertising is indispensable to modern business. Just as oxygen is one of the necessary component parts of the air which sustains life, so advertising has become one of the vital forces that sustains business. It not only breathes the breath of life into business, but it develops and regulates the wants, the habits and the life of the individual. It is largely responsible for the culture and refinement of present-day civilization.

In this Text the author has endeavored to organize and classify the principles on which the new science is founded. It is hoped that the business man will find these fundamentals of practical value in planning, creating and supervising his advertising. The application of the principles, or the art of advertising, is fully treated in a later Text.

PREFACE

In the preparation of this Text thanks are due to the successful users of advertising and to advertising specialists, many of whom were consulted and who freely contributed the results of their experience.

Especial thanks are due *Printers' Ink* and *Advertising and Selling,* thru whose courtesy valuable material has been obtained.

Thanks are also due Mr. William G. Clifford, who has rendered valuable assistance, drawn from his wide experience in handling advertising for many successful institutions, as well as editorial connection with many business magazines, and to Mr. Benjamin Sherbow, expert on type arrangement.

Acknowledgment is also made to Elon G. Pratt, formerly Vice President of Collin-Armstrong, Inc., Advertising Agents, for valuable assistance rendered at all stages in the preparation of the Text.

The author also wishes to express his appreciation to Dr. Lee Galloway, Mr. Bernard Lichtenberg and Mr. Leroy Fleck, of the Alexander Hamilton Institute, for their suggestions and help.

HERBERT F. DEBOWER.

New York.

TABLE OF CONTENTS

CHAPTER I
PRESENT DAY ADVERTISING

SECTION	PAGE
1. Economic Rôle of Modern Advertising	1
2. Early Development of Advertising	1
3. Growth of Advertising	3
4. Influence of War on Advertising	4
5. A Creator of Utility, Service to the Consumer	6
6. Assists Intelligent Selection	7
7. Improves Quality of Goods	7
8. Educates the Public	8
9. Creates New Wants	9
10. Reduces Price to Consumer	10
11. Service to Distributor	10
12. The Manufacturer's Advantage	11

CHAPTER II
FUNDAMENTALS OF ADVERTISING

1. Purpose of Advertising	13
2. Advertising as Insurance	14
3. Advertising Reduces Selling Cost	14
4. Raising Price by Advertising	15
5. Increasing Volume of Business	15
6. Sales by Advertising	16
7. Determining Advertising Appropriation	16
8. Advantages of Correct Budgeting Method	17
9. Detailed Methods Vary	18
10. Need of Careful Planning	18

ADVERTISING PRINCIPLES

SECTION	PAGE
11. Approaching the Plan from Proper Angle	19
12. Groundwork of Plan	21
13. Policy of the Firm	21
14. The Product Itself	22
15. Present Market	22
16. Potential Market	23
17. Competitive Products	23
18. Mode of Distribution	24
19. Sales Department	25
20. History of Past Advertising	25
21. Study of Similar Problems	26
22. Plan of Campaign	26
23. Survey of the Field	26
24. Continuity	27
25. Consumer's Point of View	27
26. Stocking the Dealer	28
27. Selection of Mediums	28

CHAPTER III

GETTING THE ADVERTISEMENT SEEN

1. Advertising Must Attract Attention	30
2. Elements that Secure Attention	31
3. Variation	31
4. Arrows, Darts and Designating Signs	33
5. Contrast	37
6. Illustration	37
7. Color	40
8. Position	42
9. Motion	43
10. Novelty and Uniqueness	44
11. Headlines	45
12. Teaser Copy	45
13. Favorable Impression	47

CONTENTS

CHAPTER IV

GETTING THE ADVERTISEMENT READ

SECTION	PAGE
1. Turning Attention into Interest	48
2. Connected Images Stimulate Interest	48
3. Appeal to the Imagination	51
4. Use of Proper Images	54
5. Images Should Please	54
6. Appeal to Self-Interest	55
7. Offer as a Means to Secure Interest	55
8. "Playing Up" a Hobby	57
9. Interest Value of Copy	59
10. Proper Use of Type	61
11. Emphasis Secured by Type	61
12. Breaking up the Reading Matter	63
13. Use of Subheads	63
14. Importance of Letter Spacing	65
15. Construction and Diction	65

CHAPTER V

MAKING THE ADVERTISEMENT UNDERSTOOD

1. Simplicity	67
2. Clear Sentence Structure	68
3. Length of Sentences	68
4. Coherence	70
5. Emphasis	71
6. Harmony	71
7. Copy Classified as to Form	72
8. Use of Argument	72
9. Use of Incident	72
10. Use of Monolog	73
11. Use of Dialog	74
12. Use of the Story	76
13. Educational Copy	79

SECTION	PAGE
14. News Copy	79
15. Historical Contrast	81

CHAPTER VI

MAKING THE ADVERTISEMENT PRODUCE ACTION

1. Getting Decision and Action	83
2. The Process of Reasoning	84
3. Elements of the Reasoning Act	84
4. Creating and Maintaining Confidence	85
5. Confidence thru Testimonials	86
6. Confidence thru Prestige	86
7. Securing Action thru Argument	91
8. Securing Action thru Suggestion	92
9. Suggestion by Repetition	93
10. Indirect Suggestion	93
11. Securing Action thru "Limited Time"	95
12. Securing Action thru "Free Offer"	98
13. Making it Easy to Act	98

CHAPTER VII

HUMAN APPEALS IN ADVERTISING

1. What are Human Appeals?	101
2. Appeal to the Senses	101
3. Touch	102
4. Taste	104
5. Smell	105
6. Sound	109
7. Appeal to Emotions	109
8. Reaching the Emotions	112
9. Appeal to Instinct	115
10. Feminine Intuition	116
11. Appeal to Imagination	118
12. Romance of the Commonplace	120
13. Appeal to Reason	122

CHAPTER VIII

WORD VALUES IN ADVERTISING

SECTION	PAGE
1. Words are Tools of Advertising	124
2. Economizing the Reader's Time	125
3. Clearness	126
4. Exactness	126
5. Emotional and Intellectual Value of Words	128
6. Short Words	128
7. Long Words	129
8. Idioms	129
9. Nouns and Verbs	130
10. Adjectives	131
11. Figures of Speech	131
12. Colloquialisms	132
13. Slang	133
14. Word Atmosphere or Setting	133

CHAPTER IX

"GETTING THE ORDER" COPY

1. Purpose and Scope	137
2. Typical Mail-Order Copy	137
3. Mail-Order Advertising	141
4. Catalog Type	143
5. Adaptations of the Catalog Type	143
6. Booklets and Catalogs	144
7. Appeals in Mail-Order Copy	146
8. Price Appeal	146
9. Style Appeal	146
10. Free or Trial Offer	148
11. Classified Advertising	151

CHAPTER X

"GETTING THE INQUIRY" COPY

1. Purpose and Scope of Inquiry Copy	153

ADVERTISING PRINCIPLES

SECTION	PAGE
2. Kinds of Inquiries and Copy	153
3. Why Inquiries Are Solicited	154
4. Inducement to Respond	155
5. Catalog Offer	156
6. Free Sample Offer	156
7. Booklets and Samples at Small Cost	159
8. Limiting Replies	161
9. The Idly Curious	163
10. Free Booklet Offer	164
11. Methods of Distributing Samples	164
12. Follow-up after the Sample	166
13. Function of Coupon	166

CHAPTER XI

"DIRECTING THE READER" COPY

1. Purpose and Scope	171
2. Methods of Directing the Reader	172
3. "Ask Your Dealer" Copy	172
4. "Ask Your Dealer or Write Us" Copy	174
5. "At All Good Stores"	175
6. "For Sale at Wanamaker's"	175
7. "Sold Nowhere Else"	176
8. Directing the Reader thru Display	178
9. "Take no Other Make"	178
10. Establishing New Trade Connections	180
11. Dealer Cooperation	182
12. Substitution	184

CHAPTER XII

"MOLDING PUBLIC OPINION" COPY

1. Purpose and Scope	189
2. Styles of Copy	189
3. Repetition of Name	191
4. Repetition of Name and Picture of Product	192

CONTENTS

SECTION	PAGE
5. Setting Forth a Policy	193
6. Cooperation Copy	195
7. "Creating Atmosphere" Copy	196
8. Educational Copy	198
9. Political Purpose	198
10. Legislative Purpose	200
11. Directing Public Sentiment	203
12. Advertising an Industry	204
13. Change in the Public's Attitude	207

CHAPTER XIII

PREPARING THE ADVERTISEMENT

1. Three Parts of the Advertisement	210
2. The Heading	210
3. The Body	211
4. The Close	213
5. Importance of Display	213
6. The Inclosing Shape	215
7. Size	217
8. Margins	217
9. Selection and Arrangement of Material	218
10. Appropriateness of Illustration	219
11. Importance of Headlines	221
12. Proper Phraseology	223
13. The Key	224
14. The Coupon	225
15. Grouping the Elements	226
16. Fitting the Advertisement to the Medium	226

CHAPTER XIV

LAYOUT OF ADVERTISEMENTS

1. Object of Layout	229
2. Objects of Display	232
3. The Optical Center	232

xiv ADVERTISING PRINCIPLES

SECTION	PAGE
4. Balance in the Layout	232
5. Securing Emphasis	233
6. Value of Movement	234
7. Display Type	235
8. Body Type	236
9. Illustrations	236
10. Borders and Rules	237
11. White Space	237

CHAPTER XV

BOOKLETS, CATALOGS AND FOLDERS

1. Aim of Booklets, Catalogs and Folders	239
2. Purposes of Each Form	240
3. Color and Typography	241
4. Need for Simplicity	241
5. Booklets	242
6. Catalogs	243
7. Layout	244
8. Size	247
9. Quoting the Price	248
10. Folders	248
11. The Dummy	249

CHAPTER XVI

DRAWINGS AND REPRODUCTIONS

1. Value of Illustrations	252
2. Tendencies in Advertising Art	253
3. Styles of Art	253
4. The Line	253
5. Stipple, Tones and Masses	255
6. Pen Drawings	255
7. Wash Drawings	256
8. Oil Paintings	256

CONTENTS

SECTION	PAGE
9. Retouched Photographs	256
10. Sources of Art Supply	258
11. Kinds of Engraving	258
12. Wood Cuts	259
13. Zinc Etchings	260
14. Half-Tones	261
15. Importance of the Screen	262
16. Lithography	264
17. Hand-Made Engravings	264
18. Ben Day Process	265
19. Electrotyping	266
20. Stereotypes and Matrices	266
21. Mechanical Processes	268

CHAPTER XVII

PRINTING ART IN ADVERTISING

1. Relation of Printing to Advertising	270
2. Standard Flat-Press Bed	270
3. Offset Process	270
4. Multicolor Process	271
5. Lithographic Printing	272
6. Photogravure	272
7. Copperplate Printing	273
8. The Make-Ready	273
9. Correcting the Proof	273
10. Styles of Type	275
11. Type Families	276
12. The Point System	277
13. Type Bodies	278
14. Practical Type Arrangement	279
15. Estimating Space for Copy	280
16. Figuring Stock	281
17. Selection of Material	282

CHAPTER XVIII

TRADE-MARKS, SLOGANS AND CATCH PHRASES

SECTION	PAGE
1. Origin of Trade-Marks	285
2. Purpose of Trade-Marks	286
3. Early Restrictions	286
4. Creating a Trade-Mark	287
5. Trade-Mark Individuality	289
6. Appropriate Trade-Marks	294
7. Trade-Marking Perishable Eatables	295
8. Trade-Mark as a Reminder	295
9. Preventing Substitution	296
10. Registration of a Trade-Mark	298
11. The Slogan	298
12. Catch Words and Phrases	301
13. Other Tendencies in Trade-Marking	303

CHAPTER XIX

LEGAL LIMITS AND RESTRICTIONS ON ADVERTISING

1. Restrictions of the Federal Government	304
2. State Regulations	306
3. Postal Regulations	307
4. Municipal Regulations	309
5. Constitutionality of Billboard Restrictions	310
6. Distribution of Circulars and Dodgers	311
7. Protection of Trade-Marks	313
8. Registration Regulations	315
9. Infringements	316
10. Remedy for Infringement	317
11. Deceptive Advertising	318
12. Personal Right of Privacy	319
13. Property Right in Advertisements	320

ADVERTISING PRINCIPLES

CHAPTER I

PRESENT DAY ADVERTISING

1. *Economic rôle of modern advertising.*—

Advertise: to give public notice of; to announce publicly, especially by a printed notice, as, to *advertise* goods for sale, a lost article, the sailing day of a vessel, a political meeting.
—Webster's Dictionary.

When a dictionary of recognized authority falls so far short of defining the modern significance of advertising, it is not surprising that a careful analysis and summary of the economic functions fulfilled by advertising is needed at this time. The citizen, the business man, even the trained economist have frequently been misled in their efforts to classify and interpret this tremendous force which, despite the active opposition of some powerful business factors, has grown into almost universal use within two generations.

2. *Early development of advertising.*—The advertising of the eighteenth century was merely a series of announcements. The typical advertisement of those days states that a certain product is offered for sale at a certain place. Even in such announcements

there is seen the awakening of a new force in business. The announcements acted as connecting links between consumers desiring a product and manufacturers or dealers with products for sale.

In the field of business the first half of the nineteenth century was devoted largely to solving the technical problems of production and transportation, while the latter half was concerned with problems of marketing, credits, selling and advertising. The commercial system gradually adjusted itself to the necessity of mass distribution, a necessity which the machine, the railway, the telegraph and the corporation had forced upon trade by crowding the world with excess goods. This necessity, in turn, brought about the further need for publicity.

Occasionally before the Civil War, expensive advertisements were published, such as that of the N. K. Fairbanks Company in *The New York Tribune*. This advertisement cost $3,000 and was the marvel of its day. In the main, however, the advertisements before 1860 were confined to ship and steamboat sailings and to runaway slaves.

About the time of the Civil War modern experiments in writing advertisements began. The old theory that goods were made to meet a demand was supplemented by a new and broader theory, that a producer in addition to manufacturing the goods must create a demand for them.

Shortly after the advertisements of Fairbanks came those of Pierre Lorillard, manufacturer of tobacco; Enoch Morgan's Sons, manufacturers of "Sapolio," and P. T. Barnum, of circus fame. By 1870, dealers in condiments, tea and similar commodities had adopted advertising as a necessary adjunct to their sales methods. The more staple products such as flour and sugar began to be advertised about 1890.

3. *Growth of advertising.*—During the first two years of the European war, one and a half billion dollars of European money was spent in the United States for war supplies. The effect of this enormous sum of money put into a few restricted lines was felt in all industries. Agriculture, mining, manufacturing, transportation—all felt the force of this tide of money and adjusted themselves to move with it.

Compare this spasmodic impact upon the whole body of business during the comparatively short war period with the one billion dollars—three million dollars a day—which American advertisers are pouring into every line of business year after year, and then judge of the effect which this constant pressure must have upon the marketing structure of America.

The growth of advertising is possible because of its social value, as well as of its individual value to the business using it. Society has learned that any human activity, to be economically justifiable, must produce something of value—must add some new or higher utility to the goods which comprise the wealth of society, and by this test, over the years, all institutions of economic endeavor ultimately stand or fall.

Advertising came into its own only recently, when the economic theory that only as a product can be sold is there industrial need of its manufacture, became generally accepted. It is estimated that there are today at least twenty thousand general advertisers and about one million local advertisers in the United States. The extent to which advertising counts in modern business may be gathered from an expert's figures, which place the cost of printed advertisements at seven hundred million dollars annually, and the cost of all kinds of advertising at over one billion dollars annually.

4. *Influence of war on advertising.*—The effect of the world conflict upon the conduct of advertising became a topic of special interest. One result of this unusual situation was the curtailment in production of luxuries, semi-luxuries and non-essentials. The changed conditions brought about by war gave a vastly broader view to all classes engaged in the advertising business.

The curtailment in the usual expenditure of those manufacturers who formerly were classed among the large national advertisers was attributable to various causes. For example, in the case of the candy manufacturer having a national distribution of goods, the sugar situation during the war gave him cause for worry. In the case of the piano and talking machine manufacturer, the problem of transportation was a hard one to solve.

The great tobacco industry, particularly in view of

the rapidly increasing consumption of cigarettes, may be embarrassed by a shortage of Turkish tobacco because of its lack of cultivation in Europe during the past five years and on account of the difficulty of securing bottoms in which to carry a supply to America. The uncertainties of possible future legislation or official regulation in the manufacture and marketing of many classes of commodities were but a few of the instances thru which, by reason of the war, advertising was affected to a more or less serious extent.

It is not a matter of years but really only of months since nearly every advertiser regarded his advertising as a force to be utilized for the introduction or movement of goods from the shelves of his dealers into the hands of consumers. This has always been one of the leading functions of what is termed "consumer" advertising, but many of these advertising manufacturers have now, as a result of the broadening influences for which war conditions were directly or indirectly responsible, awakened to the fact that the advantages of employing advertising space in the public prints are greater than the mere expediting of sales.

To illustrate: A large manufacturer whose product had been nationally advertised for a considerable time found himself urgently in need of additional plant facilities to care for a suddenly increased demand for his goods. Building materials were at a premium. Reputable builders were obliged to refuse further commissions. One of the largest builders was approached on the subject of building the new plant. To the surprise and gratification of the manufacturer, the builder agreed to take the contract. In a much shorter time than even the impatient manufacturer himself could expect, the new plant was built and production put months in advance of the date anticipated.

Asked the reason for the unusual accommodation, the builder replied that the erection of a plant to manufacture a product so well known and so widely used was in itself one of the most judicious advertisements of his own activities in which he could indulge, even at no small inconvenience to himself. Hence his ready acceptance of the commission.

This instance is but one of a number which might be given to demonstrate the potency of advertising for purposes other than the actual sale of merchandise.

5. *A creator of utility, service to the consumer.*— Some modern economic thinkers have accorded to advertising its rightful place with agriculture, manufacturing, commerce and transportation as one of the prominent forms in the creation of wealth. Just as "form utility" is created and added to the total utility of goods by manufacturing, and "place utility" is created by transportation, so "information utility" is created by advertising. Just as rough pig iron has only a potential value until made into a finished, usable form by manufacturing, just as the finished

article has only a potential value until transported to the place of its use, so the finished product, delivered to warehouse or store, has only a potential value until the public has been informed of its existence there, and educated to its use.

The importance of this social service of advertising can scarcely be overemphasized in view of the prevalence of the old idea that its value is to the advertiser only—its cost an unnecessary burden borne by the ultimate consumer. As a matter of fact, the consumer is not only saved time and effort in selecting what he buys, but is enabled to get better qualities and lower prices per piece by this very power of advertising. There are five distinct ways in which advertising is of service to the consumer.

6. *Assists intelligent selection.*—Advertising educates the public to better knowledge, and thus to quicker and more intelligent selection of goods on the competitive market. If the buyer does not know the relative claims or merits of the competing products, if he does not know where to find them, or if he is in ignorance of the competing prices, he cannot effectively utilize either his time, his means, or his selective ability in buying. Not knowing prices, he cannot buy as cheaply. Not knowing qualities, he certainly cannot find the best. The absence of advertising handicaps the consumer.

7. *Improves quality of goods.*—Advertising not only assists the buyer to select the best qualities, but also gives him higher and higher qualities from which

to select. Present-day competition forces the manufacturer to establish a sound claim of superiority for his article. This claim is voiced by advertising. Modern advertising of branded and labeled goods, thru their established individuality and the general knowledge of their quality by the public, has set new standards for the market. The new and higher business morality brought about by advertising makes misrepresentation unsafe and in many cases impossible of success.

8. *Educates the public.*—The social service of advertising in the introduction of new and useful devices, or of improvements on established products, need hardly be dwelt upon here. Advertising has brought new products to the consumer's attention and taught him to use them. In most cases, these products have added to the consumer's health, welfare and happiness. Soap and bath-tub manufacturers have taught the value of cleanliness in preserving the health; advertisements for tooth brushes have emphasized the necessity for care of the teeth until it is not longer considered entirely natural to lose one's teeth early in life. The makers of good food preparations have exposed many popular fallacies about eating coarse and unwholesome food, and they have spread abroad much information on the subject of pure food and sanitary cooking.

There is hardly a phase of modern life into which the influence of advertising has not entered. Railroad and steamship companies, by advertising the quality of their services, have taught travelers what to expect in convenience and in safety, and by advertising the benefits of travel have stimulated travel itself to a great degree. Insurance companies, banks and similar institutions have dwelt so strongly upon the necessity of thrift and protection of the family, that men who do not provide against the risks and accidents of life are looked upon as possessing poor judgment at least. Automobile manufacturers probably have done more to secure good roads for the farmer than have the combined efforts of all the road commissioners thruout the land. Nobody now denies the utter futility of any new product until the public knows of its existence and has been educated to its use; but few have recognized the importance of advertising in increasing the social serviceability of well-established products thru creating wider fields for their use. The intelligent advertiser devotes as much care to the education of old customers to the fullest use of his product, as he spends in attracting new buyers.

9. *Creates new wants.*—A modern development of advertising is shown in the systematic creation of demand. Products are no longer considered isolated units, but units which are closely interrelated with other products. The automobile, for instance, not only creates a number of closely related wants, but also affects remote trade lines. Moving pictures, to take another example, have, by their competition, decreased the demand for certain higher-priced amusements. If the advertiser means to hold his

place amid this shifting of wants on the part of the purchasers, he must, in many cases, create new uses for displaced products or recreate the old ideas in the minds of former purchasers.

10. *Reduces price to consumer.*—No discussion of the social and economic functions of advertising is complete without mention of its effect on production methods and unit costs of production. Advertising assures and enlarges the market for the manufacturer's goods. It thereby makes possible large-scale production from single patterns or designs which, thru reduction of the "overhead" or indirect costs per unit, brings about the low prices of most articles of standard design today. The low-priced watch, the automobile under $1,000, the cigarette, the man's collar—all these standard products and hundreds more, are a tribute to the economic power of advertising. Without the assurance of widespread demand and easy sale which good advertising alone can give, no manufacturer could dare to produce the quantities which justify these low prices.

The ultimate consumer, who, of course, pays the cost of the advertising, pays it with but a small portion of what it has saved him.

11. *Service to distributor.*—The distributor has been well served by advertising. He is, as a matter of fact, almost entirely dependent on advertising to keep his products before the public and to survive competition. The retail distributor, who is notoriously lacking in sales ability, should give to the manufac-

turers of the products he sells, credit for the consumer demand created largely by them.

12. *The manufacturer's advantage.*—By means of advertising, the manufacturer has been able to fight his way from obscurity to prominence in the field of business. In the lists of the early advertisements, there were few if any of the present well-known products. Consumers depended largely on their local dealer's judgment. The dealer, in turn, selected his stock from the wholesaler's samples or on his recommendation. The manufacturer's connection with the consuming public was, therefore, indirect. He was seldom known, and frequently was at the mercy of the distributor, when the latter wished to push a competing product.

The manufacturer took the first step in winning public recognition when he adopted a specific brand or trade-mark; the second step, when he advertised his product thru his brand or trade-mark. Not many years passed before the trade-marks were well known and millions of consumers were asking for them by name. This recognition forced the dealers to handle the goods, for unless they did, the customer would either send to the manufacturer for his supplies or encourage a competitive dealer to take up the trade-marked line. The third step was taken by the manufacturer when he put his guarantee back of his trade-mark; and a fourth step when he shifted his methods of competition from a basis of price to a basis of quality and service.

REVIEW

On what general principles is modern advertising based?

In what sense does advertising create wealth?

How does it contribute to the education of the public?

Discuss the proposition sometimes advanced that advertising is an economic waste which only enhances the prices of goods.

What are the advantages of advertising to the distributor and to the manufacturer?

CHAPTER II

FUNDAMENTALS OF ADVERTISING

1. *Purpose of advertising.*—The advantages of advertising are succinctly put in a statement made by the president of one of the largest companies of its kind in the United States, which manufactures a product of staple use no longer protected by any patent:

> Our gross sales are in the neighborhood of seventy-five million a year. We are oversold and our factories are driven to the limit of their capacity. We have been so for three years.
>
> We advertise extensively for the insurance of our investment, our good-will and the future volume of our business.
>
> I find also that it is a direct economy thru saving the time of my salesmen on the road, and the increased percentage of sales on the better grades.

Perhaps this short statement sums up the best reasons for the tremendous amount of advertising done by concerns whose strength in their fields might lead to an assumption that further publicity or educational sales effort is unnecessary.

The executive quoted here realized that the value of his business lay not so much in his fine plant and excellent manufacturing processes, as in the good-will of the public toward his product. For the maintenance of this good-will he was willing to pay a substantial insurance, and was pleased to find that it was more than repaid to him by direct facilitation of sales, and the economy of expenditure in sales effort. There are in all five results which may be secured by advertising.

2. *Advertising as insurance.*—The insurance of good-will as a measurable asset of the company, to be protected from destruction just as plant, raw materials and product should be protected from fire, is an idea which has not yet found definite form in the minds of many who regard advertising merely as a means for publicity and advance sales in the invasion of competitive markets.

The most progressive manufacturers now budget the advertising appropriation to be attributed to insurance. They base this budget on a definite knowledge of the current value of the good-will of the business.

3. *Advertising reduces selling cost.*—That the advertising done as insurance had more than repaid itself thru economy of sales effort, was of incidental interest to the manufacturer quoted at the beginning of this chapter. This fact, however, is one of vast importance to every distributor of goods. Aggressive advertising cuts down the cost of selling, thereby reducing the marketing expense.

Practically no article can be sold to the public generally unless there has been some recent review of its merits, its claims to usefulness, and notice of its presence upon the market. If this work, informative and educational, is not done thru advertising, it must be done thru personal efforts of salesmen—a vastly more expensive process.

4. *Raising price by advertising.*—Some producers whose plants are at "capacity," as well as many who offer products with interesting or unique qualities (such as motion pictures of highest grade), have found that sound profits on the old prices are impossible with rising costs of raw materials, transportation, labor or direct selling. They have accordingly employed intensive advertising as a means of increasing gross receipts thru the raising of the price without loss of sales. This experience, altho by no means general, is encountered in a surprisingly large number of cases.

5. *Increasing volume of business.*—The owner of a plant susceptible of enlargement, the product of which caters to a growing market, finds advertising of the greatest value. For such a producer advertising renders the same service which it can render to the plant running at capacity, and the further service of stimulating public interest and educating public taste.

Intelligent advertising does the missionary work for the salesman who is sent out to enlarge markets by cultivating the established trade or by sales to new customers. The rapid sales work, so essential to the development of new lines in competitive markets, can only be accomplished when the salesman has been properly and effectively introduced, and a public demand for the goods created in advance of his coming.

6. *Sales by advertising.*—The growth of gross sales of a product is usually directly proportional to the extent or persistence of the advertising, increasing when this increases, and falling off with the cessation of advertising effort. This is especially the case with products which are classified as luxuries and conveniences rather than necessities of life.

Intelligent advertising does more, however, than merely extend the sales of articles for accustomed uses in the established market. The intelligent advertiser finds in advertising a means of exploitation of new uses and new markets for his product.

An interesting phenomenon resulting from the war was the advertising of manufacturers showing the buyer how to make the product last longer. The Packard Motor Car Company advising users of Packard cars to retain them after proper overhauling, is one example. Several large clothing manufacturers followed the same general thought. One said in an advertisement: "To lengthen the life of your suit needs but a little thought and care. Neglect alone hastens the end. Brush it thoroly and frequently. Have it pressed regularly. When not in use, hang smoothly on a wooden hanger, the trousers inverted."

7. *Determining advertising appropriation.*—With the growth and recognition of advertising as a major factor both in getting and in keeping business,

the old question, "Why should we advertise?" has been replaced by, "How shall we advertise?" And this new question is the more in order as the manufacturer realizes that the exact amount and nature of his advertising must be based on intelligent calculation of the work to be done—the load the advertising is to carry.

The progressive executive now recognizes in his advertising a definite sales force which he must measure, budget and scientifically determine in each detail in advance of his advertising campaign. He further recognizes that advertising costs should be figured scientifically, and based on a definite relation to some measurable quantity in the business. For example, a definite amount per unit of estimated production, a definite percentage of current gross sales, a definite percentage of current profits, a definite amount per unit of population to be educated, a definite insurance premium on the current value of the business, or a combination of all may be the basis of the appropriation.

8. *Advantages of correct budgeting method.*—The recognition of the principle of correct budgeting has taken the advertising appropriation out of the field of sporadic or uncertain expenditures. The advertiser knows accurately from clear and scientific analysis, just what he is investing in advertising *and why;* what he will invest and why; and that the total amount so invested in any period is absolutely based on production estimates and analyses of the returns

from the advertising done in the preceding period.

Past experience thus furnishes the basis for scientific determination of the advertising appropriation as an integral part of the operating budget.

9. *Detailed methods vary.*—The details of method whereby the correct apportionment is to be fixed, will, of course, vary with every industry and with the phase of commercial development thru which the business is passing. In many cases two or more bases of appropriation must enter into the calculation. The problem is a complex one in every case, requiring an expert knowledge that is not to be expected in any but a specialist.

10. *Need of careful planning.*—In most effective advertising campaigns, the real cause of effectiveness is the care with which the campaigns have been planned—the thoroness with which every bit of detailed knowledge available has been reviewed and correlated before the first piece of advertising copy has been written, or before a single advertising illustration has been made.

To any person of even elementary education, the idea of outlining a composition before starting to write it, is an old one. To professional men engaged in research work—the preparation of legal cases, the writing of books or articles—the brief or outline is the all-important consideration. The preparation of the brief requires more time, pains and effort than the writing of the book, or the presentation of the case to the court. Yet many advertisers will enter into an advertising campaign with little or no plan, no definite idea as to how the campaign is to be carried thru, no clear outline of what points are to be brought forward nor in what sequence. They think, perhaps, that "We can afford about —— thousand dollars this year"; that "The first two or three advertisements look good, and by the time they have run we can order more."

When such advertising campaigns prove expensive in proportion to the returns secured, these men are apt to conclude that advertising is "not all that it's cracked up to be," and that personal effort of salesmen in the field is, after all, what sells the goods. It is therefore necessary at this time to discuss briefly the things that an advertiser should not do, before discussing how he should plan his campaign, and bring out some of the reasons why advertising campaigns need to be thought out carefully in advance.

11. *Approaching the plan from proper angle.*— Under the old idea of advertising as mere paid publicity, it was entirely natural that it should be regarded as something which could be carried on intermittently, on which careful planning had little effect. The repetition of a trade-mark and a few trade slogans, with a pretty girl's head or a picture of a mischievous child to attract the reader's attention, was considered an adequate advertisement. The main considerations were to get a first-class trade slogan, and to make each girl's head or small child's picture as pretty or amusing as possible. Even now some

advertisers buy space and attractive designs when good solicitation catches their fancy, purchasing the illustration and possibly the idea for an individual advertisement here and another one there. Such sporadic efforts constitute their entire advertising.

Advertising, to these men, has never attained its full significance. They have never recognized in it a real sales force. They frequently regard all advertising as an expensive necessity forced on them by competitors.

Advertising designed merely as publicity for a trade-mark may be conducted sporadically without material disadvantage. But advertising for education, for the development of public taste, or for the actual sale of the product—the kind of advertising that must be done today to drive the public thru the doors of a retail dealer—needs to be carefully planned and carried out. Each advertisement, and each detail of each advertisement, must contribute to the execution of a complete argument.

The planning of the modern advertising campaign, then, becomes a matter of primary importance, usually involving more care and pains than the writing of the copy or the preparation of illustrations.

The analysis of conditions on which the plan must be built becomes a broad and thoro search into the entire history and present status of the company, its business, the product to be advertised, and the conditions of the market which it is to reach. This analysis falls into nine main divisions which are discussed in the present chapter. The careful student will bear in mind that none of these sections is a complete statement of all that needs inquiry, but rather they are designed to suggest the kind of inquiry that should be made.

12. *Groundwork of plan.*—In mapping out the plan of the advertising campaign, an analysis should be made of the following factors: (1) policy of the firm; (2) the product itself; (3) the present market; (4) the potential market; (5) competitive products; (6) mode of distribution; (7) the sales department; (8) history of past advertising; (9) study of similar problems.

13. *Policy of the firm.*—A complete history of the firm, with that of the ideals and personalities of the owners as well as of their business and financial policy, should be known by the writer of the advertisement in order that he may have the proper background for the presentation of the product. When was the business started, and by whom? What has been its rate of growth? What changes have been made in the product, or in the business policy of the firm? Can the management be relied upon to follow out the plan consistently after approving it? Are the margins of profit large enough to warrant a thorogoing advertising campaign? Has good judgment been used in setting the retail price? Each of these questions may be of material importance in the making of the finished sales plan.

What is to be the specific object of the advertising?

Is it designed to introduce a new product or primarily for the insurance of the firm's good-will and investment? Not only should the nature of the copy be different in these two cases, but the advertising mediums to be selected will also be different.

14. *The product itself.*—What is the nature of the product? On what basis of individuality can it claim distinction? Is it really the best thing on the market at its price?

What is its design, construction, style? Of what material is it made? What are the best sources of technical information on the subject of this product? What would be the ideal product for the service to be rendered, and how nearly does this particular article approach that ideal? Is the cost of production subject to change so as to make it likely that the present price to consumers cannot be maintained? This is necessary to a complete understanding of the product.

15. *Present market.*—What is the present market of the product? By what class of people is it used? In what sections of the country? Is it bought by men or by women? Has it universal consumption, or is its use limited to those with incomes higher than $1,500 per year, for instance? Does it appeal equally to the educated and uneducated classes? What are the territorial variations in its consumption? Is it used as extensively in the North as in the South; in the city as in the country? Is the unit made for the individual or for the family? What are the present seasonal variations in the market?

Frequently the advertiser's problem is based almost entirely on this question of territorial limits. Many products are first introduced into one or two large cities, and after they have gained a foothold there, a campaign in other cities is planned. A careful study for the purpose of determining just where the product has been most successfully introduced, and what elements contributed to its success, furnishes the best possible basis for planning the campaign to introduce it into other cities.

16. *Potential market.*—What is the potential market for the product? Should it find a sale in sections of the country into which it has not yet made its way? Is it, for example, popular in the Northeast, but relatively unknown in other sections? If so, is there any good reason for this? Is it a product that should be used by all classes, but as a matter of fact, is used only by the poor, or only by the middle classes, or only by the rich? Has its market been unnecessarily limited in the past by mistaken advertising or sales policies?

17. *Competitive products.*—What is the nature and strength of the competition? Are there closely competitive products now on the market? How do they compare in quality with the advertiser's product? Is there any competition from other lines? These questions are, like many others here suggested, ones on which the judgment of the advertiser himself cannot be accepted by the men who must make the plan and write the copy.

18. *Mode of distribution.*—The channels and method of distribution need especially careful study in the preparation of the plan. Is the product sold direct to the consumer by mail, by direct solicitation, or thru "the trade"? The last usually means distribution thru a manufacturer's agent or broker, to jobbers who supply retailers, who in turn sell to the public. If sold thru the trade, then what trade—drug or grocery, hardware or dry goods?

In each trade the details of the problems will differ. Will these retailers and jobbers make strenuous sales efforts to push the product? Or are they handling a large number of lines on standardized and reduced margins of profit which makes it better policy for them to serve practically as order takers? An advertising campaign which fails to take these factors into account is foredoomed to ineffectiveness.

What is the attitude of the trade toward the product in question? Is that product one which competes with jobbers' private brands, which they are interested in pushing for a wider margin of profit? Are there competing brands that allow the dealer better discounts? Are there adverse trade prejudices which need to be overcome? What is the average stock the dealer keeps on hand? What is the average size of order received by the retailer? All of these questions vitally affect the advertising, for it is the business of advertising to send customers into the retailers' store to order the product by name, asking for that product and no other.

19. *Sales department.*—The sales department constitutes a vital link in the chain connecting the factory and the consumer. It is essential, then, to know before starting the advertising campaign what is the elasticity of the sales organization. Is it capable of responding quickly to large and sudden increases of demand? Can it back up a national advertising campaign, increasing the demand simultaneously in all parts of the country? Or are its limitations such that the advertising campaigns must be local, starting in one section of the country, then in another, gradually extending the territory? What is the past history of the sales force? Has it in the past loaded up its dealers intelligently, or has it been guilty of overloading, or of allowing the dealers to be caught short?

In this connection, a careful consideration of the factory and the shipping department is necessary. Is the factory in a position to meet sudden and substantial increases in demand? It is possible for an advertising campaign to be much too effective, if the factory, the shipping or the sales department is unable to meet the demand created.

20. *History of past advertising.*—A careful analysis of the past advertising of the company will always reveal many points of value. What were the results of the preceding advertising campaigns? If unsatisfactory, what causes contributed to their failure or success? Were the returns "spotty" and irregular? In this case many avenues for investigation and study

are opened up—avenues which one cannot afford to neglect.

21. *Study of similar problems.*—But no matter how complete the past records of the business advertised may be, no advertising plan is complete without a careful study of experiences in related fields, involving the same types of problems. This phase of preparation is frequently overlooked.

Probably no two articles on the market would seem less similar to the average mind than the silk seam binding in ladies' garments and Timken roller bearings for automobiles. Yet the advertising principles back of the exploitation of these articles are the same. In each case the article is sold as a relatively inconspicuous part of the larger article which is assembled from many parts, and the advertiser's problem is to make the public demand of the dealer that this assembled article, automobile or suit of clothes, be equipped with the Timken axle or have the seams bound with silk.

22. *Plan of campaign.*—Before a plan is definitely decided upon, the following factors must be taken into consideration: (1) survey of the field; (2) continuity of the campaign; (3) the consumer's point of view; (4) stocking the dealer; (5) selection of mediums.

23. *Survey of the field.*—In laying out any plan of campaign it is first necessary to make a complete survey of the field so that the advertiser may know its limitations and possibilities and be guided by them in making his plans. With this information carefully

analyzed, he is ready to turn to the details of his campaign.

24. *Continuity.*—Several laws limit the detailed planning of a campaign. The entire plan must be made to carry thru the ultimate purpose of the campaign. There must be continuity thruout the entire series, and whatever idea gives this continuity must be strong enough never to be lost sight of, yet not so strong as to destroy the individual values of the advertisements.

25. *Consumer's point of view.*—The most important of all rules is that every advertisement in the series should be written from the point of view of the purchaser. Many campaigns have been spoiled and their effectiveness lost thru too much emphasis on what the advertiser thinks of his product, too much discussion of mechanical detail, too much emphasis on the size of the plant, the pet hobbies of the proprietor, catch phrases or trade slogans that appeal to the owner of the business, when as a matter of fact the advertisement that sells goods is the one which presents the customer's side of the question and talks from his point of view. The prospective buyer is constantly asking, "What is there in this for me?" He cares little about where the article is made and little about the age of the firm from which he buys it, especially if it is an article for which he pays cash and on which repair service is not essential. He cares everything for the service which the article may render him after he has secured it, everything for the care with which

it has been adapted to his needs, and a great deal for its presentation in terms which he understands.

26. *Stocking the dealer.*—A definite portion of the plan is that which relates to the dealer, for a campaign cannot result in success without his cooperation. It is as important to shape the advertising so as to have the trade prepared to meet the increased consumer demand, as it is to make the advertising reach the consumer. Advertising in the trade journals to the dealers often becomes an important part of the complete campaign. Especially is it necessary in some way to make the trade, both jobbers and retailers, thoroly familiar with the fact that a general advertising campaign is coming and that increase of demand is to be expected.

27. *Selection of mediums.*—The final step in the plan is the selection of the medium thru which to appeal to the public's interest. Shall the advertisements be inserted in magazines or in newspapers, shall they appear on billboards, on painted signs, on street-car cards, handbills, circulars, or on several or all of these?

How shall the budget for advertising be apportioned among these mediums? After the advertiser has determined to use magazines as a medium, his problem of selection has only just begun. Many considerations enter in determining what magazines to use. Different magazines appeal to different classes of readers.

The territorial distribution of the magazine is also

important. One would hardly advertise heavy underwear in a magazine which has its circulation mostly in the far South, even tho it is a most excellent advertising medium for products which are of use in that section. In the case of newspaper selection also, especially in large cities, if the article to be advertised is an economically priced shoe, a set of metropolitan newspapers would be selected which would be quite different from those chosen if we were advertising a very high grade of ladies' wearing apparel.

When the mediums have been selected, the size of the space determined and all subordinate parts of the campaign completely laid out, the actual work of writing the copy and preparing the illustrations may begin. If the campaign is to be well carried forward, the series comprising the first large section of the campaign should be completed and accepted as a whole before the publication of the first advertisement. Only in this manner can a complete, comprehensive and thoroly effective campaign be put thru with maximum results.

REVIEW

Explain in what sense advertising may be looked upon as insurance, and how it reduces selling costs.

How can advertising be used to increase the price of the product?

What consideration should enter into the fixing of the appropriation for advertising? State the chief elements which form the groundwork of any advertising campaign.

How should the campaign be planned with reference to the consumer and the distributor?

What determines the value of advertising mediums?

CHAPTER III

GETTING THE ADVERTISEMENT SEEN

1. *Advertising must attract attention.*—It is the purpose of all advertising to create certain impressions in the reader's mind and to secure a favorable response. Invariably, the first aim is to bring the advertisement to the notice of the largest possible number of readers. The advertisement, then, is always striving to be seen.

The process taking place in the mind of the reader of an advertisement consists of a series of mental phenomena. There may be some variation in the degrees of intensity of the different impressions, or in the length of time that different minds give to the same one, but every mind receives more or less similar impressions from the same stimulus.

There are two kinds of attention, voluntary and involuntary. The advertisement needs particularly to evoke the latter as it is sustained the more easily.

The first task of the advertisement, then, is to meet the great competition for attention. With the large number of publications to choose from and the tendency toward the rapid reading of only selected matter, together with the increase in the number of advertisements, competition is made many times as intense as it was a few decades ago.

2. *Elements that secure attention.*—There are certain elements in an advertisement that secure involuntary attention. The degree of this involuntary attention depends on the arrangement of the copy and the illustration, color, type and spacing. Words also, in themselves, have value in attracting attention, especially if they suggest action or call up vivid images. All these are factors in getting initial attention. Action, too, has decided attention value in displays. The most important elements that secure attention are (1) variation, (2) arrows, darts, and other designating signs, (3) contrast, (4) illustration, (5) color, (6) position and (7) motion.

3. *Variation.*—Variation is the primary method of securing attention. If a hundred men of the same size and build are in line, all alike except one who is noticeably heavier than the rest, the heavy man will be brought to the attention of practically every observer. Of any group of objects, similar in general, those differing from the rest in form, size and color will attract the most attention.

One of the older types of variation in form, that of unusual shape, is shown in the advertisement of the Hazel-Atlas Glass Company. In this instance, the fruit jar advertised lends itself most effectively to what printers call "mortising," in which the copy is displayed within a representation of the product advertised. In many cases the idea of "mortised copy"

These sanitary, all-glass jars open as easy as they close

How often do you have trouble in opening fruit jars? Honest, now! Isn't it about nine times in ten? Eh?

The top sticks. You twist and turn, squeeze and squirm. It still sticks.

You get rid of that sort of thing for all time if you use

Atlas E-Z Seal Jars

A touch—so—seals them. Another touch and they are open.

E-Z Seal Jars are made of green glass —to exclude the light and prevent discoloration. Yet you can tell, by holding the jar up to the light, what is in it.

Wide Mouth—so you can put in plums, tomatoes, apples, pears, peaches, beets, string beans, etc., without cutting them in small pieces.

Most grocers sell E-Z Seal Jars. If yours does not, let us know.

Half pints, pints, quarts and half gallons.

Write for book of recipes. 20 pages; 60 recipes. Some by Marion Harland; some by famous Virginia cooks.

Hazel-Atlas Glass Co.
Wheeling, W. Va.

Hamilton Coupons packed in these jars.

Member of Rice Leaders of the World Association.

NOTE: *Shrewd housekeepers are not satisfied with putting up a few jars of cherries or strawberries. They buy beets, tomatoes, corn, string beans and other vegetables by the bushel, and put up enough to last all winter. That's one way to keep down "the cost of high living"*

This advertisement illustrates how variation in form, in this case the unusual shape of the advertisement, acts as an important element in securing involuntary attention.

is inappropriate and forced, but in this company's advertising, special attention is drawn to the principal selling point, the wide mouth of the jar, which is easily opened without twisting the cap or without risking breakage of the jar. What would otherwise be waste space in the illustration—the body of the jar—is thus effectively utilized.

4. *Arrows, darts and designating signs.*—A standard method of attracting attention to the advertisement, or more particularly to a portion of it, is by means of an arrow-like line or lines pointing to some parts of the illustration or text. The arrows not only attract attention in themselves but they also carry the eye along to the point to be emphasized. Many of the products advertised in this way are machines or appliances where the arrow is particularly valuable as a designating sign to indicate salient points. The use of this device, however, has been employed to such a large extent as to make it hackneyed and the public does not respond as readily to it as formerly.

The Western Electric advertisement offers an example of a product that is well displayed by means of the arrow. The main talking points of the product are thus brought forcibly to the reader's attention.

In the Burnham and Morrill Company's advertisement of fish flakes, the fish moving from the ocean to the can is a striking and appropriate variant of the use of the arrow idea.

In the Hanes Underwear advertisement, circles are used to bring out clearly important points in the

Western Electric
POWER and LIGHT

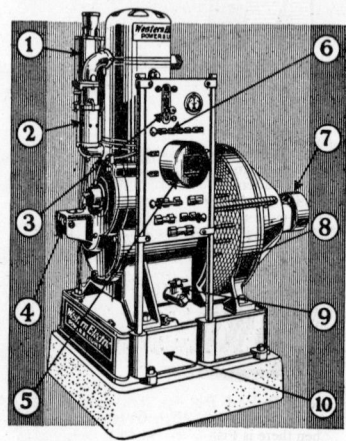

A fine piece of machinery

Fine quality is evident in every part of this Western Electric Direct Connected Plant. Its ten important features are outlined in this advertisement.

If you are any judge of machinery

—be sure to read these ten points. They will mean much to you: you will want us to tell you more about them and all about several others that make this plant distinctive in many ways.

If you buy machinery solely by name

—then consider that the Western Electric Plant is guaranteed by an organization of nearly fifty years electrical experience; one with unlimited resources for making you entirely satisfied long after the sale.

A Western Electric man near you will demonstrate this plant and explain how easy it is to have the safety and convenience of electric light and the dollars-and-cents help of electrical power for farm work.

Write for booklet No. N F 15, giving full details

WESTERN ELECTRIC COMPANY
INCORPORATED

Ten Features that Make This Plant Dependable

1. Vacuum feed system; same as on high grade automobiles.
2. Air preheater; completely vaporizes the kerosene.
3. Pushing this switch down starts the engine.
4. Throttling governor; keeps the engine speed practically constant at all loads.
5. This device automatically stops engine when battery is fully charged.
6. Moving this switch makes all the engine power available for operating other machinery.
7. Pulley; for operating other machinery.
8. 1500 watt generator direct connected to engine.
9. Oil for splash-lubricating system supplied here.
10. Kerosene supply kept in this tank. Entire plant stands about 4½ feet high. Storage battery consists of 16 cells.

The arrows secure attention to this advertisement and indicate the most vital parts of it in an attempt to develop the attention into interest.

LENT

The one food you depend upon to round out the home bill of fare during Lent is FISH. You may have such a delightful variety of fish dishes by using Burnham & Morrill Fish Flakes. Open a tin—combine the contents any way you like—heat them a few minutes—and the most delicious fishfood is ready to grace the table and delight the family—the marvel is that food so tempting may be so quickly served.

Creamed Fish on Toast **Fish Croquettes**

Creamed Fish on Toast or served with **Baked Potato**, makes a most wholesome and appetizing dish for breakfast or luncheon. **Fish Croquettes** for dinner are hearty, also satisfying. Then there is Fish Hash, Codfish Balls, Fish Souffle, Fish Chowder, Fish Salad, Curried Fish, Fish Timbales, Fish Omelette—a score or more dishes to choose from—dishes so easily made that you will welcome them three times a day.

Burnham & Morrill Fish Flakes
10c—Sizes—15c (*Except in Far West*)

are the finest codfish and haddock, fresh from the sea, cleaned, boned—cooked in our seaside kitchens—immediately sealed in airtight, parchment-lined tins. Only a little salt used in cooking—no preservative—no bones—no skin—no waste. All sweet, white meat—the finest lenten food at smallest cost. B. & M. Fish Flakes save time, eliminate trouble—add greatly to the pleasure and satisfaction of the home table.

INTRODUCTORY OFFER
Most grocers have Burnham & Morrill Fish Flakes or will get them for you. If not mail us $1.00 and we will send you **ten 10c tins**, prepaid anywhere east of the Missouri River.
Our Recipe booklet "Good Eating" free for the asking
BURNHAM & MORRILL CO.
42 Water Street
Portland, Me.

An interesting variation of the arrow device in order to secure attention.

Greatest winter underwear at popular prices

HANES

Buy None Without It

GUARANTEE — We guarantee Hanes Underwear absolutely — every thread, stitch and button. We guarantee to return your money or give you a new garment if any seam breaks.

You know Hanes Underwear is right the instant you rig up in a suit!

Put that fleecy warmth of Hanes Winter Weight Underwear next to your skin—and, you're fit to face the stiffest blast the north can let fly! Get the friendly hug of the elastic knit, long fibre cotton; and, strain in any direction, and prove how perfectly Hanes gives-and-takes with every body movement! If you'll pass-up the fuss-frills in high priced underwear, then add these fine service-features, you'll know what Hanes Underwear offers at a popular price. *Follow every fact*—guaranteed unbreakable seams; elastic tailored collarette that cannot gap; pearl buttons that are sewed on for keeps! And, behind them all stands Hanes workmanship! An unbeatable combination!

Hanes Heavy Winter Weight Underwear comes to you in Union Suits and Shirts and Drawers—the utmost extra value your money can buy.

Illustrated above is the Hanes Heavy Winter Weight Union Suit. The Closed Crotch *stays closed;* the elastic knit ankle cuffs assure snug fitting. In every way these Union Suits are perfection.

Shirts and Drawers **HANES** Union Suits
ELASTIC KNIT
UNDERWEAR

Hanes Heavy Winter Weight Shirts and Drawers have for many years been the American Standard at popular prices!

Greatest Underwear for boys!

Hanes Boys' Union Suits exceed in quality, workmanship and service any boys' underwear we have ever seen. They are superbly made with an unusual finish and combine the features of the men's garments with cozy warmth so ideal for youngsters. In reality, they are men's suits in boys' sizes. *If your dealer does not have Hanes Underwear write us immediately.*

P. H. HANES KNITTING CO., Winston-Salem, N. C. New York Office 366 Broadway

WARNING TO THE TRADE— Any garment offered as Hanes is a substitute unless it bears the "Hanes" label.

Securing attention by designating circles

product which immediately attract the reader's attention.

5. *Contrast.*—When it is possible to throw into sharp contrast the faulty or ordinary, and the perfect or new, one of the most successful principles of advertising is observed. This is strikingly done by means of illustration as in the Duofold advertisement.

Another good illustration which effectively shows contrast is the advertisement of the Warner Lenz.

In some cases it is possible to contrast products of the same manufacture which differ in some important particular. The G. & C. Merriam Company employs a suggestive contrast in picturing the difference in bulk and weight between the regular and India paper edition of Webster's New International Dictionary. The difference between the 16 pounds of the one, and the 7½ pounds of the other is brought out sharply by the representation of weighing a volume of the India paper edition, the heavier volume being shown in contrast to the lighter.

6. *Illustration.*—By the term "illustration" is meant anything from photographs to decorative lines or borders. People see a picture before they see a word. The picture language is universally understood and is grasped more readily than the printed word. Accordingly, the attention value of the illustration is a matter of great importance to the advertiser. One of the chief reasons why people peruse the advertising pages of a magazine is that they like to look at pictures.

Securing attention by means of contrast

Which for You?

The Man-Made Daylight of Warner-Lenz—or

The Dangerous Glaring Shaft of Ordinary Lens?

Warner-Lenz brings the final solution of night-driving problems to all who motor. At last here is a lens that gives a _perfect_ driving light for both country and city.

This wonderful new Warner-Lenz—176 lenses in one—announces the end of old-style, hazardous lighting. No need now to "feel" your way on difficult country roads or crowded city streets. Nervous tension ends. No more guesswork.

Over 250,000 automobiles have been equipped with Warner-Lenz. What greater endorsement? This means that Warner-Lenz has undergone the severest tests. This means that automobile manufacturers, police officials and motor experts—in addition to owners—will have no other lighting methods—once they know Warner-Lenz. They are bound to become universal.

Warner-Lenz positively does away with the blinding glare prohibited by law. It eliminates the necessity of dimmers that make your light dangerously weak and confusing.

Warner-Lenz bring man-made daylight for motoring at night. Your lamps give forth as much light as ever, but it is properly diffused. The road is brightened up on both sides of your car and ahead of you —from 300 to 500 feet.

The road is seen _as it is_, without exaggerated dips and bumps. Lurking dangers on both sides and ahead are disclosed, _before_ you get to them.

The wide-angle Warner-Lenz lights up the turns and the corners before you reach them and while you are turning. Safety, pleasure, and motoring etiquette all demand the Warner-Lenz in your automobile lamps. It's a courtesy you owe to "the other fellow." Let yours be the light of safety and the light of a gentleman.

WARNER-LENZ

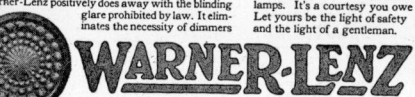

ADOPTED AS STANDARD EQUIPMENT FOR PACKARDS AND MARMONS

The Warner-Lenz is not a lamp. It is a lens, and is easily attached to any automobile lamp of any size. Anybody can attach Warner-Lenz. You merely take out the glass now in your lamp and insert the new Warner-Lenz. Nothing mechanical about it—nothing to adjust or get out of order. Once on —there to stay.

One dark night's use is convincing thousands that they can't get along without this great invention, which bears the personal guarantee of Mr. A. P. Warner, of Auto-Meter fame. You, too, will be convinced.

So wait no longer. Equip your car now with Warner-Lenz.

Accessory dealers throughout the country will supply you with a pair of Warner-Lenz. And put them on your car in a jiffy. If your nearest dealer should not have a supply just now, we will ship direct, if you use the coupon.

THE WARNER-LENZ COMPANY
S. Michigan Avenue, CHICAGO

Price of Warner-Lenz Per Pair	
Diameter in inches	Sell of Beckies
5 to 9, inclusive,	$3.50
9¼ to 10, inclusive,	4.00
10¼ to 12, inclusive,	5.00
West of Rockies 50c per pair extra	

Please Read These Directions Carefully
Merely send us the name and model of your car with the diameter of your present lens.

Money-Back Coupon
THE WARNER-LENZ CO.
S. Michigan Avenue, Chicago

Inclosed find check, money order or cash, for which please send me prepaid one pair of Warner-Lenz, with a guarantee that if not satisfactory money will be refunded upon return of the lenses within ten days.

Name ....

City .... State ....

Name and model of car ....

Dealer's name ....

Address ....(42)

Another use of contrast to secure attention

40 ADVERTISING PRINCIPLES

In the Duofold advertisement on page 38, no words could make as effective an appeal thru contrast as does the illustration.

In the Whitman's Sampler advertisement below, the first thing that attracts attention is the picture of the child, then the box of candy, then the words "Whitman's Sampler," because of their size and prominent location. Next we notice the words at the top, "A Sweet Surprise." The quaintness of the picture has an interest value, too, because the picture, the thing advertised and its name are in harmony.

7. *Color.*—The use of color as an attention-getter has long been recognized. Like many other good

Novelty of illustration and border in this advertisement helps to secure favorable attention

things, however, it has been overdone by many advertisers who do not clearly understand the principles of color attraction and the effect on the reader of the use of color in an advertisement.

The practical advertiser will use color with discretion, making his choice of color to harmonize with the object advertised or with the effect he wishes it to produce.

In general, color is used for two purposes: (1) To reproduce the package or product as it is sold. This helps in identifying the product; as a rule, the nearer the colors in the advertisement can approach the actual colors of the package the greater the advertising value. (2) To attract attention and appeal to the emotions. Its value in the latter use is dependent on the effect of various colors on the human mind. Red, for example, is suggestive of warmth, excitement and passion. It is said to reach the eye thirty per cent faster than any other color. Hence it is used for attracting the eye quickly or for intensifying an effect. Yellow suggests light and is an effective color as a background; blue, cold, reserve and dignity and is also used as a background; purple, mystery and darkness; orange suggests flame; green suggests coolness, repose.

No intense color should be used for backgrounds. For this purpose it is best to use a neutral color, light gray or buff, for example.

Again, dark type on a light background is usually more effective and always easier to read than light type on a dark background. Black type on a field of white is decidedly more effective than white type on a black field.

The greatest abuse of color lies in overdoing it and in employing two or more colors that do not harmonize. Care should be taken to avoid poor combinations of color. The effect is irritating, and the reader is likely to pass on without reading the advertisement.

8. *Position.*—It takes but a few simple experiments to demonstrate the fact that points in a line vary in attention value. Similarly—and of even greater importance to the advertiser—on any page or signboard, certain portions of the area are much more easily brought to the attention than others.

Objects at the beginning and end of a series are more quickly distinguished than are other similar objects in the series. Of a line of soldiers of the same height and similarly equipped, those at the end are most easily distinguished. In a newspaper or magazine page, the areas about the margin line compete in attention value with a small area at the center.

Position values are studied carefully by the advertiser in his desire to have his advertisement seen. Give an experienced advertiser his choice of position and he will usually select the top of a column, the right hand page, next to the reading matter associated with the advertisement. If he uses a full page magazine advertisement, the back cover, the inside front, or the inside back would usually be chosen, in

THE ADVERTISEMENT SEEN

the order given. Right hand pages, near the beginning of the magazine, stand high in favor. "Spreads" or "double trucks," advertisements occupying two opposite pages, are thought by some advertisers to lack the distinction that should come from space, as it is possible that the reader may pass by opposite pages without even glancing at them.

9. *Motion.*—There is nothing so interesting in life as motion. That is why anything in motion involuntarily attracts attention. This is also the basic reason for the success of many advertising displays which not only attract the attention but impress the value of the product upon the customer.

Motion is suggested in an illustration by making the reader imagine that the article is moving. The ideal advertising display is one in which the motion features some exclusive characteristic of the product advertised. The figure of a man using a safety razor attracts attention, but it advertises all safety razors, not merely the particular one. The figure of a doll apparently running a sewing machine approaches the ideal display more closely, as it advertises an "easy running" sewing machine. The representation of steaming water running out of a faucet to advertise an instantaneous water heater; of a neatly dressed woman with a cheerful face, ironing with an electric iron, and many others of this sort, are made effective by suggested action.

One method of indicating "movement" is to draw white lines across black letters, the latter being set at an obtuse angle. This idea is brought out in the illustration which follows:

BLUE STREAKS

A similar effect of speed can be shown by having letters lean forward, that is, toward the right, and then blearing these letters as if a blotter had been rubbed across them from right to left.

Puffs of dust shown at the rear of a vehicle will give the effect of motion. Straight lines across the body of a vehicle will also show movement. In the case of simple objects like a wheel, speed can be indicated by omitting the spokes, showing merely the rim and the axle, and by drawing a few horizontal lines across the wheel and a few more very short horizontal lines ahead of the rim to represent the surface over which it is traveling.

Many automobile advertisements suggest action rather than repose. This not only attracts attention but is a means of emphasizing many points of superiority—hill-climbing power, speed on rough lanes or mountain roads, stability or freedom from jar under adverse conditions and the like.

10. *Novelty and uniqueness.*—Anything that is different from the ordinary will attract attention by stimulating curiosity. If this attention can be converted into genuine interest in the product, then it succeeds in its purpose. The quaintness of the cos-

tume of the child in the Whitman's Sampler advertisement, on page 40, stimulates the curiosity to ask what is in the box.

The unusual position and the lighter color of the circles in the underwear advertisement on page 36, will stimulate the curiosity to find out why the circles are brought out so prominently.

11. *Headlines.*—The headline is designed to attract attention. If it is well conceived it will lead the reader on to find what the advertisement is all about. The headline is usually short, containing four or five words. If it is longer, it should be put in two or three lines. The following headlines are illustrative of good attention-getters:

"Corns Check the Salesman," to advertise Bluejay Corn Plasters.
"The $100,000 Man Who Went to School Again," to advertise the Alexander Hamilton Institute.
"The Hog Slanders the Hen," to advertise Sawtay Shortening.
"Tea for the Troopers," to advertise Lipton's Teas.
"Ditched by the Glare," to advertise Osgood Deflector Lens.
"Once in Every Woman's Life," to advertise Colt's Firearms.
"Good Food to Study On," to advertise Campbell's Soups.
"Henry M. Stanley Went 30 Weeks Without a Shave," to advertise Gillette Safety Razors.

12. *Teaser copy.*—The designation "teaser" is given to a class of advertising whose full meaning is reserved until a time after the appearance of the advertisement. The teaser appeals openly to curiosity.

Teaser advertisements, rightly written, make it possible for the advertiser to turn one of the most powerful of human instincts to his own account. Such advertisements have the disadvantage that curiosity has little power to persist, diminishing rapidly as the exciting power is removed.

The common method of employing teaser advertising is to display a puzzling statement or question. This may, and commonly does, border on the bizarre or grotesque, as in the forerunner of a series of breakfast food advertisements which asked, "What did the woggle-bug say?" It may seek to place the reader, in imagination, under the stress of some unusual or thrilling environment. It may take the form of a rhythmic jingle, as in the street-car card announcing: "We should worry, we should care; we'll be there, we'll be there! Where?" This was used to precede an advertisement for an amusement park.

One of the most striking advertisements employing suspense was the series featured by the Sterling Gun Company. Individual advertisements featured six points of the product in detail. For guessing the seventh point, a first prize of $1,000 was offered. Lesser prizes ranged from $500 down to a box of 10 five-cent packages of gum. The announcement stating the conditions under which prizes were to be awarded said in part:

> From Maine to California, from Texas to Hudson Bay, millions of people have been asking, "What is the seventh point in Sterling Gum?"

In practically every town, city and village in the United States and Canada, the published six points of superiority have brought Sterling Gum fast-growing popularity.

But the seventh point still remains a riddle. Point 7. What?

13. *Favorable impression.*—An advertisement may attract attention and yet utterly fail to interest the prospective customer. If his attention will lead him to look upon the thing advertised with disfavor, it is of no value. An umbrella over the driver of a garbage wagon may be a conspicuous place upon which to advertise, but it would hardly attract favorable attention to a brand of men's hats. A man cutting himself with a razor will not attract attention of a favorable sort either, as this idea will not further any contemplation if that special razor is the article advertised.

Attention, then, is valuable only if an advertisement suggests an attitude that is favorable to a consideration of the goods. This sort of attention leads to interest.

REVIEW

Discuss the various devices used in advertising to attract attention, and explain their value and their limitations.

Recall other instances besides those mentioned in the text, in which advertisements excel thru their unique character.

Can you remember the effective headlines named in the text, and suggest others which you have seen?

Give one or more illustrations of "teaser" advertisements.

Why should an advertisement produce a favorable impression?

CHAPTER IV

GETTING THE ADVERTISEMENT READ

1. *Turning attention into interest.*—Attention is the first in a series of mental processes which the successful advertisement must induce in the reader. The advertisement which attracts the initial attention only and fails to gain interest has left work unfinished at the very start.

We continually follow in thought a successsion of images that are associated with something in our own experience. Experiments prove that forced or voluntary attention cannot be sustained for more than a few seconds at a time. For this reason an advertisement must suggest images that will hold the interest by the association of other images in the reader's own mind.

In the series of images or mental pictures thus produced, there must be gradual and certain progression from the first image to the one which causes the product advertised to be favorably considered. The mind constantly selects certain impressions from memory, combines these with the mental pictures suggested by the description, and thus produces the final image conveyed by the advertisement.

2. *Connected images stimulate interest.*—If an ad-

Big Ben

A *Westclox* Alarm

4 a.m.

The Gift of Time

BIG BEN'S the only time-clock the modern farmer knows—he helps the farmer beat the sun to work.

Four a. m., in growing time, starts the farmer's day—brings a bumper crop of hours, for chores and in the field.

That's why Big Ben goes to the farm, at Christmas every year—to lend a hand in preparing for planting days. Now'days there's business-like system on the farm.

Where Big Ben's wound up every night, the farm cannot run down.

So it's Big Ben for Christmas, wherever you go—the gift of time that means good-will all year.

You'll like Big Ben face to face. He's seven inches tall, spunky, neighborly—downright good all through. He rings two ways—ten half-minute calls or steadily for five minutes.

Big Ben is six times factory tested. At your jeweler's, $2.50 in the States, $3.00 in Canada. Sent prepaid on receipt of price if your jeweler doesn't stock him.

Westclox folk build more than three million alarms a year—and build them well. All wheels are assembled by a special process—patented, of course. Result—accuracy, less friction, long life.

La Salle, Ill., U.S.A. **Western Clock Co.** Makers of *Westclox*

Other *Westclox*: Baby Ben, Pocket Ben, America, Bingo, Sleep-Meter, Lookout and Ironclad

The logical succession of thoughts or images is used in this advertisement to develop attention into interest

vertisement starts one on a train of images toward a desired result and then introduces irrelevant ideas, the interest will be killed. When statements are so disconnected that we can hold them in mind only by effort, we let them go while we attend to something else. Notice that in the advertisement on page 49, the suggestions are pleasant, they are closely connected and follow each other in logical order. The illustration is pertinent; the man at the plough directs the eye to Big Ben which stands out in almost life size. "Four a. m. in growing time starts the farmer's day—brings a bumper crop of hours, for chores and in the field."

The train of images suggested by text and display leads the interest up to the climax in which conviction is secured—"Big Ben is six times factory tested." "Westclox folk build more than three million alarms a year—and build them well." Type, arrangement, illustration, headline which is specific and unique, and the text it-

The copy in the bristles helps to connect the mental images

THE ADVERTISEMENT READ

self, all hold the interest to the very end. One reads it involuntarily.

The Prophylactic Tooth Brush advertisement, opposite, suggests connected imagery. The copy within the part that does the brushing contains only two ideas: "The shape fits your jaw—the bristles fit your teeth," while the slogan "A clean tooth never decays" is particularly apt.

To create involuntary interest, an advertisement must present connected imagery and make one or two things prominent so that a definite conclusion may be formed. Otherwise there will be no stimulus to decision and action.

3. *Appeal to the imagination.*—One of the chief purposes in advertising is to evoke pleasing images in the mind of the reader.

Success in moving audiences depends upon the ability of the speaker to suggest only a part of the picture he desires his audience to see, but to do so in such a way as to cause them in imagination to reproduce the complete picture.

This is exactly what an advertisement should do. If the reader's imagination is stimulated to follow out the line of images suggested, either by reason or thru the emotions, the battle is more than half won. The factors of reason and emotion will be treated more specifically in later chapters.

An illustration of appeal to the imagination is the Globe-Wernicke advertisement, on page 52, which features the sectional bookcase—"the heart of the

Appeal to the imagination thru copy and illustrations representing various periods in history

THE ADVERTISEMENT READ 53

home"—as the modern substitute for the minstrels, troubadours, jesters and tutors of earlier days. A heart-shaped illustration of each of these has an inscription beside it. The pictures alone stimulate the imagination pleasantly, but the text makes them even more interesting and ties up with the purpose of the advertisement—to show that the Globe-Wernicke is "the center of the family's intellectual life, a hall of learning and a theater of amusement." The text reads as follows:

The Bards of Ancient Greece

Homer, the greatest of these minstrel-historians, is preserved to us in the Globe-Wernicke Sectional Bookcases.

The 11th Century Troubadours

They were the Globe-Wernickes of their day, human fiction shelves, traveling tellers of tales and singers of romance.

The 14th Century Jester

He was the companion of the greatest nobles' idler moments—their uninspired substitute for the volumes of Mark Twain, Swift and Molière, in our Globe-Wernicke Sectional Bookcases today.

The 19th Century Tutor

He was in every wealthy household—the companion and preceptor of every youth; seldom a genius and never so many geniuses as are today within reach of every student, in the Globe-Wernicke Sectional Bookcase.

The pleasant series of images brought up by the text emphasizes the point "Growing as the book collection grows, section being added to section as required, it is the outward symbol of your inward growth."

4. *Use of proper images.*—As images are recalled and reshaped from our previous experiences only, an advertisement should create in the mind of the reader an image of something that lies within his experience. Most society women would not be interested in an analysis of a storage battery, nor would farmers be interested in the mechanical explanation of gas as industrial fuel in a candy factory.

Therefore a universal appeal in an advertisement should be planned so that sufficient numbers of images are created to come within the experience of all prospective readers in order that their imaginations may be stimulated. If the appeal is directed to a certain class only, then the range of appeal need not be so inclusive.

5. *Images should please.*—There are certain images of thought from which we shy like frightened horses. We dislike gloomy suggestions; we do not like to be reminded of pain, of illness, of death. The more pleasant a suggestion is, the more likely is it to get a hearing. A disagreeable image should be suggested only to contrast a pleasant one. The slightest competing mental image will distract the attention from an advertisement that is unpleasantly suggestive in its general tone or makeup.

6. *Appeal to self-interest.*—Primarily every act is based upon self-interest. Of the success of advertising that appeals to self-interest there is no doubt. Convince a man that he will better himself by taking a certain step and, in a great majority of cases, he will do it.

Universal appeals, so called, are appeals to self-interest. An appeal to the desire either for health, honor, fame or a future secured against care or want is one of the strongest pleas for action. Because of the universality of the purchasing power of money, the appeal to self-interest, by showing how it is possible to make, save or employ money more effectively, is one of the strongest. This is shown in the advertisement of the Ætna Casualty and Surety Company on page 56.

Greater salary or income thru education or investment is often featured in a manner to appeal to even the most sluggish minds. Greater comfort coming from the use of some appliance; greater respect from better clothing; greater security because of some form of insurance—these appeals to self-interest stand out among weaker appeals on the advertising pages of every periodical.

The appeal to self-interest may be subtle or open; it may appeal to the emotions or to the pocketbook. No matter to what element of self-interest the advertisement makes its appeal it is reasonably sure to meet with response.

7. *Offer as a means to secure interest.*—Latter-

One of Every 7 Men Is Killed or Injured by Accident Each Year.
Which Will It Be?

YOU may be the one. Your chance is no better than those of the other six. Protect yourself and your family now—while you can. *Three cents a day* will do it if you are in a "Preferred" occupation. The cost of a couple of newspapers brings $1250 to $3250 in case of death by accident, $5 to $10 weekly income, $1,000 to $3,000 for loss of two limbs or eyes, $500 to $1,500 for loss of one hand, foot or eye, $250 for death from any cause. (50 added to the above payments for death if you insure while under forty years of age.)

Larger amounts at proportionate cost.

ÆTNA-IZE

If you have other policies, add this because it's so good. If you have no other policy, get this one now. You're in danger every moment. Send the coupon for the whole story and protect your family while you can.

You get a weekly income when disabled by accident. It isn't only railroad wrecks, shipwrecks and falling elevators you have to fear.

One man was hit in the eye by a snapping rubber band. It put him in bed for six weeks. He was Ætna-ized, so he drew his weekly indemnity.

One man was struck in the head with a baseball. He had to have a surgical operation and was unable to leave his home for three weeks. He drew his weekly Ætna benefit and Ætna paid for his operation.

One man tripped on a flight of stairs, fell, broke his ankle, went to bed for two months. He was Ætna-ized, so he drew a weekly income and turned his hospital bill over to Ætna.

To Ætna-ize means much more than to insure. It means a constantly evident personal interest in the problems of the assured on the part of a great institution. The Ætna is maintained for the service of the policy holder, to advise and aid as well as to protect him, working always for his best interests, and for his complete satisfaction.

Check the coupon and let us tell you all about the kind of insurance in which you are interested.

1. Accident, Health and Disability Insurance of all kinds. *2. Combination Automobile Insurance*—most completely protects car owners against theft, fire, collision, property damage, liability, and includes daily indemnity to owner for loss of use of car—issued for complete or partial coverage of above as desired. *3. Fidelity and Surety Bonds*—for all court proceedings; public and federal office; probate; customs and internal revenue; contracts; bank deposits; license franchise and indemnity; and miscellaneous indemnity bonds of all kinds. *4. Combination Residence Policy*—completely protects home against burglary, glass breakage, water damage, loss of use, and provides liability for personal injuries to guests, public or servants on premises. *5. Burglary Insurance*—moderate cost, covering all types of theft, even by servants, and permitting residence to be unoccupied during four months of the year. *6. Payroll Insurance*—absolute protection at small cost of payroll cash, from bank to distribution.

ÆTNA LIFE INSURANCE COMPANY
with which are affiliated
Ætna Casualty and Surety Company
Automobile Insurance Company of Hartford, Conn.
The largest Institution in the world for the fulfillment of every Insurance need of Society

ÆTNA LIFE INSURANCE COMPANY, Hartford, Conn.
I have checked the kind of insurance I wish to know about:
① ② ③ ④ ⑤ ⑥
(Note: if accident or health, give age)
Name..
Occupation.....................................
Business Address...............................

In this advertisement the appeal to self interest is particularly strong, as shown in the stories relating the experiences of other men

day methods in advertising often economize time, space and attention by using the offer as a means of attracting attention and securing interest. By appealing directly to the desire to obtain a "present" without having to pay for it, the advertiser may throw the offer well to the fore instead of reserving it until the last. "Gift" headlines read as follows: "Music Lessons Free"; "Crochet Book Given!"; "10 Sample Packets of Flower Seeds Free"; "$2.00 and You Get This Superb Cornet"; "Would Shakespeare's Works at One-Fourth Regular Price Interest You?"

These gifts not only suggest the proposed basis for business directly but secure attention and interest from the start.

8. *"Playing up" a hobby.*—Favorable attention is quickly attracted when the subject treated is one which the reader associates with past pleasurable impressions. Common ground is one of the best of introductions.

The hobby or "suppressed function" as a means of securing preliminary interest has provided more than one good opening in the past. In advertising, the catch line which has to do with a hobby will often attract attention as will nothing else.

Sports and pastimes may be systematically "played up." Golf, boating, canoeing, yachting, fishing, bathing and the like are shown by means of attractive crayon and word pictures. The pose of the golfer who has just made a telling stroke or the "fore" of the

Even if You do not Play Golf

—it is great to spend the winter where golfing is good—where all the snow you see is on the tops of mountains far away. It is great to bathe in the ocean in January.

With the lid on the Mediterranean, Southern California has become, more than ever, the Winter Playground of the world—there is no question of that. The only question is how to get there, and

UNION PACIFIC SALT LAKE ROUTE

is Wisdom's answer. This is the warm winter way to Southern California—traverses broad expanses where snow blockades are impossible.

EXTRA-FINE TRAINS BUT NO EXTRA FARE

—Los Angeles Limited and Pacific Limited from Chicago every day, straight to Los Angeles, the Gateway to our American Riviera.
Ask for Set No. 000 of descriptive booklets. Address

W. S. Basinger, G. P. A.
Union Pacific
Omaha, Neb.

T. C. Peck, G. P. A
Salt Lake Route
Los Angeles, Cal.

A good illustration of the "hobby" appeal

player about to drive makes a strong appeal to devotees of the game.

To extend the appeal of the "hobby" advertisement, a double appeal is often made, as in the advertisement of the Union Pacific on the opposite page. In this, the drawing makes a golf "hobby" appeal, while the copy suggests ocean bathing in January.

9. *Interest value of copy.*—Generally speaking, the narrative or dramatic form of copy has more attention and interest value than any other form. We are all fond of a story and an advertisement that is dramatic in its appeal has more chance of being read than a dry recital of facts. Under the dramatic form may be classed the incident, the monolog, the dialog and the story. These will be discussed in a later chapter.

The following lines have decided interest value because of the incident form:

> Napoleon was deathly afraid of a Razor.
> The Emperor Napoleon never permitted anyone near him with an open razor. He did his own shaving and, owing to a sensitive skin, never could get a razor that pleased him. The one that annoyed him least was picked up during the Peninsular Campaign and had a blade of Saracen steel.
> Today nearly all the World's Rulers use a Gillette Safety Razor. The latest convert is Yuan Shih-kai, the great man of China.
> Another is the Premier of New Zealand.
> In the present war the Gillette was used by the leading Generals and by some 3,000,000 men in the trenches and on all fronts.

THE POSTMAN'S PAY

Crane's Linen Lawn
[THE CORRECT WRITING PAPER]

has beauty as well as style. A girl may be beautiful in any costume. She will be smart only when stylishly gowned.

The beauty of Crane's Linen Lawn is inherent in the paper. The style is the result of our knowledge of what is correct and appropriate in fine stationery.

All good stationery departments can show you the five new, smart envelope shapes—Whitley, Premier, Intervale, Geraldine and Copley—any one of which you can select with confidence. Also three new colors—Mignonette, Laurel and Forget-me-not—as well as white.

Usable samples sent on request for twenty-five cents

Intervale   Whitley
Premier   Geraldine
Copley

EATON, CRANE & PIKE COMPANY, *New York, Pittsfield, Mass.*

The type used above is not only pleasing and readable, but its design and arrangement suit the product and lend a tone of quality and distinctiveness to the whole advertisement.

10. *Proper use of type.*—A great deal of advertising matter which is interesting in itself fails to get attention; its type is difficult to read. Type must not only be pleasing in appearance but must be decidedly legible. Every stroke and every letter must be not only instantly visible but instantly readable with normal eyesight.

The type should be made to emphasize the important matter and subordinate the less important part of the text by variation. In the advertisement of Crane's Linen Lawn, on page 60, notice how easily the variety in the kind and size of type leads the eye on to read the entire text.

11. *Emphasis secured by type.*—An advertisement that employs type which emphasizes too many things is not easily read. If everything is emphasized, the result is no emphasis at all. The eye and mind are confused. On the other hand, if nothing is empha-

---

FIRST

In 1915, under the sixteen classifications listed below, The New York Times published 4,764,143 agate lines of advertising—2,464,148 lines, or 1,026 pages, more than any other New York morning newspaper:

CLASSIFICATION.	AGATE LINES.	CLASSIFICATION.	AGATE LINES.
Automobiles	529,953	Men's Furnishings	314,092
Boots and Shoes	76,115	Musical Instruments	261,269
Charity and Religious	63,037	Books	344,581
Druggist Preparations	174,035	Railroads	68,960
Financial	947,579	Steamship and Travel	296,509
Hotels and Restaurants	253,910	Tobacco	144,023
Jewelry	69,861	Women's Specialty Shops	434,746
Beverages	105,864	Miscellaneous	679,609

The circulation of The New York Times (over 320,000 copies every day, including Sunday) represents in one grouping the largest number of discriminating, intelligent and prosperous readers ever recorded by a newspaper.

> ## First!
>
> IN 1915, under the sixteen classifications listed below, The NEW YORK TIMES published 4,764,143 agate lines of advertising—2,464,148 lines, or 1,026 pages more than any other New York morning newspaper:
>
> | CLASSIFICATION | AGATE LINES |
> |---|---|
> | Automobiles | 529,953 |
> | Boots and Shoes | 76,115 |
> | Charity and Religious | 63,037 |
> | Druggist Preparations | 174,035 |
> | Financial | 947,579 |
> | Hotels and Restaurants | 253,910 |
> | Jewelry | 69,861 |
> | Beverages | 105,864 |
> | Men's Furnishings | 314,092 |
> | Musical Instruments | 261,269 |
> | Books | 344,581 |
> | Railroads | 68,960 |
> | Steamship and Travel | 296,509 |
> | Tobacco | 144,023 |
> | Women's Specialty Shops | 434,746 |
> | Miscellaneous | 679,609 |
>
> THE circulation of The NEW YORK TIMES (over 320,000 copies every day, including Sunday) represents in one grouping the largest number of discriminating, intelligent and prosperous readers ever recorded by a newspaper.

sized and the type is the same thruout, the most important matter does not dominate sufficiently and will lack distinction.

Mr. Benjamin Sherbow in his book "Making Type Work" gives a good illustration of securing emphasis and readability by rearrangement of type, design and the use of initials to add color.

Notice, in the illustrations given, that the single tabulation of the items makes the advertisement much more readable than when the items are arranged as in the first example. The greater use of capitals and the heavier border give distinctiveness and consequently greater interest.

12. *Breaking up the reading matter.*—In the rearrangement of the text, notice that the meaning is grasped the more readily because the eye immediately takes in the gist of matter that is broken up. The text but not the sense is broken up.

In the following illustrations the second is much more easily read:

> Style with us means beauty plus
>   A dash of
> Daring—the type
>   of clothes that appeal to young
> Women of Spirit and
>   Taste.

> Style with us means
>   Beauty plus a Dash of Daring
>   the type of clothes
>   that appeal to Young Women
>   of Spirit and Taste.

13. *Use of subheads.*—According to Mr. Sherbow, subheads in advertising print are used for the following reasons:

1. To accent the natural divisions of the story
2. To present a quick summary
3. To put more life and sparkle into a plain type page
4. To avoid monotony
5. To increase the number of places in the text at which the interest of the indifferent reader might be aroused.

The variety of type and arrangement of headings make this advertisement particularly interesting

Subheads should be so spaced that there is no question as to which section or paragraph of the text they belong, whether above or below. In the Systems Bond advertisement opposite, the headings are arranged with proper and pleasing emphasis. The variety of type puts interest into the whole advertisement and accents the chief points. The same is true of the Crane advertisement on page 60.

14. *Importance of letter spacing.*—By spacing is meant "the placing of pieces of type metal of varying degrees of thickness between single letters of type, between words, between lines and between paragraphs." A word or phrase should not suggest a collection of single letters thus:

ALEXANDERHAMILTONINSTITUTE

but should suggest whole words thus:

ALEXANDER HAMILTON INSTITUTE

There should not be too wide a space between words. The spacing employed in this book is correct from the point of view of ease in reading. This is true, too, of the spacing between lines and paragraphs. The spacing employed in the advertisements displayed in this chapter is such that the text reads easily. The subheads, where they appear, are also properly spaced.

15. *Construction and diction.*—Besides the factors already touched upon, the construction of sentences and paragraphs and the choice of words are of great

importance in getting an advertisement read. Short sentences, short paragraphs, the use of simple words that create definite images—all help to stimulate interest. These will be considered more fully in the chapter on "Word Values in Advertising."

REVIEW

How do you distinguish between attention and interest?

Why is it necessary to insure interest in advertising?

Give instances in which the advertiser plays upon the imagination. What are the limitations of this appeal?

What forms may the appeal to self-interest take?

Explain how incident and narrative can be utilized to sustain interest.

Explain the various ways in which typography will enhance or deaden interest in advertisements.

CHAPTER V

MAKING THE ADVERTISEMENT UNDERSTOOD

1. *Simplicity.*—An advertisement must not only attract the reader's attention and secure his interest but, to get results, it must also be so clear that he will understand exactly what it is all about.

If the reader is confused as to what the goods advertised really are and what they are to be used for, he will not be stimulated to decide and act. Simplicity, which of course implies clearness, is particularly necessary in advertising a new product or a new use of a known product. Simplicity means also economy of time and energy. The usual advertisement is read rapidly; the eye runs down the page or sign and catches the words and phrases that stand out plainly as a key to the meaning of the whole. In some department store advertisements simplicity is furthered by the use of short headlines which tell in a few words what the advertisement is about. This gives it "news value" to the reader.

Of all kinds of writing, advertising matter should be the least intricate, cumbersome or involved. Simplicity of style makes for sustained interest, and anything that sustains the interest in an advertisement leads the reader to decision and action.

2. *Clear sentence structure.*—To write clear sentences, the advertiser should know definitely what he wants to say. If he is muddled and is not sure of his ground, he cannot make things clear to the reader.

Again, the explanation must be adapted to the thing advertised. Simple, familiar products admit of brief and simple explanation, while new, unfamiliar and intricate products require greater elaboration.

The third consideration is the choice, number and arrangement of words. The choice of words will be considered in detail in a later chapter. The manner of expressing the thought must be so simple that the reader need spend no time on anything but the thought itself. A sentence should contain every word necessary to convey the idea of the advertiser but not one word more. Each sentence must have unity; that is, there must be one central thought and the subordinate ideas must be related closely to the main thought.

3. *Length of sentences.*—The eye has its own peculiar construction which permits it to perform its functions easily within certain limits, but with increasing effort beyond these limits. If the eye finds that the length of sentences is such that it requires a maximum of effort to focus upon them, it will turn away and select an advertisement which will allow it to function more readily.

Examples of the best prose writing today indicate that to hold the reader's attention the average sentence should not exceed twenty-five words. Varia-

THE ADVERTISEMENT UNDERSTOOD 69

tions, however, are permissible. In fact, variation is necessary in order to produce a pleasing and natural effect.

Compare the following sentences taken from recent advertisements as regards their power of holding attention and the effort required to read them:

> 1.—Out of a realization of the tremendous annual waste of money in freight shipments on the part of the railroads and the shippers due to inefficiency and lack of knowledge came a new era in freight transportation.
> THE IDEA fathered a great commercial organization of 300 railroad and industrial traffic experts banded together to disseminate knowledge to increase efficiency in the handling of freight transportation problems in such a manner as would make this waste no longer possible.
>
> 2.—Here is an opportunity of a lifetime for the young man who can qualify. Tree surgery is remunerative. Tree surgery is healthful, because it supplies an abundance of fresh air and exercise. Tree surgery is fascinating. It is a profession that commands respect.
> Untrained men won't do. Tree surgery as Davey experts practice it is a real science—as difficult and precise in its way as medicine or dentistry.

Few people will grasp all that the first example contains at the first reading. Apart from any other consideration, there are too many words in a sentence for the eye to function easily and for attention to be attracted.

In the second illustration, each sentence suggests

only one idea. The "thought groups" correspond to the sentence structure and the eye functions more easily.

4. *Coherence.*—Coherence means "sticking together." The skilled and experienced advertiser sees that his copy is coherent thruout—that his facts and purposes stick together. He arranges facts in the order in which they occur; he arranges his material so that the ideas follow one another in natural sequence to a climax.

The following advertisement illustrates coherent arrangement. Each paragraph has some connection in thought with the one before and the one after it. There is no sudden transition; the sentences progress logically. The advertisement begins by stating a difficulty; it progresses by suggesting a remedy and explaining its operation; it ends by telling the reader how to secure the thing advertised:

> When a workman without any electrical knowledge starts a motor thru a hand starter he almost invariably starts either too slow or too fast.
>
> In the first case he loses time and burns the contacts on the starter.
>
> In the second case he overloads the motor and blows a fuse or burns up the motor.
>
> E. C. & M. Automatic Motor Starters are built to give the motor-driven machine absolute protection and to minimize the amount of time required to start, without exceeding a safe limit.
>
> As the name implies, E. C. & M. Automatic Motor Starters are absolutely automatic.
>
> To start the motor it is only necessary to push a button or close a small switch.

To stop the motor, push another button or open the switch.

Mail the attached coupon NOW to the nearest branch office and receive a copy of Bulletin 1016, which describes the E. C. & M. Automatic Motor Starter in detail.

5. *Emphasis.*—When the advertiser has chosen his material, he will see that it is not all of equal importance. This must be made evident to the reader. Emphasis is given to the important points by detailed explanation and by prominence of position. Emphasis by prominence of position is generally obtained by placing the most important subject matter at the beginning or the end. An advertisement that begins and ends weakly with matter of minor importance fails to make a clear impression and to get maximum results.

6. *Harmony.*—Copy that is arranged and worded so as to be in harmony with the thought and with the medium in which it is presented, is easily grasped. If it is started in the "ginger" style, this must be maintained thruout. If it opens in a serious tone, the same tone must be maintained thruout. If it is started in a confidential heart-to-heart style, this should be kept up to the close.

The purpose for which copy is prepared is of prime importance. Signs, billboards, back pages in colors, newspapers—all should be considered in relation to the goods advertised, the people to whom the appeal is to be made and the general purpose of the advertisement.

7. *Copy classified as to form.*—Various forms of copy are employed by up-to-date advertisers. They include the argumentative, the descriptive and the narrative forms.

8. *Use of argument.*—In argumentative copy, the advertiser's purpose is to convince a reader of the truth of a proposition. Statements which are not self-evident should be supported by proof. Sometimes this proof consists only of illustrative facts, showing like conditions, or causes that produce similar results.

Arguments should develop readily and easily and should follow each other naturally and with increasing force. Argumentative copy which precludes any question of appeal or reply belongs to the peremptory type. Still other argumentative copy is designed to set at rest any doubts in the reader's mind, by conceding as well as contending. Both methods have their strong points.

9. *Use of the incident.*—The simplest form of the narrative method is the incident. The use of an incident as illustration often serves to make an advertisement much clearer and stronger. The following short incident in the advertisement of the Colt's Patent Fire Arms Manufacturing Company indicates the use of the narrative form:

THE JEWELER'S STORY

"No, Captain, I wasn't afraid—a jewelry store is always liable to holdups. I've had two 'Colt's'—

one in the safe and one behind the counter—for years. I knew my store would be 'picked out' some day. Now that the thief has 'gone up' for five years, I guess they won't mark my front door 'rich pickings—no gun' for some time to come."

A different method of using the incident is illustrated in the following advertisement which, moreover, has news value:

TEA FOR THE TROOPERS

When the Illinois cavalry started on a hike, their canteens were filled with tea and in each soldier's knapsack was a tin of tea. This idea was borrowed from the Japanese. In their war with Russia, every Jap carried a little tea-making outfit. Then, no matter how polluted the water he could be sure of a safe, sterile drink after boiling it, then brewing a tasty, refreshing draught of tea. And what was left he could carry with him, for tea is the one drink that's good hot, cold or in-between—when properly made.

When thus made and served with sugar and cream, LIPTON'S TEA is an excellent FOOD as well as a harmless stimulant.

10. *Use of the monolog.*—Sometimes the article which is advertised is personified. This method is exactly like that of the well-known "Adventures of a Penny" of our early school days. One of the best illustrations is the following:

A Leaf from the Diary of a Cake of Soap
(Being a day's adventure with "Packer's")

8 A. M. THEY started me early this morning, shampooing tiny Ethel. Naturally! Regular shampooing with me means healthy, beautiful hair in after years. Little Ethel will thank her mother then. Thousands of little Ethels have.

11 A. M. I'M in demand. Sixteen-year-old Elizabeth's using me—and you can't see her hair for the foam she's raised! Mother knows that particular care now will help Elizabeth's hair safely through a critical time—and make it silkier and softer, too. If *all* mothers only knew.

3 P. M. FATHER'S home from a dusty train and makes a dash for the bath-tub —and me. Father says I'm too good to be used for shampooing only; he likes me, too, as a bathing soap—for use all over.

5:30 P. M. MOTHER says, "Time for my own shampoo now." So she changes part of me into a beautiful, refreshing lather. She rubs it in. Afterwards she smiles when she sees the pretty lights I've brought to her hair—and the fluffiness and softness, too! Why not?

11. *Use of dialog.*—The dialog furnishes a variation of the narrative form. The danger in its use lies in the tendency to make the dialog too long and

THE ADVERTISEMENT UNDERSTOOD

the attempt to present too many opposing views. The extract given below is taken from an actual advertisement and is a good illustration of the use of the dialog as a form of advertising copy:

A talk with Leopold Godowsky, world-famous Pianist, Composer, Teacher, concerning the remarkable new Duo-Art Pianola

For awhile he sat silent as if adjusting himself to the tremendous import of what he had heard. . . .

And then he spoke.

"It is truly a remarkable experience," he said at length, "to hear the Duo-Art mirror in every essential quality of tone and expression the Fantasie as I played it a week ago!

"It would be inconceivable if I had not actually heard—if I had not recognized my touch, my characteristics, my art itself.

"It is as if," he continued, "I looked at a color photograph not of my face, but of the music-self that is within me!"

"Are you content that your performance shall go down to posterity, represented as it must be, on a record-roll of this Duo-Art Pianola?" I asked. "Don't hesitate to state a doubt if you feel one."

"I recognize the fact that it will be so—and I am satisfied that it SHOULD be so," replied he simply.

The shorter form of dialog is illustrated by the following lines which are indirectly suggestive:

"Will you tuck these into your coat?" said our host. "Will a duck swim?" chuckled Mr. Leaming in reply as he eagerly took the Virginia cigarettes.

12. *Use of the story.*—The story is the most dramatic and perhaps the most useful of narrative appeals. Like any other story, the advertising story is strongest when it has a good plot and a logical succession of incidents that will suggest a final outcome while it conceals what that outcome is to be. The story must arrest the attention at the beginning and hold it to the end. There must be little description; if description is used at all, it should be made subordinate to the narrative.

The story form is best adapted to advertisements of educational courses, text-books and goods that are high priced. The National Commercial Gas Association uses a twenty-page pamphlet entitled "The Story of Nancy Gay" to advertise all-gas kitchens and house heating and lighting by gas. It is a love story much like those of the popular magazines; it holds the interest to the end and impresses the necessity of the use of gas in the home. An excellent use of the story form is made by the company advertising the Grinnell Sprinkler System in their copy "The Watch That Caused a Fire," on the opposite page.

Another use of the story form is shown by the Alexander Hamilton Institute advertisement "At 36—General Manager of a factory and President of a bank." (See page 78.) In this copy is featured the story of a successful business man, and the means by

The watch that caused a fire!

With the help of a snow-storm, the sun, a microscope, a price-tag, and a day of the week.

This is the true story of a queer fire in a jewelry shop in Norwich, Conn.

Could anyone foresee the net result of such a combination of circumstances?

The jeweler put a watch in his window.

Attached to the watch was a celluloid price-tag, lying on crape-paper.

In front of the watch was a small magnifying-glass.

The day was Saturday; the season, winter.

On Sunday morning the sun's rays struck the magnifying-glass and were focused on the celluloid tag, which burst into flame and set fire to the crape-paper. No one saw the fire starting, because—

Snow had fallen, making foot-passage unpleasant and discouraging the usual Sunday procession through the downtown streets.

So a fine blaze was well under way before a passer-by came along and turned in an alarm.

If a chain of circumstances like this can be set up to destroy a man's business, why is everyone so cocksure *his* place can't burn up?

For instance, think how many business men lull themselves into fancied security because their business is housed in a fireproof building. They look at their concrete floors, steel pillars and iron window casings, and say, "Nothing to burn here; nothing *can* catch fire." Then some day they pay a costly price—perhaps the loss of human life—just to learn that a fire will burn in a fireproof building as easily as in a stove.

Others rely on the watchman or the firemen. Fires start and gain headway between the rounds of the watchman. Moreover, the best fire department in the world can hardly get to the scene of a fire in less than five minutes. Delayed alarms often make it much longer. And five minutes is usually enough to give a fire a deathgrip on the vitals of any business.

But the whole business world knows that a plan or system has been worked out by which *any* chain of circumstances starting out to trim up a man's business will be sure to wind up in fore-ordained failure, wind up at a Grinnell Automatic Sprinkler Head and end there with a loud fire-gong and a deluge of spray.

Usually a single sprinkler-head is enough to control the situation. But sometimes when the fire is of an explosive nature, starting in a widespread area simultaneously, as many heads automatically open as are necessary to subdue the blaze.

The chief advantage of the Grinnell System is that it keeps your going business going. Fire insurance reimburses you for your physical losses—your equipment. But the Grinnell prevents the vastly greater loss in the form of unfilled orders, canceled contracts, broken trade connections, loss of trade, profits and prestige, due to the interruptions of business by fire.

And that is the thing you want to think about.

The Grinnell System is manufactured by the General Fire Extinguisher Company, 289 West Exchange St., Providence, R. I. Write to them for their Question Blank and they will help you find out what you can save reducing your insurance rate. The saving ranges from 40 to 90 per cent. It is enough in many cases to pay back the cost of the sprinkler equipment within a few years.

The story form of advertisement used in an effective way

At 36—General Manager of a factory and President of a bank

He rose from machinist's helper to General Manager of the Salem branch of the Manhattan Shirt Company

He increased the business of the Peoples National Bank of Salem 250%, in the face of great difficulty

Mr. Henry A. Spallholz

He says: "The greatest help rendered me by your Course is the way it has broadened my business vision."

Mr. Henry A. Spallholz lives in a small town in New York State. His start in life was about the same as any other young man. His business career began as an errand boy.

He became a machinist's helper—then inspector—then foreman—then assistant superintendent. He is now General Manager of the Salem branch of the Manhattan Shirt Company.

Reorganized a bank

As a bank director, he reorganized the Peoples National Bank of Salem after three examiners tried to close it. He increased the bank's business two hundred and fifty per cent. And, this tremendous increase was made in spite of exceptionally keen competition.

This is what Mr. Spallholz says of the Modern Business Course and Service of the Alexander Hamilton Institute, for which he enrolled in November, 1916:

He sends for information

"Your Course was brought to my attention in November, 1916. I read the booklet, 'Forging Ahead In Business,' carefully, and I knew at once that the Course was just what I needed. So I subscribed.

"As I proceed with my reading, I begin to regret more and more that the Course could not have been placed in my hands a dozen years ago. The time I would have saved cannot be estimated. *And the money value of the information*, had it been in my possession during these years, could be expressed only in large figures.

Makes rapid strides since enrolling

"When I stop to consider the immense amount of time I spent in reading for information before taking the Modern Business Course and Service, and compare it with the rapid strides since enrolling with you, I am surely grateful to the Institute for pointing out this royal road to business fundamentals.

"I believe that the greatest help that the Alexander Hamilton Institute has rendered me is the way it has broadened my business vision."

Every business man should know the fundamentals of his business. A general knowledge of the basic principles underlying *all* businesses is essential to further growth. The *greatness* of a man depends upon the size and soundness of his knowledge.

What is your business problem?

If your problem is self-advancement, if you are now employed where business problems relating to production, finance, accounting, marketing, shipping, exporting, etc., come up for accurate, profitable solving, then you need the help which you will get from the Modern Business Course and Service.

If you are ambitious for the executive's place ahead of you—there is no better way to qualify yourself for that place than equipping yourself with just such an understanding and grasp of fundamentals as you get thru the basic facts you thus acquire.

If you would be a *better* executive—learn from the experience of others those fundamentals that your own work and association have not acquainted you with.

The sooner you enroll, the sooner there is brought to you the very business information and knowledge you need.

Thousands upon thousands of men—just like yourself—have realized their need for just such a training in business fundamentals as the Alexander Hamilton Institute gives. And they have subscribed for the Course.

Among the names of the men enrolled are hundreds of leaders in American business.

A few of the men enrolled

William C. D'Arcy, President of the Associated Advertising Clubs of the World; Melville W. Mix, President of the Dodge Mfg. Co., E. R. Behrend, President of the Hammermill Paper Co., N. A. Hawkins, Manager of Sales, Ford Motor Co., W. H. Ingersoll of Ingersoll dollar watch fame.

Get further information

The head of a large manufacturing plant—a broad-gauged, high-caliber young executive, the President of a bank—tells you in this advertisement how *you* can reach success—if you will profit by his experience and the experiences of thousands of other men whose findings have been similar.

Do as Mr. Spallholz did—get the 112-page book, "Forging Ahead In Business," which we will send you free. It shows you how you can develop yourself for the bigger responsibilities in business—how you can be a better executive—a better leader.

Every person with a career or business to guide, to a bigger, surer success should have this free book and read it carefully.

Fill in and mail the coupon.

Alexander Hamilton Institute

000 Astor Place   New York City

Send me "FORGING AHEAD IN BUSINESS"—Free

Name _____
Print here

Business Address _____

Business Position _____

MODERN BUSINESS

An advertisement in which the success of a young business man is presented in story form

which he achieved his success are described. The story and the Modern Business Course and Service, which the copy advertises, are well tied up.

13. *Educational copy.*—In a broad sense, all copy is educational. This designation is, however, commonly restricted to copy which replaces wrong ideas of a product or service with accurate ideas, or copy that tells one exactly why an article is of value or how to use it to the best advantage.

Educational copy that is specific in its why, how and wherefore, makes an advertisement understood. It can be presented in the narrative, argumentative or descriptive form. The "Tea for the Troopers" advertisement on page 73, and that of the E. C. & M. Motor Starters on page 70, are both educational. The New York Telephone Company's advertisement on page 80 illustrates a method of educating the public to a new use of the telephone.

14. *News copy.*—The advertiser takes advantage of the human interest in what is new when he uses "news" copy. The opening of a new tract in a city gives the real estate advertiser a chance for news copy. The invention of an improvement on a well-known article permits the news element to dominate the copy.

A striking series of advertisements illustrating news copy features the electrically operated trains of the Chicago, Milwaukee and Puget Sound Railway. Waterfalls along the route furnish motive power for these trains for 440 miles. The route is fixed in the

Emergency
Telephone Calls

WHEN SUMMONING HELP by telephone in cases of *fire, lawlessness,* or *accident,* give your call to the operator in such a way that the nature of the emergency will be clearly understood.

Say to the operator, for example:
 "I want to report a fire."
 "I want a policeman."
 "I want an ambulance."

If you are compelled to leave the telephone before the called telephone is answered, tell the operator where help is required.

In other words, give your call to the operator in such a way that she will be able to appreciate the urgency of your message and so make every effort to render aid.

NEW YORK TELEPHONE CO.

The copy here explains the use of the telephone in cases of emergency

THE ADVERTISEMENT UNDERSTOOD

reader's mind, and a novel and interesting trip is suggested.

15. *Historical contrast.*—Historical reference is used effectively by the American Telephone and Telegraph Company in its advertisements to contrast present day facilities for rapid transmission of messages with conditions in past days. The advertisement copy reproduced below is one of the best of this company's advertisements:

ONE NATION; ONE PEOPLE

When Patrick Henry declared that oppression had effaced the boundaries of the several colonies, he voiced the spirit of the First Continental Congress.

In the crisis, the colonies were willing to unite for their common safety, but at that time the people could not immediately act as a whole, because it took so long for news to travel from colony to colony.

The early handicaps of distance and delay were greatly reduced and direct communication was established between communities with the coming of the railroads and the telegraph. They connected places. The telephone connects persons irrespective of place. The telephone system has provided the means of individual communication which brings into one national family, so to speak, the whole people.

The Hartford Fire Insurance and Accident and Indemnity Company began one of its advertisements with a reference to a fact of naval history, and followed this with a reference to a more recent occurrence which fixed the attention and awakened the interest of the reader:

> When the famous frigate *Constitution* fought and captured the *Guerrière* in the War of 1812 the Hartford Fire Insurance Company of Hartford, Conn., was already well established in business. When a submarine sank the *Lusitania* in 1915 the Hartford had maintained for many years a position of supremacy in fire insurance written in the United States. Founded in 1810, the Hartford has progressed in spite of every war.

REVIEW

What are the chief requirements of the language of effective advertisements?

Illustrate the distinction between disjointed and coherent advertisements.

When is argument usefully applied?

Examine the advertising pages of a current magazine and classify contents according to the form of matter, using the classifications given in Sections 7 to 10 of this Chapter.

CHAPTER VI

MAKING THE ADVERTISEMENT PRODUCE ACTION

1. *Getting decision and action.*—An advertisement may perform merely the preliminary functions of securing attention and interest, or may do even less. It may succeed simply in laying the groundwork; that is, it may be placed where it will be seen and read. In a magazine having one hundred pages of advertising, it is possible that fully one-half of this matter will attract the attention and even hold the interest of a reader. He may write for circulars of half a dozen products advertised. His buying capacity, however, may limit him to the selection of one. Obviously, without regard to the advertising value of the impressions the reader receives, only one advertisement in the lot which attracted his attention has actually performed its function by making a sale. Thousands will read where one will buy.

It has been customary to assert that whether or not an order is received, considerable influence—the influence coming from publicity—has been exerted by an advertisement upon the minds of the people. With the growth of advertising, the study of its laws and the making of careful estimates of its cost compared with its returns, has come the realization that the only goal of the advertisement is *favorable action* on the part of the reader.

While occasionally an advertisement "happens" to pull apparently for no definite reason, yet out of a thousand advertisements which have shown remarkable pulling power it is more than probable that nine hundred and ninety-nine conform largely to certain more or less definite laws and principles in securing favorable decision and action.

2. *The process of reasoning.*—Experiments with the working machinery of the minds of men show that there are certain stimuli to which all minds will respond similarly. Human nature is not so difficult to analyze as it was thought to be in the past.

People reach decisions by one of two methods or a combination of the two; they are, reasoning and suggestion.

People, as a rule, are more susceptible to suggestion than they are to reasoning; consequently, action is produced thru suggestion more frequently than thru reasoning. An advertisement should generally make an appeal to the emotions even tho it contains "reason-why" copy. Men who arrive at a decision by the deliberative method are somewhat more difficult to convince than those who respond to suggestion. A person who reasons is one who has a store of stable and definite purposes and who does not decide on an action until he has ascertained whether it is in line with these purposes.

3. *Elements of the reasoning act.*—A deliberative

act in response to an advertisement consists of the following elements:

1. A questioning as to whether the qualities claimed for the goods are really plausible.

2. A feeling that the goods are desirable.

3. A comparison of the desirableness of the advertised goods with the desirableness of other goods.

4. A choice of one or the other and an act to obtain the goods, i.e., the sending of an inquiry, signing an order or going to the store.

Before action comes decision. As there can be no action before one decides to act, the important thing is to secure decision.

4. *Creating and maintaining confidence.*—Practically all action is based upon confidence. With the growth of cooperation, confidence has become enormously strengthened. Daily we buy advertised articles, feeling sure that they will come up to certain standards and having confidence that they would not be advertised so strongly were they not worthy of securing this belief. In this trustfulness, habit plays a great part. If a woman is not in the habit of buying household appliances which revolutionize her work, such as a suction cleaner, a considerable basis of confidence must be laid before she will become a purchaser. If a laborer, whose daily work is confined to physical activities, is solicited to purchase a set of books, a strong basis of confidence must form the root of this act.

In general, the more unusual the proposed course

of action, the greater the necessity for providing a basis of confidence. Hence, the newer the product the greater the time, energy and money which must be spent in establishing confidence by means of advertising. To a prospective purchaser of jewelry, the words, "Tiffany—Diamond—$2,000," may establish practically all the confidence necessary for making a sale. The house of Tiffany is known to be entirely reliable; and diamonds are practically standardized as to price, particularly when guaranteed by a jeweler whose honesty and skill are unquestioned. Confidence may be secured in two ways, thru testimonials or prestige.

5. *Confidence thru testimonials.*—The advertiser views the field, and judges the amount of confidence that buyers must have before they will exchange their money for something that, from their point of view, may or may not be good. Sometimes indorsements are used freely at the beginning of the advertisement, forming a background of confidence. Again, indorsements are brought to the notice at the very time that decision and action are to be impelled. Such advertising proceeds on the basis that not until the reader is asked to part with his money will he really be able to employ confidence-getting references to the best advantage. Advertisers take advantage of this principle when some impelling phrase, backed by an unquestioned testimonial, is placed above the coupon that is to be filled out in ordering.

6. *Confidence thru prestige.*—If testimonials are

given by the unknown or the unimportant members of a community they will have little or no effect. When the suggestion that neighbor Brown has just installed an all-gas kitchen may secure no favorable action on the part of the prospect, the suggestion that the Reverend Dr. Smith or Mayor Grant has done so, may lead him on to do likewise at once. The power of prestige lies in its ability to excite admiration and therefore imitation.

A good illustration of securing confidence thru prestige is found in the advertisement of Community Plate, page 88 which emphasizes a list of prominent women who are users. The fact that so many of the best known hostesses use this plate is enough to lead many purchasers of table silver to ask for the particular kind advertised.

The Pantasote advertisement, page 89, is another illustration of confidence thru prestige.

Other factors that may be classed as means of securing confidence by prestige are: (1) age, as "Rogers Brothers—1847"; (2) size or location of plant or buildings, illustrated in the H. W. Johns-Manville Company advertisement, which gives the location of all its factory branches, number of employes and selling agencies; (3) the guarantee, as illustrated by the advertisement of "Vul Cot" Waste Baskets on page 90; (4) plausibility in the advertisement which in itself invites confidence. An advertisement that rings true is not flamboyant and avoids gush of any sort.

The Vogue of Community Plate

THE BARONESS de MEYER is the daughter of the Duke of Caracciolo of Naples, and the Goddaughter of the late King Edward VII. Her dining room is furnished with the Patrician Design in Community Plate.

A FEW DISTINGUISHED PATRONS of COMMUNITY PLATE
(By Permission)

Mrs. O. H. P Belmont,
  New York
Lady Randolph Churchill,
  London
Baroness de Meyer,
  New York
Mrs. James B. Haggin,
  New York
Mrs. Oliver Harriman,
  New York
Duchess of Rutland,
  London
Mrs. F C. Havemeyer,
  New York
Mrs. Robert Jordan,
  Boston
Mrs. Honoré Palmer,
  Chicago
Princess Troubetzkoy,
  New York
Countess Cadogan,
  London
Mrs. Reginald C. Vanderbilt,
  New York

BREAKFAST ROOM *of the* BARONESS *de* MEYER

in her Venetian Palace, the Palazzo Balbi-Valier

When it comes to silverware, even the staunchest American is an aristocrat at heart. Surely no one could resist the charm and distinction of the Patrician design in Community plate. A chest containing a complete outfit for the table can be bought at prices ranging from $50.00 to $300.00. Or in individual sets; for instance, teaspoons $5.00 the dozen. At your service for 50 years.

ONEIDA COMMUNITY, LTD., ONEIDA, N. Y. CANADIAN PLANT NIAGARA FALLS, ONT Also makers of ONEIDA COMMUNITY RELIANCE PLATE (его Teaspoons, $1.10) and ONEIDA COMMUNITY PAR PLATE

The use of well-known names lends prestige to the product and induces action thru imitation

SWITZERLAND

The Castle of Chillon

The most expensive of all Top Materials — the quality product backed by a quarter century's service and reputation

Genuine Pantasote Top Material

is standard equipment on America's finest cars.

PIERCE ARROW	MARMON	MERCER	WHITE	COLUMBIA
SCRIPPS BOOTH	PREMIER	REO SIX	COLE	CADILLAC
LOCOMOBILE		HUDSON		CHALMERS

Look for Pantasote Label inside the top—it protects you against substitution which is not uncommon

The Pantasote Company · Bowling Green Building, New York City

Names of well-known firms are often used for prestige

This Insures You Against Waste Basket Renewals

THE guarantee which is attached to the bottom of every Vul-Cot Waste Basket is in reality insurance against wear. It guarantees you at least five years' service from every basket, and provides for free replacements, should any fail to give that amount of service.

Large concerns are now buying their waste baskets this VUL-COT way—for instance the Union Central Life Insurance Company of Cincinnati and the Western Electric Company both have over 500 in use.

Buyers figure that at a dollar each for the popular size, waste basket expense can never amount to more than 20c per year.

VUL-COT Waste Baskets
GUARANTEED 5 YEARS

Will not rust, corrode, crack or peel. They will not dent or get jagged edges to scratch other furniture and catch clothing. The solid sides and bottoms prevent small particles from sifting through to the floor, and lastly, they are fire-resisting.

You can see the Vul-Cot Waste Basket at most high-grade stationery stores, or if you write us we will tell you, without any obligation on your part, which of our dealers is nearest you.

American Vulcanized Fibre Co.

540-545 Equitable Bldg.
Wilmington
Delaware

An advertisement which invites confidence thru the use of the guarantee

7. Securing action thru argument.—Briefly, argument has three phases: firstly, the statement of a part of or the whole case that it is desired to prove; secondly, the arguments more or less intimately associated to prove the leading statement or proposition; thirdly, the summary which is substantially a restatement of the proposition as given at first. In advertising, the "offer" or the statement of what the advertiser will do, commonly follows.

Altho clearness and logical arrangement toward a climax are necessary in presenting arguments, the chief thing is to emphasize a supreme point by which, so to speak, a prospect is "swept off his feet." An extended argument should have some point that will turn the scale.

For example, an advertisement of an automobile, designed for a reasoning man, will dwell upon its commercial value, stability, durability and simplicity of mechanism, but will emphasize a certain factor which distinguishes it from others, e.g., its speed or its economy of fuel. Any play upon the emotions such as pride, self-esteem or prestige in owning a car would be folly, and so would the recommending of joy rides or running races on impulse, for a reasoning man who is in the market for a car will understand the danger of loosened bolts, of clogged spark plugs and other disorders.

When the price of milk was raised recently in New York State, Borden's Farm Products Company issued "reason-why" copy in various New York City newspapers. A diagram showed "What Becomes of Your Milk Dollar." The conclusion was that only $3\frac{1}{4}$ cents were retained as profit to the distributor. There were eight paragraphs of copy dwelling on the expense of inspection, of handling the milk in a sanitary way, but the chief point thruout was service. There was no play on the emotions, simply an appeal to the reason, a demonstration that Borden's is the kind of milk to buy because of the *service* that you get all along the line and that Borden's has a reason for existing because your dollar is spent for *your* benefit.

8. *Securing action thru suggestion.*—Few of our actions are the result of a carefully reasoned decision. Most of our acts are the result of imitation, habit, suggestion or some related form of mental phenomenon which is inferior to the reasoning processes. Our most important moves and our most sacred conceptions are reached by means of the merest suggestion. The majority of people are largely influenced by suggestion.

Suggestion has a further value in leading people to a decision in that considerably more time is required to follow a line of reasoning than to follow a series of suggestions. An advertisement may argue the necessity of buying a new suit without eliciting any response, but when the suit is seen on a living model, a woman can easily imagine herself wearing it with consequent improvement in appearance, and most likely she will decide to buy one.

The chief point, then, in the use of suggestion as a

factor to secure decision and action is that it must be put so strongly that competing or adverse ideas are not awakened, or if they should arise, they immediately vanish.

There are three general methods of making a person susceptible to suggestion: (1) by securing his confidence; (2) by repetition; (3) by a device known as indirect suggestion. The first one has been discussed in sections 4, 5 and 6 of this chapter.

9. *Suggestion by repetition*—By continued repetition the advertiser is often able to bring about the state of mind which must precede a purchase. There must be repetition in suggestion; either the suggestion must be repeated in the advertisement or the advertisement must be repeated in the medium. The amount of direct suggestion that it is necessary to use varies directly with the difficulty of the act to be performed. In advertising, where it is admittedly difficult to get the reader to act, direct suggestion may appear again and again thruout the copy.

10. *Indirect suggestion.*—The imitative faculty constantly compels imitation of a suggested course. The well-to-do society reader of *Vogue* or *Vanity Fair,* would, for example, most certainly resist any direct command in an advertisement that she wear a certain fabric or garment. Yet she may be influenced greatly by an illustration featuring the Duchess of Marlborough or the Princess Troubetzkoy in a becoming gown of the advertised material.

Indirect suggestion is employed in the advertise-

In this advertisement a photograph of Mary Garden is used to convey a suggestion

ment of Corticelli dress silks which features a photograph of Violet Heming, and in the advertisement of Mary Garden Perfume which uses a photograph of the noted singer.

An interesting variant of the use of the indirect suggestion may be seen in the advertisement of Weed Chains on page 96. One of the strongest objections the American Chain Company has to overcome in selling its auto-skid chains is that non-skid tires perform the same function and chains are therefore unnecessary. The illustration showing all the well-known non-skids encased in Weed Chains, and the caption "Weed Auto-Skid Chains make all tires BEHAVE," is an indirect suggestion to all car owners to protect themselves with chains even tho they may have non-skid tires.

11. *Securing action thru "limited time."*—A method based on one of the most valuable principles of selling is employed extensively by insurance agents. Learning when a prospective insurer's birth-date will call for an increased rate, the agent points out how money will be saved by taking insurance on or before a certain time. The advertiser conforms to a similar principle in limiting the time in which a certain offer is left open.

"Do it now"; "Act today"; "Sign the coupon"; "Don't delay"—these and hundreds of other direct commands look out from the pages of every newspaper and magazine, and strike the observer's eye from every billboard. Sometimes these phrases are

Weed *Anti-Skid* Chains
Make All Tires Behave

THE ABOVE ADVERTISEMENT WAS SUGGESTED BY A CAR OWNER who has the best interests of motoring at heart. Experience taught him that tire chains are the only mechanical device yet invented that is absolutely dependable to make slippery roads safe.

We want more suggestions for the chain campaign to insure motoring safety for everyone. The campaign which is of immediate, personal concern to every man who wants to protect himself, his wife, his children—from the driver, always ready to take the gambler's chance. We want *your* ideas.

Help Us Insure Motoring Safety for Everyone

AMERICAN CHAIN COMPANY, Incorporated
BRIDGEPORT, CONNECTICUT

In Canada: Dominion Chain Company, Ltd., Niagara Falls, Ontario

Largest Chain Manufacturers in the World

THE COMPLETE CHAIN LINE—ALL TYPES, ALL SIZES, ALL FINISHES—FROM PLUMBERS' SAFETY CHAIN TO SHIPS' ANCHOR CHAIN

The indirect suggestion from an angle different from that in the preceding advertisement, is given here

used as headlines; at others, they form the backbone of the advertisement. Often imperative phrases or sentences are placed above the order coupon. Sometimes they are presented in the form of a rhymed jingle that sticks in the memory like a burr in a coat.

Note this coupon, taken from an advertisement

*Why Wait to Answer a
Later Advertisement?
Clip the Coupon of This One*

INFORMATION COUPON
The Oliver Typewriter Company
108-B Oliver Typewriter Bldg., Chicago, Ill.
............Ship me a new Oliver Nine for five days free inspection. If I keep it I will pay $49 at the rate of $3 per month. The title to remain in you until fully paid for.
My shipping point is..
............Do not send a machine until I order it. Mail me your book—"The High Cost of Typewriters—The Reason and the Remedy." Your de luxe catalogs and further information.
Name
Street Address
City   State

An effective use of the coupon in a way
to bring quick results

of the Oliver Typewriter Company. The question above the coupon "Why wait to answer a later advertisement? Clip the coupon of this one," altho not featuring a "limited time" appeal, tends to secure action because of its direct suggestion.

Restrictions upon anything usually make that thing desirable. This tendency has been turned to constructive use in advertising, by limiting the time in which a given offer will stay open. Usually the offer has to do with a "special" price which is to be raised after a certain period of time has elapsed. The advertisers of the new Encyclopedia Britannica published the date on which the price would be materially advanced, thus automatically stimulating orders.

12. *Securing action thru "free offer."*—There is in all of us an inherent love of "getting something for nothing." Anything offered free, therefore, always attracts, aside from the immediate consideration that it appeals to our natural cupidity. The basic fact that the prize must often be paid for indirectly does not usually detract from its value. The advertiser who makes a bid for action by means of free samples, booklets or service is, therefore, conforming to an important psychological principle. The free offer that he makes may not actually sell the goods, but as a means of getting a reply, it is of rare value.

The "free offer" may secure a position as an attracter of attention at the beginning of an advertisement. Many advertisers, however, prefer to use it chiefly in inducing decision and action. In this case, the free offer is featured in the close of the advertisement, often with such skill that a high percentage of favorable decisions is bound to result.

13. *Making it easy to act.*—The advertisement that requires a minimum of thinking effort on the part of the prospective customer stands the best chance of getting the order. But the sale is by no means made at the instant the mind decides. There are certain mechanical operations which are necessary before the purchaser is really in possession of the thing he decides to buy. When it is necessary to write a letter, to inclose check, draft or money order, to stamp and mail the envelop, many sales are lost. These obstacles are guarded against when the number of mechanical processes which must be performed is cut down to a minimum. Suggestions, both direct and indirect, reduce the mental effort required, while definite, easily-carried-out directions reduce the physical effort.

"Fill in your name and address on the attached coupon. Place it in an envelop and mail to us," is not only a definite direction, but calls attention to the ease of the necessary operations. "Check the booklet you want," not only induces action by direction, it makes it easy to act. The corner coupon, needing but a single clip to separate it from the rest of the advertisement, was a long step forward in reducing obstacles to a decision which is the final factor in producing action.

Direct and indirect suggestion, carefully and logically worked out arguments that aid in deliberation, combined with mechanical ease of response are to be sought in the preparation of advertisements. The barrier between the suggested act and its performance must be made as slight as possible, no matter whether the argumentative or the emotional appeal is used.

REVIEW

Outline the steps thru which the decision to act upon an advertisement is reached.

Describe the different means thru which confidence is gained and maintained, and action stimulated.

Why is it important to make the buyer's action easy? Describe some of the devices used to attain this end.

CHAPTER VII

HUMAN APPEALS IN ADVERTISING

1. *What are human appeals?*—Under human appeals in advertising we may include any appeal to the consumer which arouses his interest thru sentiment, emotion or any one of the senses. For example, the appeals to fear, or to love, or to taste are human appeals. It may be said that practically all advertising which gets results is human appeal advertising; advertising which lacks that appeal lacks human interest and where there is no interest there can, of course, be no inducement to action.

The advertiser requires an intimate knowledge of the operation of the human mind. Advertising has, in fact, been defined as "the operation of one mind upon another in marketing a product or service." This definition, while general, is fairly accurate. Thoughts arising in the mind of one person are communicated in advertising to another mind or minds. Obviously, when the first mind can induce the second mind to act according to the desires of the first, the object of advertising has been fulfilled.

2. *Appeal to the senses.*—The study of human appeals is, in part, a study of certain states, impulses, propensities and faculties. Briefly, sensation is the

response to a stimulus. The sensations of the eye differentiate the colors, forms, shapes and sizes of things; those of the ear are aware of sounds; those of the skin are conscious of warmth, coldness, sharpness, lightness and heaviness; then there are the body currents that make us aware of pain, pleasure and so on. Sight is a sense which acts as interpreter to all the other senses. Only thru what we see in an advertisement can we recognize the appeal to other senses—touch, taste, smell and sound.

The advertiser would have no difficulty usually in making a sale if the prospective buyer could see, feel, hear, taste or smell the object he desires to sell, instead of having to depend on the printed word or illustration. However, it is possible by word and illustration to picture other people enjoying, *thru their senses,* the product advertised.

Because of the law of suggestion, and because human beings readily imitate what they see, i.e., carry out in action what is suggested to them, the advertiser is able to appeal to the senses of his readers. Imagination and the desire to imitate others experiencing enjoyment makes possible an appeal to the eye which spreads to the other senses.

3. *Touch.*—The appeal to the sense of touch is well brought out in the advertisement of Woodbury's Soap under the caption "A Skin You Love to Touch." Here the suggestion that by the use of Woodbury's Soap the complexion becomes greatly improved and the skin smooth to touch makes an appeal which is

A skin you love to touch

Painting by
CHARLES CHAMBERS

You, too, can have the charm of
"A skin you love to touch"

YOU, TOO, CAN HAVE THE CHARM of a skin that's soft, clear, radiant. Everyone admires it. Every girl longs for it. To have your skin as lovely as it ought to be—soft, clear, colorful—all you need is to give it the proper care for its needs.

No matter how much you may have neglected your skin, you can begin at once to improve it. New skin is forming every day as old skin dies. If you give this new skin the right care *every day*, you can keep it fresh and radiant. Such things as blackheads, blemishes and unsightly spots, you can, with the proper treatment, correct.

Begin today to give your skin the right treatment for its particular needs. You will find the famous treatments for all the commoner skin troubles in the booklet wrapped around every cake of Woodbury's Facial Soap.

You will find that a cake of Woodbury's lasts for a month or six weeks of any treatment and for general cleansing use. It sells for 25c at drug stores and toilet goods counters throughout the United States and Canada.

This beautiful picture for framing
Send for your copy today!

Picture with sample cake of soap, booklet of treatments and a sample of Facial Powder for 25c

This picture is Charles Chambers' interpretation of "A Skin You Love to Touch." It has been reproduced from the original oil painting, in full colors and on fine quality paper, expressly for framing. No printed matter on it. Size 15x19 inches.

For 25c we will send you one of these beautiful reproductions with a trial size cake of Woodbury's Facial Soap—large enough for a week's treatment—also the booklet of treatments—"A Skin You Love to Touch," and a sample of Woodbury's Facial Powder. Thousands will want this picture. Send for your copy at once.

Write today to The Andrew Jergens Co., 1903 Spring Grove Avenue, Cincinnati, Ohio. *If you live in Canada, address: The Andrew Jergens Co., Limited, 1903 Sherbrooke Street, Perth, Ontario.*

Both the illustration and the copy make a strong appeal to the sense of touch

103

hard to resist. The illustration, too, is in harmony with the text and further carries out the suggestion of this appeal. Other products in which this appeal is used are underwear, shoes and clothing where the "comfortable feeling," "non-irritating to skin" is featured.

The suggestion of the lightness of touch with which a razor may be used after the application of the foamy lather made by a certain cream, "the Gillette shave is velvet-smooth, no matter how wiry the beard," furnishes further illustration.

4. *Taste.*—The sense of taste has a wide range of practical use in making an appeal, because of the comparative ease with which memories of taste are reawakened. Food products and beverages whose principal selling point is based on taste, are often advertised in this way. It is not easy by means of words alone to make a reader imagine the taste of a thing. An illustration usually makes it much clearer. If words only are used, they must furnish a vivid stimulus to the imagination.

The following description appears under an illustration of vegetables grouped around the well-known "Campbell Kid." It is not only appetizing but gives properties, spiciness and variety of ingredients.

> The stock, made from selected beef, is of remarkable strength and fine flavor. You could not have a more nourishing foundation for vegetable soup.
> The white potatoes, sweet potatoes, carrots and yellow turnips give both substance and flavor.

HUMAN APPEALS

> These we cut into attractive little cubes—or "dice" as they are called.
>
> We include "baby" lima beans, tender peas, tomatoes, sweet corn, cabbage and juicy green okra.
>
> We add rice and barley, celery, parsley and other delicate herbs, also a hint merely of leek and onion. And we blend in a sprinkling of "alphabet" macaroni with just a touch of sweet red peppers to give a pleasing snappy effect to the combination.

In the Crisco cut, on the next page, there is a picture of an appetizing pie made with Crisco. The knowing smile of Grandmother and the expectant look of the rest of the family make a good appeal to the sense of taste.

The Royal Baking Powder Boy furnishes an excellent illustration of plain, direct suggestion. The picture, on page 107, speaks for itself and needs no amplification by means of words.

5. *Smell.*—The sense of smell is closely related to the sense of taste. Therefore in advertising edible products, a combined appeal may be made to both taste and smell. In advertising coffee, the suggestive steaming of the liquid from the cup, pot or percolator is the usual method employed to make this appeal.

Odors have a wonderful power to reawaken memories. The scent of a flower often brings back the most vivid recollections. Because of this, an appeal to the sense of smell may be effectively made by the skilled advertiser. The choice of words in the

The copy and the illustration harmonize well in bringing out an appeal to taste

THE APPETIZING FLAVOR

reaches perfection in cakes, biscuit and muffins made with

ROYAL BAKING POWDER

Made from Cream of Tartar, which is derived from grapes, a delicious, wholesome fruit, Royal Baking Powder adds none but healthful qualities to the food.

Many baking powders contain materials derived from mineral acids, which are used instead of Cream of Tartar because they are cheaper.

The label on the baking powder can gives the names of all ingredients. Read it carefully and remember it never pays to sacrifice quality and healthfulness for low price.

The illustration in itself makes an unusually strong appeal to the sense of taste

COLGATE'S

CASHMERE BOUQUET
TOILET SOAP

In its flower-born fragrance Cashmere Bouquet Soap suggests the rifled treasures of an old-fashioned garden. Delicate, yet lasting; piquant, yet refined, reminiscent, yet elusive; favored by those of particular taste today, as it was in Grandmother's time.

Nor is that exquisite perfume its sole attraction, for Cashmere Bouquet Soap is luxuriant in its lather and so wholesomely pure that it is safe for baby's delicate skin. It is an economical soap too, wearing down thriftily to a tissue-like thinness, and "hard milled" so that it does not soften and waste as do some soaps when left wet in the soap dish.

Medium Size
10¢ a cake

Large Size
25¢ a cake

Large size cakes, 3 in a box
Medium size cakes, 6 in a box

COLGATE & CO.   Established 1806   NEW YORK

An appeal to the sense of smell

Colgate advertisement together with the illustration of the basket of flowers and the butterflies makes the copy pleasantly stimulating.

The American Tobacco Company has been advertising its "Tuxedo" brand tobacco almost entirely on the appeal to the sense of smell. A typical advertisement from the campaign is reproduced on page 110.

6. *Sound.*—Sound, "the most vibratory of the senses," is one to which the appeal is usually made by picturing results. Advertisements of phonographs, depicting upon the faces of the hearers the pleasure of the music being produced, make a "result appeal." The Grafonola advertisement, on page 111, suggests the sound of music by the position of the lips and the expression on the faces of the ministrels.

In general, appeals to the sense of sound in advertising lack force because of the difficulty in representing volume and quality which are so essential in suggesting musical tones.

7. *Appeal to emotions.*—Emotion is defined as any strong movement or perturbation of the conscious mind. The aphorism that emotion is "thought in a glow," is a particularly happy one. If we think of an ordinary steel bar as being simply warm to the touch, and another steel bar heated until it glows and sparkles, we have a fairly correct analogy between ordinary thought and emotional thought.

Among the primary emotions are love, hate, joy, grief, anger, fear, pride; and these make the sounding board of human nature vibrate most intensely.

Illustrating an appeal to the sense of smell

"Ye Olde Minstrelle Outdone"

Let a COLUMBIA sing the *Christmas Carols* in your home

The minstrels who sang of the "tidings of great joy" in the days of long ago are supplanted by the minstrel of modern days—the

COLUMBIA GRAFONOLA

The Columbia Grafonola truly brings "tidings of great joy" at Christmas-tide. There is no gift quite like it, no gift so welcome, no gift that could bring a more lasting joy. The Columbia Grafonola is the "gift supreme"—a gift around which more dreams are woven, which brings more pleasure day after day, than any other gift you may give or receive—and it is a gift within the means of all.

Prices from $15 to $350—*on special Christmas terms*

Columbia Records
Grafonola

Illustrates an appeal to the sense of sound

The secondary emotions have less intense bodily reactions; they include numerous shadings of the primary emotions—such as dislike, spite, jealousy, distaste, resentment and so on.

8. *Reaching the emotions.*—A successful insurance man says: "In selling accident insurance, a well-drawn picture of your prospect's friends passing the hat for him when he is laid up, is worth a hundred pages of fine-type specifications." Even discounting this statement liberally, it is true that the emotions count greatly in the appeal.

The emotions are much more easily played upon than reason. Fear, hatred, prejudice may be aroused instantly while the reasoning faculties are left cold.

There is always the danger of carrying the appeal to the emotions to the extreme. The bank advertiser who devoted considerable space in a newspaper telling how a man was frightened into becoming a bank depositor because he found himself without money to bury his baby is an example of a suggestion that is too direct.

While now and then a skilled advertiser is able to make a satisfactory negative, nonconstructive appeal, as that referring to death, dishonor, loss and the like, yet it can be safely set down as a principle that usually only the positive side of appeals to the emotions should be used. If there seems to be no positive appeal, or if the positive appeal fails to produce results, only then may it be necessary to try out a conservative emotional appeal from the negative angle.

> **WESTERN UNION TELEGRAM**
>
> NEW YORK CITY JAN 19 1916
>
> MRS L H HILL
> 1063 NEWTON AVE
> CHICAGO ILL
>
> All SAFE AND SOUND WAS NOT NEAR
> SUBWAY DISASTER
>   TOM

THIS telegram is reproduced to show how easy it is to care for the feelings of the women folks at home. They have a habit of worrying, even when there is very little cause.

If you happen to be near an accident or a catastrophe of any kind, think how much worry and anxiety a telegram will save.

Western Union carries your thoughtful message to the folks long before the scare-lines in the newspapers have had time to set them worrying.

THE WESTERN UNION TELEGRAPH CO.

Illustrating a positive and direct appeal to the emotions

Gillette Safety Razor

The Gillette is the Service Razor

UNCLE SAM wants his boys to be comfortable—healthy men and healthy surroundings—alert, set-up, fit, and *clean shaved.*

Trim, time-saving men in every branch of the Service—have tested out all the razors there are—and settled on the Gillette.

In nearly four years of the Great War the Gillette has made good with every shaving problem a man can put up to it—met every condition of face and skin—delivered the velvet-smooth shave in the worst possible conditions.

It's always on the job—with hot or cold water—in cold or hot weather.

It's the razor that ten million up-and-coming men—the men who are doing the big things in all parts of the world—find 100% dependable.

Hundreds of thousands of fighting men who know the value of time, comfort, and soldierly appearance won't have any other razor. Blades are always sharp—always ready. No strops or hones to clutter up the kit. It can be tucked away in the breast pocket, the pack, or the ditty box. No Stropping—No Honing.

Have you seen the New Gillettes specially designed for the Fighting Man?

THESE models were designed by members of the Gillette Organization who have seen service with the Colors and know what the soldier is up against.

Hundreds of officers and men are buying them—the U. S. Service Set in metal case, and the new Khaki-covered sets for Uncle Sam's soldiers and officers.

The Gillette is the one razor for the man who is doing things—the one razor with world-wide use and reputation.

When a man wants new Blades he can get them at any Post Exchange or Y M C A Hut—here in America or Overseas.

Our Paris Office carries stocks—is constantly supplying the American Expeditionary Forces. Gillette Safety Razors and Blades on sale everywhere in France, England, Italy and the Eastern battle fronts.

GILLETTE SAFETY RAZOR COMPANY
BOSTON, MASS., U. S. A.

GILLETTE SAFETY RAZOR COMPANY, OF CANADA, LTD
73 ST. ALEXANDER ST., MONTREAL

GILLETTE SAFETY RAZOR SOCIETE ANONYME
17 BIS, RUE LA BOETIE, PARIS, FRANCE

VEDOVA TOSI QUIRINO & FIGLI
VIA SENATO, 18, MILAN, ITALY

GILLETTE SAFETY RAZOR, LIMITED
200 GREAT PORTLAND ST., LONDON, W., ENGLAND

A. G. MICHELES
52 LITEINY, PETROGRAD, RUSSIA

This advertisement appeals directly to a man's pride—to his desire to look well

HUMAN APPEALS

The Western Union Telegraph Company's advertisement on page 113, illustrates a positive, direct appeal to the emotions. Notice the telegram reads, "Am safe and sound. Was not near subway disaster." The advertisement then goes on: "Think how much worry and anxiety a telegram will save." The suggestion is constructive and positive and the reader feels kindly toward the telegram and kindly toward the company that can help to keep off thoughts of anxiety.

The Gillette advertisement is a positive, constructive appeal to the universal emotion of pride and the desire to look well. The statement that Uncle Sam wants his boys to be fit and *clean shaved* is joined to the positive, direct suggestion that the Gillette delivers the velvet-smooth shave in the worst possible conditions.

9. *Appeal to instinct.*—Instinct is a natural, spontaneous impulse to act in a certain way. The strongest human instinct of all, perhaps, is the mother impulse. In the term, mother impulse or instinct, is included the intense inclination of every woman to protect the child. It is to this passion that the advertiser may appeal most effectively when dealing with women. The slightest suggestion will call forth not only strong emotion, but the desired act itself.

What woman is not interested in the following text whose strongest point is the appeal to instinct?

WHAT COCOA FOR BILLY'S BREAKFAST?

> Billy is just a rosy-cheeked, freckle-nosed boy. He's all boy, too, and don't you forget it.
>
> Billy is blessed with a whopping big "boy" appetite, coupled with an utter disregard of what he eats or drinks or when or why.
>
> For a good many mornings now Billy has been starting off to school or play with a good warm cup of LOWNEY'S Cocoa under his little belt.
>
> Perhaps you ask, "Why LOWNEY'S?"
>
> Quite a while ago Billy's mother found that a lot of cocoas had been selfishly "robbed" of the nutriment her boy needed—a large percentage of the nutritive butter fats had been removed.
>
> Then she found that LOWNEY'S Cocoa contained just 25% of these "child-helping" butter fats. She learned that this correct proportion gave her "Billy-Boy" all the good, wholesome nourishment he could assimilate, yet taxed his young digestion not a bit. That is why so many mothers say, "for your children's sake—LOWNEY'S."

The appeal in the "Reznor" Gas Heater advertisement is made to the mother instinct. The illustration of Big Sister playing with Baby as Mother comes to give him his bath in a room warmed by the gas heater, taken together with the headline, instantly registers the sense of protection and comfort for the baby which all mothers feel.

10. *Feminine intuition.*—There are a few other points to be kept in mind when preparing advertising for women. Because of the primitive instinct to protect and foster children, women have developed quick and accurate judgment as to what course to pursue

Heats the Whole Room

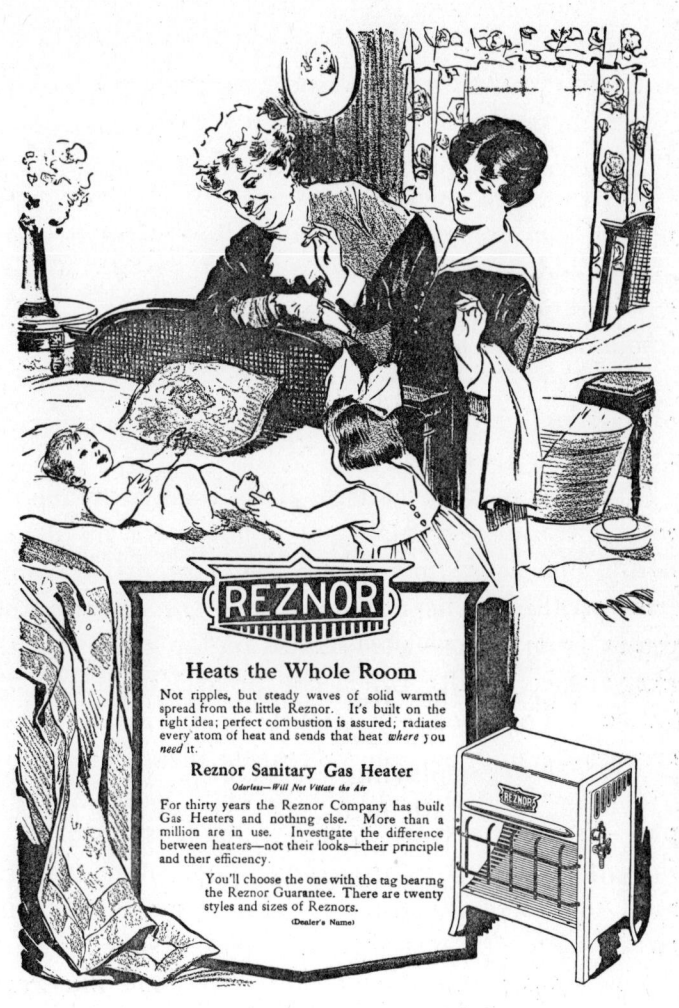

Not ripples, but steady waves of solid warmth spread from the little Reznor. It's built on the right idea; perfect combustion is assured; radiates every atom of heat and sends that heat *where* you *need* it.

Reznor Sanitary Gas Heater
Odorless—Will Not Vitiate the Air

For thirty years the Reznor Company has built Gas Heaters and nothing else. More than a million are in use. Investigate the difference between heaters—not their looks—their principle and their efficiency.

You'll choose the one with the tag bearing the Reznor Guarantee. There are twenty styles and sizes of Reznors.

(Dealer's Name)

A direct appeal to a mother's instinctive love for her children when these children are in peril. This is expressed by what we call feminine intuition. A woman's caution leads her to conservatism, timidity, apprehensiveness and a natural disinclination toward innovations. When an innovation is introduced, it should be explained upon a basis of existing and tried out things and fortified by a direct appeal to her instinctive love of the child. In their preparation of copy for women, advertisers have not paid sufficient attention to this fundamental and passionate impulse.

11. *Appeal to imagination.*—The "picturing power of the mind" is one faculty to which the advertiser can invariably appeal.

Thru the magic of imagination, the man without a college training sees himself honored for his education. The poor man senses the power that comes from wealth. The unknown feels the prestige that comes from fame—all because of the power of the imaginative faculty which can project itself into the future. That peculiar quality of description which arouses the imagination, recreating pleasurable recollections, even adding to the pleasing pictures of the past—is a valuable asset, one of the most valuable to the advertiser who is appealing to any other than the most matter-of-fact trade. This is more fully discussed under "Word Values in Advertising."

The Paramount Pictures advertisement illustrates an appeal to the imagination. Notice how it carries the reader out and beyond the immediate limits of his environment with these statements:

Let's live a life in two hours—

OUT goes the library lamp.

Be sure you have the key!

We're bound for a chair in a theatre that *knows* and *shows* what we want to see in photoplays.

We don't have to hunt for it—don't even have to take a chance on what we'll see. The name of the play? Who cares? It's a Paramount or Artcraft picture; and that's saying we'll see foremost stars, superbly directed in clean motion pictures.

* * * *

Time! Who counts the time of clocks in this wonderful land.

Our heart is the time-table of our emotions. A magician somewhere waves his wand, and we're off on our travels into the realms of laughter and tears; of sighs and regrets; of love and adventure.

(Please be reminded that these are Paramount and Artcraft motion pictures, not just "motion pictures.") We're heroes; we're against the villain and all his wiles; we're lovers, hanging on the "yes" of the heroine; we're fond mothers and stern fathers; we're ambitious youths; we're struggling girls; we're Cinderella and Prince Charming; we are the king and we are the beggar—we are all things and all men.

We are not forty or eighty or sixty-two during those magical hours we watch Paramount and Artcraft stories on the screen. We are youthful romancers living in another world.

* * * *

And when those two absorbing hours have flitted past—we rouse ourselves and readjust our viewpoint to taxes and potatoes.

But we can't forget the pictures that work such a happy transformation in us—we remember they're Paramount and Artcraft pictures—

the ultimate in the genius of great stars
the ultimate in directing craft
the ultimate in character of their stories

all combining to produce *better* pictures, *clean* pictures—pictures worth your while and mine.

Paramount and Artcraft Pictures
"FOREMOST STARS, SUPERBLY DIRECTED, IN CLEAN MOTION PICTURES"

Three Ways to Know how to be sure of seeing Paramount and Artcraft Motion Picture

one By seeing these trade-marks or name in the advertisements of your local theatres.

two By seeing these trade-marks or names on the front of the theatre or in the lobby.

three By seeing these trade-marks or names flashed on the screen inside the theatre.

FAMOUS PLAYERS–LASKY CORPORATION
ADOLPH ZUKOR *Pres.* JESSE L.LASKY *Vice Pres.* CECIL B. DE MILLE *Director General*
NEW YORK

An advertisement which appeals strongly to the imagination

119

> A magician somewhere waves his wand, and we're off on our travels into the realms of laughter and tears; of sighs and regrets; of love and adventure.
>
> We're heroes, we're against the villain and all his wiles; we're lovers, hanging on the "yes" of the heroine; we're fond mothers and stern fathers; we're ambitious youths; we're struggling girls; we're Cinderella and Prince Charming; we are the king and we are the beggar—we are all things and all men.

An appeal like this sets one's imagination to work picturing himself in the condition which the advertising suggests.

12. *Romance of the commonplace.*—One way of arousing the imaginative faculty is by glorifying the commonplace. This is analogous to "thought in a glow." Put life into dry facts and you have a strong appeal to the imagination. One of the finest illustrations of this is found in the series of advertisements of Revillon Frères, in which is told the whole story of the fur industry as carried on by this company thru its traders and trappers. One illustration of the series is shown on page 121. In it, the "romance of the commonplace" is well emphasized.

In the following advertisement of the Hampton Shops, sentiment is woven around matter-of-fact furniture:

> In those delightful old English Rooms, whose quiet dignity carries us back to the spacious days of Queen Elizabeth, the harmony between the centuries-old Furniture and its surroundings is so intimate as to be difficult of attainment in our own day.

THE STORY OF REVILLON FURS

© 1918

A Trading Post and Trader

THE post trader is absolute ruler in his little world. He has his Indian dog driver, and helper, and in the larger posts an assistant to keep his accounts. He must be a shrewd merchant and an excellent judge of furs, since he is responsible for the commercial success of his post. As he can buy stock only at stated and very infrequent intervals, he must be thoroughly acquainted with the needs of his customers.

The Revillon post store is an interesting place, with a curiously mixed stock of dry goods, fire arms, tools and provisions. This merchandise is exchanged by the trader for the furs which eventually supply our New York workrooms.

Revillon Frères
ESTABLISHED 1723
Fifth Avenue at 53rd Street

How advertising can be used to tell most interestingly the story of commonplace products, is well illustrated by this piece of copy

122   ADVERTISING PRINCIPLES

13. *Appeal to reason.*—Altho emotional appeals are likely to be more popular than appeals to reason, yet certain things because of their mechanism, price and general utility lend themselves easily to the reason-why argument.

> ## Would you name a friend as trustee?
>
> Often it is desired to keep an estate under the supervision of a friend or member of the family, and yet not burden him with its management.
>
> If you appoint a friend or relative as co-executor and co-trustee with the Bankers Trust Company, your estate will have the desired personal attention and he will be relieved of most of the burden of work and responsibility. Caring for estates and trusts is the primary object of the Trust Company, and it has every facility for managing them safely and advantageously.
>
> The officers of this Company will be glad to confer with you, or to send you information regarding any trust or banking business you may have in mind.
>
> **BANKERS TRUST COMPANY**
> 16 Wall Street   New York
> Resources over $250,000,000
>
> *Bankers Trust Company's Building*

Illustrating the "reason why" type of copy

Appeals to reason are particularly potent in those matters where saving of time, labor or energy are effected. The Bankers' Trust Company's advertisement shown here is a good illustration of "reason-why" copy. When the advertiser for the business phonograph states that there is no reason why letters should be written twice, first in shorthand and later in typewriting, he is making a definite appeal to reason into which sentiment need not enter. When the tailor, disregarding all other factors, shows that a tailor-made suit costs less than two or three ready-made suits, he appeals to reason. By shutting out the entire emotional side of the argument and keeping the reader's mind on the plane of reason, it is occasionally possible to make a sale when the emotional appeal would be valueless.

REVIEW

Describe the means employed by the advertiser to secure an appeal to the senses of touch, taste, smell and sound, and name instances illustrating this point, adding some not mentioned in the Text.

Why is the appeal to the emotions stronger than the appeal to reason? Give illustrations of an effective emotional appeal.

How is the appeal to the imagination employed in advertising articles of comparatively common use?

Give illustrations of the use of "reason-why" copy. To what class of products is it best adapted?

CHAPTER VIII

WORD VALUES IN ADVERTISING

1. *Words are tools of advertising.*—In the mechanism of advertising there are three factors: 1, the words and illustrations which are the tools; 2, the layout which is the framework; 3, the balanced arrangement of the whole advertisement, which includes the illustration, the decoration and the copy.

The words are the tools by which the advertiser conveys certain ideas of his own to the prospective customer. The larger the number and the greater the variety of words he has at his command the more readily can he "put across" his thoughts into the minds of others.

The question of word values is of tremendous importance in advertising. The use of the right word, that is, the word that has the greatest suggestive power for the particular instance, is a matter requiring close study.

As men have greater demands made on their time, word values take on a new significance. The style of successful authors today is as different from the stiff, roundabout, elaborate phraseology of even two generations ago as our modes of travel are different from those of the stage coach era. New words are coined, sentences and paragraphs are shorter, and our phrases are concrete. Nowhere is conformity to these modern standards more necessary than in the writing of advertisements.

2. *Economizing the reader's time.*—In this complex age, economy of the reader's time must be considered in wording an advertisement. This factor is of importance no matter to whom the message is addressed. In his "Philosophy of Style," Herbert Spencer gives us the fundamental reason for making language clear and simple:

> Regarding language as an apparatus of symbols for the conveyance of thought, we may say that as in a mechanical apparatus, the more simple and better arranged its parts, the greater will be the effect produced. In either case, whatever force is absorbed by the machine is deducted from the result. A reader or listener has at each moment but a limited amount of mental power available. To recognize and interpret the symbols presented to him requires part of this power; to arrange and combine the images suggested requires a further part; and only that part which remains can be used for realizing the thought conveyed. Hence, the more time and attention it takes to receive and understand each sentence, the less time and attention can be given to the contained idea, and the less vividly will that idea be conceived.

Consequently, if the language and the sentence structure of an advertisement are such that the message is quickly grasped, the more likely is it that the appeal will effect a sale of the thing advertised. The ideas must be simple, they must be well arranged and they must be vividly presented. All of us like to avoid the labor of useless thinking just as much as we like to escape avoidable physical drudgery.

3. *Clearness.*—Simplicity of language implies clearness. There must be no doubt as to what is meant. An error of any sort not only distracts the attention from the subject matter, but also irritates those who know better. Errors of number in nouns and verbs, the omission of a necessary apostrophe, disagreement of pronouns, the misuse of adjectives for adverbs, improper tense sequence, incomplete comparisons and other errors are inexcusable in advertisements unless colloquialism is introduced for a purpose, and when it is perfectly evident that it is meant as humor. Sentences such as "Food bakes *quicker* and more *uniform*"; "Each food cell is blasted by steam explosion, thus all are *fitted to digest*," detract from the effect of an advertisement.

Loose construction, too, is harder to understand than unified, coherent structure. "These rain-coats carry with them a powerful selling argument because they are rain-repellent and still they don't even suggest this tremendous advantage in trade in their classy appearance." Such muddled construction and indefinite phraseology do not produce conviction and desire on the part of the reader.

4. *Exactness.*—Exactness is a factor in securing simplicity. Words must be accurate and appropriate. It is a good idea to put the following test to the choice of words: 1. Does the word express what you have in mind? 2. Will it convey the same idea

to your reader? 3. Will its impression upon your reader be such as to aid in the acceptance of your ideas?

Words that are not exact in their meaning are vague, ambiguous or obscure. If the writer of an advertisement is not sure of what he wants to say, he is vague. If he is not extremely careful in his phraseology, he is ambiguous, that is, his meaning may be interpreted in more than one way. If he does not have a sufficiently extensive vocabulary to say what he wishes to say, he is obscure.

In order to secure accuracy in expression, the thought must be clear in the writer's mind. In almost any advertisement it is possible to tell whether or not the writer's grasp of his subject is clear. As in photography, where a blurred negative is sure to produce a blurred print, so in writing advertisements, hazy mental images cannot be made to produce an exact description. As there is bound to be some loss in force when thoughts are transmitted from one person to another, the importance of clear imagery on the writer's part is emphasized.

There are two ways of avoiding ambiguity. One is to learn the exact differences in meaning between words whose significance is similar; the other is to arrange words in logical order. As the transposition of figures in a number may affect the entire import of a statement, so wrong order in the arrangement of words affects the meaning of the sentence.

The use of a large vocabulary tends to remedy obscurity of expression. As words are the working tools of "ad" writing, familiarity with all kinds of words is necessary—Anglo-Saxon and classical derivatives, technical and non-technical terms—so that the writer may have a big stock from which to choose.

5. *Emotional and intellectual value of words.*—All words are not equally serviceable. Some from their derivation or association suggest more to our minds than others. Some have greater value in stimulating thought and the reasoning process; others have greater value in suggesting images or creating emotions. If the emotions are to be aroused, words that appeal to the sensibilities must be used; if the intellect is to be appealed to, the phraseology must stimulate thought. The use of the right word is a matter of primary importance.

6. *Short words.*—The simplest words of the English language are Anglo-Saxon in origin. When Old English or Anglo-Saxon became a written language the people were not far advanced in civilization, consequently they had no great range of ideas to express and they did not develop an extensive vocabulary. They used words which express the ideas and feelings that are common to all humanity. Thus, words expressing elementary relationships as *father, mother, son, daughter, heat, cold, light, dark, fear, love, hate,* are Anglo-Saxon in origin. As a rule, the short Old English words express greater emotional force than derivatives from the Latin and are more generally understood. It is not considered effective to say of

tooth paste that "the constituents of this remarkable detergent compound have been assembled with such scientific accuracy that the savor with which the gustatory sensations are awakened is a pleasure long to be retained in the memory." How much more striking is the sentence, "Russian soldier finds Kolynos so good he eats it."

7. *Long Words.*—When an advertising appeal is directed exclusively to the well-read, or is primarily technical, it is perfectly safe to use long words that express fine shades of meaning. However, it is always bad taste to use long words when they appear pretentious. To explain the technical structure of complex mechanisms long words of classical origin are often absolutely necessary. For example, there is nothing pretentious or pedantic about the following description of the Willard Storage Battery:

> The *electrical system* in your car is as near as man can come to perpetual motion. . . . Your *battery* is *chemical* not *mechanical*. It *accumulates energy* but does not *originate* it. As the *current* flows out of it to the lights, starting the *motor* and other parts, it grows weaker because the *elements* of its plates are *changing* into different *substances*. But when a *current* is sent thru it in the *opposite direction* by the *generator* these *elements change* back to their former *condition* and the *battery* is said to be *charged*.

8. *Idioms.*—By idioms we mean those expressions which have grown up with the people from early times and which cannot be translated. Idioms are the life

and spirit of the language. Their very ruggedness gives them strength. The English expression "How do you do?" cannot be translated word for word into any other language and make sense. Neither does the French idiom *"Comment vous portez-vous?"* make sense when translated word for word.

"Cherish the homely idioms of the language" we are told by Genung, the author of a book on rhetoric that is in wide use. Idioms are brief, often figurative and vigorous and are used by advertising men in preference to more pretentious equivalents.

9. *Nouns and verbs.*—Dr. Frank Crane has drawn the following analogy: "Nouns are bullets, verbs are powder and adjectives are smoke." Nouns and verbs, without doubt, are the most impressive parts of speech and carry the weight of meaning. Nouns must be used accurately. As an illustration, the word *theory* means a supposition in accord with all known facts, but how often it is used to express *guess, opinion* or *idea*.

The verb is particularly impressive since it usually indicates action. It should give the exact shade of meaning and if it is intended to convey the idea of motion, the particular motion should be specified. "He *dashed* out" or "*crept* out" or "*staggered* out" are more expressive terms than "he *went* out." "Don't *tie up* capital in a coal bin" is more suggestive than "don't *put* capital into the coal bin." In the following sentences we find suggestive verbs. "This tractor doesn't *eat* one-fourth of the crop in

return for cultivating, as will a team of horses."
"The National *guards* your money." "Dioxogen *hits* hard ... and it *hits* so well that germs never get a foothold to *work* hard."

10. *Adjectives.*—The chief objection to the use of adjectives is that they are so frequently over-used that they lose their effectiveness. Commonplaces are described by the terms *awful, tremendous, huge, splendid,* when much milder and more accurate terms will do. These adjectives are so frequently misused that the concrete meaning that they had at one time is almost entirely lost. This is also true of *fine, best, first-class,* and others. If an article is *best* in the sense that it ranks high in convenience, why not confine the adjective to a definite concrete suggestion? If it is a labor-saving device why not bring out that idea specifically instead of saying that it is a "splendid thing"?

The following sentences taken from current advertisements are definite and bring out specific ideas. "Her kitchen was equipped with an ordinary sink encased in *vermin-inviting, moisture-holding* woodwork. The old outfit was *dull, dreary* and *unsanitary.*" "This elongated shape in the picture makes possible a *slim, thin, easily-pocketed* camera."

Unless adjectives make a definite, vivid, concrete impression they are nothing more than smoke.

11. *Figures of speech.*—When figures of speech are in keeping with the goods which they are used to describe they are much more impressive than a bald

statement of facts. However, a figure of speech should be only an aid to the thought and fails in its purpose if it diverts attention from the message of the advertisement.

The apt comparison is particularly effective and is one of the most useful tools at the command of an advertising writer. A paper dress-pattern in itself is not stimulating to the imagination, but notice how in the following lines, the implied comparison makes an appeal to every woman's instinctive desire to be well dressed. The paper dress-pattern becomes more than an inert bit of flimsy paper.

THE TISSUE OF DREAMS

> Around it are woven the dreams of fair women,
> By means of it dreams come true.
> The paper dress-pattern is the magic key to the goal of heart's desire,
> The Butterick pattern has made style international and simultaneous.

Other strikingly implied comparisons are: "It is the nightingale of phonographs." "This delivery car is a whale of a one-ton truck." "Lucky Strike is packed full of the tang and rich savor of the out-o'-doors."

12. *Colloquialisms.*—Colloquialisms are those forms of speech which are found in common, rather than in literary speech; in fact, "Speech below literary grade," is one definition of a colloquialism. The advertisement for the Owl cigar, given on the next page, is an illustration of a colloquial usage:

"ZAT'S ZE STUFF"

"Oh, 'twasn't much. Something gave me a wallop over the head. When I came to, I was riding on the seat of my breeches over No Man's Land—but in the wrong direction."

The position of such colloquial language is often on the sporting page flanked by items which also are expressed in colloquial language.

13. *Slang*.—Slang, as defined by the authorities, has two shades of meaning. In one sense *coarseness* or *rudeness* is the distinguishing characteristic. In the second sense—*forced usage*—as when words of the prize-ring are made to serve in the description of an afternoon tea—is the distinguishing mark. These two shades of meaning are illustrated in the advertisement.

There is no doubt that current slang is usually spicy, forceful and often convenient. But those who resort to its use have, as a rule, a limited vocabulary. Much slang means looseness of expression and it is therefore dangerous to resort to it except in rare cases. Slang, as employed by the advertising writer, is a means of securing raciness of description and picturesqueness in appeal. It is suited only to advertising addressed to men, to a certain, limited class of goods, and preferably in the more informal methods of advertising. Even then, if colloquialisms of equal force are available it is better to use them than slang.

14. *Word atmosphere or setting*.—The suggestion

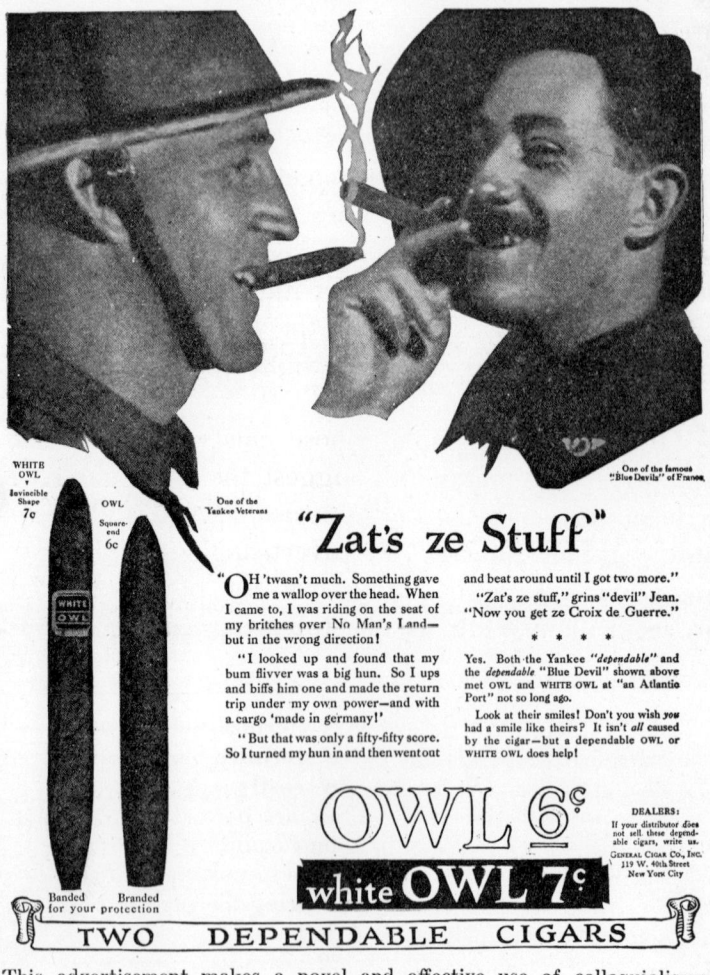

"Zat's ze Stuff"

"OH 'twasn't much. Something gave me a wallop over the head. When I came to, I was riding on the seat of my britches over No Man's Land—but in the wrong direction!

"I looked up and found that my bum flivver was a big hun. So I ups and biffs him one and made the return trip under my own power—and with a cargo 'made in germany!'

"But that was only a fifty-fifty score. So I turned my hun in and then went out and beat around until I got two more."

"Zat's ze stuff," grins "devil" Jean. "Now you get ze Croix de Guerre."

* * * *

Yes. Both the Yankee *dependable* and the *dependable* "Blue Devil" shown above met OWL and WHITE OWL at "an Atlantic Port" not so long ago.

Look at their smiles! Don't you wish *you* had a smile like theirs? It isn't *all* caused by the cigar—but a dependable OWL or WHITE OWL does help!

WHITE OWL
Invincible Shape
7¢

OWL
Square-end
6¢

One of the Yankee Veterans

One of the famous "Blue Devils" of France

OWL 6¢
white OWL 7¢

Banded Branded for your protection

TWO DEPENDABLE CIGARS

DEALERS:
If your distributor does not sell these dependable cigars, write us.
GENERAL CIGAR CO., INC.
119 W. 40th Street
New York City

This advertisement makes a novel and effective use of colloquialisms and slang phrases

134

of mood, place, surroundings, or the atmosphere created by words in their concrete, specific usage has not been sufficiently emphasized by the writer of advertisements. If an advertisement is to arouse the desire to *want* a certain thing, then the imaginative faculty must be stimulated. Atmosphere is gained by an understanding of word values and by definite, suggestive imagery. The specific imagery stimulates the imaginative faculty, the reader fills in his own experiences and emotions between the lines. This factor will put the reader in the right mood for being convinced.

Objects, for example, whose chief merit is their sanitary value might well suggest the atmosphere of a hospital, perfectly sterile surroundings, and absolute, rigid cleanliness. In advertising surgical dressings, first-aid outfits, fumigators and objects needed in accidents and illness, the following setting is convincing:

> We depend on no ordinary sterilization. B & B surgical dressings are twice sterilized—once after being sealed. It is done by costly apparatus, in the most efficient way. They are packed in rooms filled with washed air, in rooms equipped like operating rooms. The workers are in uniform. Then we take extreme measures to bring the products to you sterile—just as they left us. . . . They are made by chemists who for 22 years have been serving physicians and hospitals.

In the following advertisement, atmosphere is secured by means of strikingly suggestive adjectives:

California offers you this, from her *sunlit valleys*—California Raisin Bread, made with Sun-Maid Raisins. Plenty of these *deep-juiced, full flavored, sugar-laden nuggets* of energy make this the true fruit food.

Sun-Maid Brand Raisins are choice California white grapes—*too delicate to ship*—*sun-cured* in the *open* vineyards. Nowhere else do such grapes grow, and no other grapes yield such a flavor in their *sun-brewed* juices.

REVIEW

What do you consider the most important factor in the advertising mechanism?

Why is clear and exact diction of prime importance in advertising? How can clearness and exactness be secured?

Do you consider the use of slang or colloquialisms permissible in advertising?

What is meant by "word atmosphere"?

CHAPTER IX

"GETTING THE ORDER" COPY

1. *Purpose and scope.*—Copy which is intended to sell goods direct to the consumer, without the help of any other marketing agency, is known as "getting the order" copy.

Not all products can be successfully advertised by direct mail-order copy. This type of advertisement is usually confined to medium priced products, and to articles of personal consumption whose nature is easily explained.

Usually a fitting illustration is used in combination with a suggestive headline to attract attention. Then follows a paragraph designed to inspire a wish for the article, the descriptive matter, the offer and the address. The whole advertisement is crowded with information.

2. *Typical mail-order copy.*—The preparation for a mail-order campaign involves more than the mere writing of copy for magazines and newspapers. It includes the preparation of catalogs, folders and a proper follow-up system.

To overcome the prestige of the local store having a personal contact with customers, a favorable location, counter and window displays, is the supreme test

A magazine page of typical mail-order advertisements

of mail-order copy. It must, with the same words, awaken the impulse to buy and create confidence. It must tell an interesting and plausible story connected with the product that will bring enough orders to prove profitable.

A single word in the advertisement of a mail-order campaign may affect the results favorably or unfavorably. To no one is the subject of word values of more

RIDER AGENTS WANTED
Everywhere to ride and exhibit the new **Ranger "Motorbike"** completely equipped with electric light and horn, carrier, stand, tool tank, coaster-brake, mud guards and anti-skid tires. **Choice of 44 other styles,** colors and sizes in the famous **"Ranger"** line of bicycles, all at *Factory-to-Rider* prices.
DELIVERED FREE on approval and **30 DAYS TRIAL.** Send for big **free** catalog and particulars of our *Thirty Days Free Trial* offer and marvelous offers and terms.
TIRES Lamps, Horns, Wheels, Sundries, and repair parts and supplies for all bicycles—at half usual prices.
SEND NO MONEY but tell us exactly what you need. Do not buy until you get our *Factory-Direct-to-Rider* prices, terms and the big FREE catalog.
MEAD CYCLE COMPANY DEPT. CHICAGO, U.S.A.

importance than to the man writing mail-order copy. "Increase your salary" proved to be twice as effective as "increase your income," and the word "rider" before the stereotyped phrase "agents wanted" turned the latter from a formal, unproductive insertion into a business-building advertisement for the Mead Cycle Company.

It is sometimes assumed that mail-order copy must be "snappy" and "smart" in order to be productive. But experience has demonstrated that this is not the case. The many successes of the past prove the efficacy of appeals in plain tales unadorned. The copy must, however, combine human interest with clear description.

Occasionally mail-order advertisers use a simple form of copy, year after year, without any change whatever. The Press Company's copy, "Print Your

Print Your Own Cards, Circulars, programs, labels, books, newspaper. $6. PRESS, Larger $20. Rotary $70. Save money. Print for others, BIG PROFIT. All easy, rules sent. Write factory TODAY for catalog presses, TYPE, paper, cards etc. IT WILL PAY YOU.
THE PRESS CO. D-49, MERIDEN, CONNECTICUT

Own Cards" is an example of a successful advertisement of this kind.

Maher and Grosh Company's advertising, as an example, has changed but little in ten years or more. This company uses two-inch, double column advertise-

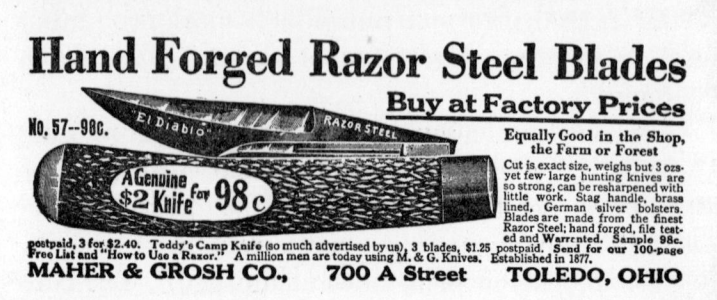

Exact Size

$1.00 KNIFE for 78c
Postpaid. 3 for $2.10. Best 7-inch shears, 85c. This Knife and Shears, $1.50. Best hollow ground razor, with strop, $1.65, postpaid. Every M. & G. blade is hand-forged from razor steel, file-tested, warranted. Send for 100-page free list and "How to Use a Razor."
MAHER & GROSH CO.
636-A Street,
TOLEDO, - - OHIO

Hand Forged Razor Steel Blades
Buy at Factory Prices

NO. 57--98c. "El Diablo"

A Genuine $2 Knife for 98c

Equally Good in the Shop, the Farm or Forest

Cut is exact size, weighs but 3 ozs; yet few large hunting knives are so strong, can be resharpened with little work. Stag handle, brass lined, German silver bolsters. Blades are made from the finest Razor Steel; hand forged, file tested and Warranted. Sample 98c.

postpaid, 3 for $2.40. Teddy's Camp Knife (so much advertised by us), 3 blades, $1.25 postpaid. Send for our 100-page Free List and "How to Use a Razor." A million men are today using M. & G. Knives. Established in 1877.
MAHER & GROSH CO., 700 A Street TOLEDO, OHIO

GETTING THE ORDER

ments, and the quality of the offer is varied to suit the medium. The farmer is offered a substantial knife at a low price; the business man is solicited to buy a high-grade penknife, prices being quoted in each case. Not only are Maher and Grosh advertisements simple, but it has been possible to use the same catalog, practically unchanged, for a number of years, thus cutting advertising expense to a minimum.

3. *Mail-order advertising.*—The high commercial value of mail-order advertising as a means of building business is seen in the growth of many concerns from obscure beginnings to an assured position.

In the simplest form of mail-order merchandising there is frequently some manufacturing done, but the business usually places the stress upon selling, preferring to buy what it sells, rather than to manufacture.

In a large mail-order business a predetermined market is supplemented by quantity buying. The entire output of factories is purchased; surplus stocks are bought at bargain prices. Goods bought at a low price cut down the advertising expenditure proportionately, so that the amount of periodical advertising these houses do is really not at all proportionate to their volume of business.

Extensive periodical advertising has been done away with by the "giants." But houses without the prestige of age and size must still advertise heavily. Their problem of getting names, preparing lists, diverting business, adding to the prestige of the house

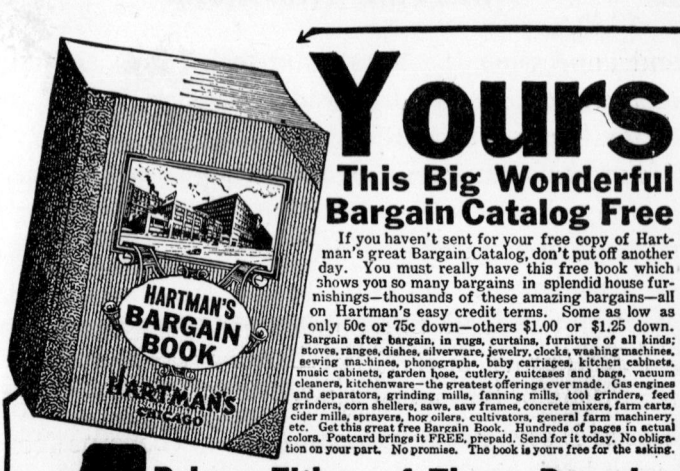

A typical example of "mail-order house" copy. The fundamental appeal is to the pocketbook. Note the strong drive made to the reader to send for the catalog.

and impressing the lines upon which they specialize on the public's mind, is considerably greater than that of the big and successful houses.

4. *Catalog type.*—For mail-order houses the catalog page has in a sense acted as a mold in which the style of copy, illustration and make-up have been cast. When possible—and as a rule it is possible—the article is pictured, because therein lies a large part of its selling power. Mail-order advertisers realize that more than a quarter of a million dollars are paid for drawings and engravings in each of the leading mail-order catalogs. The description follows a set style, tho the present tendency is to make it replete with selling quality, if not with human interest.

5. *Adaptations of the catalog type.*—Altho the leading houses focus their attention upon the catalog type of advertising, there are signs that some of the smaller houses are breaking away from this style of copy. They are breaking the catalog up into seasonal booklets, divisional books and "flyers," and are putting more individuality into their literature.

These smaller houses show a strong tendency to drop the blanket method of offering many lines in one advertisement. Small individual advertisements, scattered thruout the same periodical, are now used. This method is particularly applicable to lines made up of large items. The Galloway Company specializes on cream separators, gasoline engines and farm machinery in its advertising, tho it sells a fairly complete line of standard mail-order products.

144   ADVERTISING PRINCIPLES

The advertisement of the Ohio Carriage Company presents an example of personality mail-order advertising, restrained in tone, advertising the product rather than the man. More personality is put into

Only one product featured in the advertisement of a mail-order house selling a general line to farmers

the catalog and correspondence than into the advertisement.

6. *Booklets and catalogs.*—Complementary to the individual advertisement are the seasonal and divi-

sional books which are sent out to prospects in place of the big catalogs. In the spring, catalogs containing descriptions of seeds, plants and other things associated with this time of the year are sent out. These are known as seasonal books. A somewhat similar principle underlies the catalogs called divisional books.

Another typical mail-order advertisement of a rather personal conservative type

These books are prepared on the basis of certain natural divisions in the organization rather than on the seasons. Thus the hardware division may have a special catalog separate from the clothing division. Frequently, too, it may be necessary to inform customers of a special stock which the concern has on hand. A small catalog called a "flyer" is prepared and distributed.

7. *Appeals in mail-order copy.*—There are two distinct appeals in mail-order copy. The first is the *price appeal;* the second the *style appeal.* There is still another appeal made, which in reality includes either the price or the style appeal or both and which is known as the *free or trial offer appeal.*

8. *Price appeal.*—The price appeal has been and is used with great success because it touches a fundamental chord in human nature and in a great majority of cases brings a response. The method of appeal is always in the form of a bargain offer. This may take one of several forms. It may be a special sale of goods marked down temporarily from standard price. Another form shows a low price with a statement that the price will be advanced within a short time. The time when the advance will become effective may be stated definitely or not.

The Bedell advertisement is a typical illustration of copy used by mail-order houses selling wearing apparel. This puts direct emphasis on the catalog by featuring it prominently and giving accurate reproductions of some of the dresses described therein. Stress is laid on the thousands of beautiful styles shown in the catalog, to arouse the curiosity and interest of the reader and induce her to send for the book. The advertisement offers an absolute guarantee of satisfaction or a refund of money.

9. *Style appeal.*—The center of style in this coun-

Selling wearing apparel by mail by means of the price appeal

try, particularly for women's wear, is New York. This accounts, in part, for the fact that there are so many women's wear houses that sell by mail from New York. One or two of the large mail-order houses have their main plants in the Middle West but operate a special branch for women's wear in New York.

The appeal of style is very often fully as strong and more successful than the price appeal. The advertisements with this appeal feature the product and give a detailed description of all its fine points. The products are often pictured in luxurious surroundings and thereby make a distinct appeal to love of good style.

The Sears, Roebuck advertisement is a good example of "style appeal" and shows a new departure in advertising women's gowns. This method is a recent development and features garments created by a designer of national reputation.

10. *Free or trial offer.*—The free or trial offer may be made in connection with either one of the preceding appeals, and states the company's willingness to send the product to the consumer's home or office for trial.

An analysis of trial-offer copy shows most of the advertisements to be frank in spirit. The advertisement of the Typewriter Emporium, on page 150, is typical. It says in effect: "We trust you; we will make it as easy as possible for you to get this machine; all the risk is assumed by us; we have so much confidence in our typewriter that we are willing

"My Dream Girl Frock"

WHEN I was designing this model I had in my mind a picture of the bright eyes, red lips and flushed cheeks that go with youthful happiness. I could see this girlish figure appearing among her young friends in lovely unconsciousness of her charm, yet all the time making a fascinating picture in her dainty frock so perfectly suited to her individuality.

"My Dream Girl" is made in softest shades of silk taffeta, with beautiful lace outlining sleeves and corsage and the point of the fitted bodice. Filmy chiffon covers the neck and shoulders and a band of silk ribbon follows the edge of the V-neck and peeps from under the lace cascades.

The full skirt has just a suggestion of draping on the lower edge at each side. The graceful panniers are faced with soft satin of a darker shade and caught up with perky little bows. A light hoop holds the skirt out over the hips.

This is a very youthful model and is most becoming for young, slim figures. "My Dream Girl" is very lovely made up in shades of pink, light blue, maize or the exquisite orchid tints with touches of contrasting color. A little French corsage bouquet of vari-colored flowers completes the picture.

Lady Duff Gordon

115 Fifth Ave.,
New York

The "Dream Girl" Model in blue, pink, maize or orchid silk taffeta. Sizes 14, 16, 18 and 20. Order by number 31A105. Price, $32.00.

Lady Duff Gordon's
"My Dream Girl Frock"

LADY DUFF-GORDON, the world's greatest fashion creator, has perfected her plan for designing clothes for *all* the women of America who are interested in being correctly and beautifully dressed. The "Dream Girl" frock, shown in the illustration above, is one of twenty charming models which she has just completed under this plan and which are pictured in a luxurious "Lady Duff-Gordon Style Book," just published. This is for presentation, without charge, to all who fill in the coupon printed below.

Up to this time, Lady Duff-Gordon's remarkable genius has been available only through the "Lucile" establishments in London, Paris, New York and Chicago, of which she is the head. From now on, the thousands of American women who have been attracted by the beauty and distinction of the "Lady Duff-Gordon" creations, will be able to get them at very moderate cost. Original "Lady Duff-Gordon" designs, made up in beautiful materials, will cost no more than you have been accustomed to pay for ordinary dresses. To make these designs available to women in all parts of the country, the Sears-Roebuck organization will distribute them for Lady Duff-Gordon under her personal direction. All orders should be sent to the Chicago office of Sears, Roebuck and Co.

Each garment is guaranteed to meet the entire satisfaction of the purchaser, or it will be altered as wanted—or, if preferred, the purchase price will be refunded without question. The designs are all made, under Lady Duff-Gordon's supervision, from materials of her own selection.

Lady Duff-Gordon's Style Book, which is now ready and which you may have for the asking, shows the beautiful designs created by her for the season of 1916-1917, photographed on living models. There are tailored suits—including her famous "Curate" costume—afternoon dresses, dancing frocks and house gowns, models for all ages, at prices ranging from $20 to $45.

In the Style Book there is also a clothes talk by Lady Duff-Gordon and an intimate story of her life and work. This is accompanied by a beautiful photograph of Lady Duff-Gordon suitable for framing. Style Book and photograph will be sent without cost, if you fill in and mail the attached coupon to the Chicago office of Sears, Roebuck and Co.

SEARS, ROEBUCK AND CO., Homan Avenue at Arthington Street, CHICAGO

Please send me without charge, copy of Lady Duff-Gordon's Style Book and Autographed Photograph

Name _____ Street Address _____

City _____ State _____

Selling gowns thru the mail by means of the style appeal

This advertisement shows the use of the trial offer appeal

to put it into your hands for an examination. Call in experts if you like—we sell at less than manufacturers' prices. We offer you a free trial and a five-year guarantee. If you decide to keep it, there are no interest charges, no red tape, no salesmen, no collectors, no bother. All your trouble is reduced to signifying your desire on the coupon."

11. *Classified advertising.*—Perhaps the most distinctive form of copy which bases its style upon getting orders is found in the small classified advertisements. With the growth of all kinds of advertising, the "classified" has experienced a corresponding development. This has been brought about mainly by the rivalry of newspapers in building up their classified columns.

While the comparatively low cost of service was a reason for the growth of classified advertising in the past, this is no longer true.

As the classified columns of periodicals were first used for "help wanted" and "situation wanted" advertising, it is to be noted that this kind of advertising has held its lead to a remarkable degree. In nearly every classified department, the columns under the headings "Positions Wanted" and "Help Wanted" exceed those of any other class of classified advertising. "Furnished and Unfurnished Rooms," "Furnished and Unfurnished Houses" and "Real Estate for Rent and Sale" are usually next in order of importance. "Business Opportunities" is another group of importance. In the better-class periodicals, a large percentage of "Business Opportunities" advertisements may be actual opportunities. In periodicals whose advertising standard is low, these may be merely disguised canvassing or investment advertisements.

The principles governing classified advertising are those which aim to secure conciseness and suggestive power. Since there is no opportunity for either illustration or display—tho some magazines encourage capitalization or the use of type up to 12-point—the story must be told in the advertisement itself. The following advertisements are typical and illustrate well the style of copy which must get the order and yet be brief as a telegram:

> Great bargains in handkerchiefs. 3 Ladies' beautifully hemstitched fancy handkerchiefs done in embroidery and lace, all for 25 cents.
> Try 3 and you will want more. Address ———— Mail Order Co. ————.

> Patents Manufacturers Buy are the kind we get from Inventors. For proof and reliable free book, write ————.

REVIEW

What are the characteristic features of "getting the order" copy?

In what special phase of his art must the writer of "getting the order" copy be skilled?

How can a mail-order house keep down its advertising appropriation?

What advantages has the catalog type of advertisement?

How may this type be varied?

What do you consider the strongest appeal in advertising women's clothes? Typewriters? Automobiles?

CHAPTER X

"GETTING THE INQUIRY" COPY

1. *Purpose and scope of inquiry copy.*—An advertisement that seeks to attract attention, arouse interest, establish conviction and persuade the prospect to buy, all at once, has a big task to perform. For this reason many advertisers prefer to divide the burden between two or more processes. They put upon the advertisement the task of attracting attention and of interesting the public in their product, and depend upon either the follow-up letter or the salesman to close the sale. Copy, therefore, that seeks to arouse the interest of a reader in the product only to the extent of drawing an inquiry from him may be termed "inquiry copy."

2. *Kinds of inquiries and copy.*—The advertiser seeks to induce prospects to make inquiries about his product. Ultimately, of course, he expects to turn these inquiries into orders. In some cases it is desirable to persuade the prospect to go in person to a dealer and ask for information, and in other cases to send a coupon or postal card direct to the advertiser.

There are many and varied appeals used to get inquiries. In some cases a catalog or booklet is featured; in others samples of the product are offered, and in still others the product itself is offered on free trial. Experience has shown (1) that where the advertisement depends entirely upon its own power to persuade readers by purely educational copy, a minimum of inquiries may be expected; (2) that where free offers of booklets and the like are featured the inquiries increase materially; and (3) that where the free offer is featured in a way that arouses curiosity to a high pitch, the maximum inquiries result.

3. *Why inquiries are solicited.*—The purpose in seeking inquiries is to locate possible customers. Most people hesitate to part with their money on the first appeal. On the other hand, they are willing to investigate if the process is made easy and the risk reduced to the mere sending in of their names and addresses. Even very weak interest in a product may thus induce a reader to send in an inquiry. Curiosity alone may be enough; but most advertisements of this nature do not rely solely upon curiosity to supply the necessary motive for action; they include a "free offer" of some sort. Inquiry copy, therefore, is usually enhanced with a strong appeal to those motives in human nature which make one dislike to lose a chance to get something for nothing, or to discard a coupon or other evidence of value.

Having located prospective customers, the company seeks to make them actual customers. The simplest way of doing this is by the use of the direct order appeal. The advertiser asks a reader to send for information and with the prospect's name and address

GETTING THE INQUIRY

as a basis seeks to persuade him thru direct mail solicitation or by a visit from a salesman.

Another method is closely associated with the copy designed to direct the reader. A manufacturer may wish to show the dealers in a particular community that there is a demand for his product. The list of inquiries would be used as evidence of this demand and hence would influence the dealer to handle his goods. It is important to keep the motives distinct, for upon the motive depends the selection of the point of appeal and degree of emphasis to be put upon the selling qualities in the advertisement.

4. *Inducement to respond.*—The gradual change in the point of view in all parts of the advertising field is reflected in the means of getting inquiries from prospective readers. At first the catalog was used almost exclusively, and in accordance with prevalent ideas, the product was made the sole basis of the appeal. Long technical descriptions predominated. Then came the coupon as an adjunct in obtaining inquiries for catalogs and as a basis for the more complete follow-up system which was added to the catalog and coupon methods. But finally there came a complete change in the conception of advertising appeal, the adoption of the "you attitude." Hence the catalog which had featured the product and which had been the mainstay in getting the inquiry, was superseded by a booklet which contained not merely a technical account of the product, but suggestions and information of real value to the reader. Thus an office device

was not explained as a piece of mechanism in the booklet, but as a part of an office system. The excellence of its descriptions raised the booklet from the rank of a catalog to the rank of a reference or textbook upon the subject of office systems. The booklet of today makes, therefore, a double appeal since it offers information about the product and is in itself a valuable acquisition to the reader's library.

5. *Catalog offer.*—To introduce a product whose general qualities are well known may depend more upon the outside inducements offered than upon the direct appeals based upon the product itself. There are several coal crushers on the market. In general, their qualities are well known to the users of such machines. The Jeffrey advertisement is a good illustration in which the emphasis is put upon the book, altho to feature the virtues of the Jeffrey Single Roll Crusher is the final objective.

Little attempt is made to describe the coal crusher other than by the descriptive name on the cover of the bulletin and in the argument showing why the bulletin should be sent for. The product appeal is submerged in the free catalog appeal.

6. *Free sample offer.*—A variation from the style of copy used in the Jeffrey advertisement, yet one which resembles it, is the advertisement on page 158, of the Minute Tapioca Company. Here is offered not only a free book but a free sample package upon which the emphasis of the entire advertisement it put.

There is no description that can equal a test of the

The Coupon
Brings This Bulletin
Free

SINGLE ROLL COAL CRUSHER

for service at the
MINE AND POWER HOUSE

THE JEFFREY MANUFACTURING CO
COLUMBUS, OHIO. U.S.A.

Contains Full Description and Illustrations of the

Jeffrey Single Roll Crusher

The machine that will Crush More Coal with Less Power, Expense and Trouble, Than any other on the Market.

If your Power Plant is equipped with Stokers, or if you use Crushed Coal for any purpose, you ought to have a copy of this important book.

The Jeffrey Manufacturing Co.,
922 North Fourth St., Columbus, O.

Please send me, without obligation, copy of Bulletin No. 141.

Name ....

Address ....

....

The free booklet is featured here,
rather than the product

158   ADVERTISING PRINCIPLES

**New Minute Cook Book FREE
With Generous Sample
of Minute Gelatine**

Minute Gelatine

Measured for Use

Four envelopes to each package, 1 pint of jelly to each envelope. Promptly dissolves in hot milk or water. Makes light, tempting, transparent desserts.

Sample package of Minute Gelatine, enough to make a pint of jelly, sent free with Minute Cook Book. The Minute Cook Book gives a choice from 124 delicious Tapioca and Gelatine recipes which you can make in a few minutes. Use coupon.

MINUTE TAPIOCA CO., 000 East Main St., Orange, Mass.

Another example of an advertisement which features a free booklet but which also offers a free sample

goods themselves. Particularly where the value of the product depends upon one main appeal, made perhaps to the sense of taste or smell, a small sample is sufficient to give a clear idea of the product. The advertiser of a new food product, for example, could spend much money in description and yet not succeed in giving so good an idea of how his product actually tastes, as could a sample costing less than a cent.

Fabric products lend themselves in most cases to sample offers. One of the most familiar advertisements, changed little from year to year, is that of a collar company which offers a liberal supply of collars in return for the names of those who might be interested. A manufacturer of underwear is able to show the superiority of his fabric over others by a sample not over an inch square. "Tailoring-by-mail" firms not only supply their agents with samples of goods from which the clothes are to be made, but often furnish the prospective customer with fabric samples as well.

The advantages of an efficient sample-offer plan may be summarized as follows:

(1) Increased number of inquiries.

(2) Increased value of inquiries thru elimination of requests of idle curiosity seekers.

(3) Since the goods are in the prospective buyer's possession they will do their own advertising.

(4) Superiority of demonstration over verbal description, in such matters as the taste of a food product, the sound of a talking machine or musical instrument and the like.

(5) Aiding distribution, thru dealers or agents.

(6) Furnishing new names that may be used in future advertising campaigns.

7. *Booklets and samples at small cost.*—Altho it is necessary to write copy that will get results in connec-

tion with free offers of booklets and samples, some check must be put upon inquirers who are merely curious.

The copy of the Crisco advertisement on this page is particularly strong in its appeal to housewives and even to professional cooks. Since the purpose is not to sell directly, the advertisement strikes at a particularly vulnerable spot by suggesting a problem in cooking in the very first phrase—"Whys of cooking." This in itself would be enough to stimulate the action of asking for a free book. Curiosity and interest are evoked at once. But those who are merely curious are usually not desirable as prospects, hence the ten-cent charge. By putting in this element, the free offer is changed into an "offer at small cost"; therefore it is necessary to add more force to the appeal. The copy speaks of the authority back of the authorship, the Principal of the Boston Cooking School and publisher of "American Cookery"; it appeals also to woman's desire to get this cooking information in the

> YOU can learn more about Crisco in Janet McKenzie Hill's "Whys of Cooking" which we have published as the successor to "A Calendar of Dinners". Every woman interested in cooking will be interested in this splendid addition to the important literature of domestic science. It is an authoritative text book, for the author is Principal of the Boston Cooking School and Publisher of American Cookery. It gives in the form of questions and answers just what *you* may want to know of puzzling problems in cooking. It is handsomely illustrated in colors and contains many new and hitherto unpublished recipes.
>
> Of course, this book is published to gain the good will of our customers, and therefore further advance the sales of Crisco, but it is a book which is worth five times at least what we ask for it. The cost is but five two-cent stamps. Address your request to Dept. H-9, The Procter & Gamble Co., Cincinnati, Ohio.

simplest form—question and answer. It stimulates the desire to possess the book by saying "It is handsomely illustrated in colors and contains many new and hitherto unpublished recipes." Finally, it skilfully leads up to the small cost by taking the reader into the company's confidence, for, of course, "this book is published to gain the good-will of our customers, and therefore further advance the sales of Crisco, but it is a book which is worth five times at least what we ask for it." The last paragraph skilfully builds up the confidence of the reader while telling her, "The cost is but five two-cent stamps."

Another excellent example of this type of advertisement may be seen in the "Jim Henry" copy of the Gerhard Mennen Chemical Company, shown on page 162. An indication of how successful such copy can be made is the fact that one insertion of this advertisement brought 10,000 replies. W. A. McDermid, advertising manager of the company, says:

> No advertisement we ever ran has created so much interest as this one. We attribute its success to the headlines in the first paragraph which caught the average man's interest. It induced him to read a straight story about our product in the belief that it was a man-to-man, informal talk.

8. *Limiting replies.*—Charging a small price for a booklet or sample automatically cuts out the cheaper class of inquiries that are the bane of so many advertisers. Such a course is founded on well-known principles that what is paid for is esteemed more highly

"My English may not be there, but the facts are straight"

A Salesman's Story

Jim Henry, who is selling you

THE boss said the other day, "Jim, I want you to sell Mennen's Shaving Cream to every man who reads the *Post*. You tell our story in a way that sells druggists everywhere. There's no reason why those same facts shouldn't sell the druggist's customers. He put it up to me, so here goes—and all I ask is that you men sink your prejudices for the moment. I have a real story to tell, and you needn't take the statements on faith. You can demonstrate for yourself the accuracy of what I say.

The Chemistry of Shaving

There are differences in chemical composition between "hard" soaps and cream soaps; between other shaving preparations and Mennen's Shaving Cream.

Now, the composition of your shaving preparation determines, more than anything else, whether or not you get the "head barber" shave.

If your skin burns and smarts after shaving and little pin-pricks of blood cover the face; if the lather dries quickly, making you relather several times; if you have to "rub in" to soften the beard—you can blame it all on the soap.

Mr. Mennen experimented three years to perfect a formula for a preparation that would eliminate these nuisances. The result was Mennen's Shaving Cream.

Some real dope on lather

Have you ever tried to shave without soap—with water alone? You found it as pleasant as pulling out hairs with pincers. Well, you undergo almost the same torture if your shaving preparation does not give a full, firm, creamy, beard-softening lather.

Now, it is a fact—attested to by all chemists—that "hard" soaps give a different character of lather from a preparation like Mennen's. The composition of Mennen's is such that it absorbs much more water than "hard" soaps. This gives it the quick, profuse, creamy lathering qualities, and the high percentage of water held in the lather makes it moist and cooling.

Because the lather of Mennen's absorbs so much water, it does not dry quickly on the face. It remains moist at least ten minutes. *No need to be constantly relathering in the middle of a shave.* That's one thing that rings the bell with every man who uses Mennen's.

Again, the peculiar properties of this cream enable it to soften the hair, so that "rubbing in" (which brings the blood to the surface and makes the skin tender) is totally unnecessary.

Here is something so revolutionary that most men balk at believing it. They are so used to shaving the way Father taught them that they persist in "rubbing in" even when they use Mennen's. But take our word for it. You *don't* have to "rub in" when you use Mennen's—save your time and your skin—see whether this isn't a straight tip.

"Hard" Soaps Contain Little or No Glycerin

In making soaps, glycerin is formed—and glycerin, you know, is worth money. So in "hard" soaps it is usually extracted and sold as a profitable by-product. In making Mennen's, we not only leave the glycerin in, *but we add more.*

You know how soothing glycerin is. Your mother used it on your chapped hands when you were a kid. Doctors prescribe it for its skin-softening and emollient properties. It gives the skin that velvety soft "feel."

Mennen's takes the sting out of shaving. Wonderful, you say, but it's a fact, and the main reason is that there is no "free caustic" in it. Those words "free caustic" don't sound very dangerous, but believe me, I know all about it. I stuck my finger in a caustic tank one day, and I don't want any more on my skin, "free" or any other way.

It's the "free caustic" in soaps that causes the thousand stings on your face after shaving, and draws your skin all up. Don't blame this torture on the razor. The razor is second fiddle.

Get a trial tube Now—Prove these facts yourself

You may discount my enthusiasm, you may want to check me up. Well, there's nothing in the world we want more. Let us send you a medium-sized trial tube.

When you get this tube, follow the directions for use in the package. You remember the story of the painter who put on his signs, "Wet paint—believe the painter." Believe us when we tell you how much cream to use for every shave—not to "rub in" the lather—simply work it up on the face with the brush. Remember, it took three years to perfect Mennen's and we know *how* it should be used to get the best results. Follow our directions, and you'll boost it as whole-heartedly as I do.

Tear out the coupon now, fill it out, wrap up a dime in a piece of paper, and mail. With the medium-sized tube of Shaving Cream we will send, free, a trial can of the Mennen Talcum for Men, described below.

Cap can't be lost
Notice how big the cap on this regular-sized tube is. It is too big to fall down the drain-pipe, or to be lost on the floor, when you drop it. The tube is sealed when you buy it, so that the cream comes to you absolutely fresh and pure.

The Talcum for Men

Most men like to use a talcum after shaving but object to appearing in public with a "flour-face." The Mennen Talcum for Men avoids this. It's a neutral tint and doesn't show. A trial can of this talcum will be sent free to every *Post* reader who sends for a tube of shaving cream. Mail the coupon

MENNEN'S SHAVING CREAM

GERHARD MENNEN CHEMICAL COMPANY
LABORATORIES, 1403 ORANGE ST., NEWARK, N. J.

This coupon brings you two samples for 10 cents

Gerhard Mennen Chemical Co.,
Laboratories, 1403 Orange St.,
Newark, N. J.

Enclosed is 10 cents, for which please send me a medium-sized tube of Mennen's Shaving Cream, and a trial can of Mennen's Talcum Powder for Men.

Name _____
Address _____
City _____ State _____

This advertisement offers a sample of the product at small cost—only ten cents for both the shaving cream and the talcum powder

162

GETTING THE INQUIRY

than what is given free. The practice, therefore, of limiting the distribution of booklets or samples by charging for them, in many cases aids markedly in securing a much better class of inquiries than is secured when the distribution is free. If the advertiser can manage the cost of the offer so as to shut out the curious while not repelling actual, prospective customers, he has reached high efficiency in getting returns.

The growth of the "small cost offer" has been limited as it is not adapted to every line. It helps to eliminate those who inquire merely from curiosity. Finally, great value is attached to the names of staple purchasers as possible steady customers. When the advertiser has a varied line of goods, the customer for one commodity may be circularized from time to time for other commodities.

9. *The idly curious.*—Many persons send for expensive booklets or samples of products in which they are not at all interested. Most prospects are drawn to a product first thru curiosity, but there are some prospects who since they have not even a potential purchasing power may be classed as purely curious. Children who seek catalogs and the like for the pictures are a good illustration. One successful method of selecting the right kind of prospect is to stipulate that the request for the free book be sent, "upon your business letterhead." In other cases the inquirer is asked to furnish further information besides his name before a valuable book or sample is sent him. Thus

the curious seeker is headed off while the really interested prospect is not repelled.

10. *Free booklet offer.*—There must be some inducement offered to the reader of an advertisement to get him to send in his name and address. The Atlas Powder Company's advertisement, shown on the opposite page, illustrates a type of copy built around the free booklet offer.

To introduce a product whose general qualities are well known may depend more upon the outside inducements offered than the direct appeals based upon the product itself. There are many powders on the market. In general, their qualities are well known. The Atlas advertisement is a good illustration in which the emphasis is put upon the "Better Farming" book, altho the announcing of the virtues of Atlas Powder is the final objective.

11. *Methods of distributing samples.*—Offering the sample "on request" is the standard method for systematic distribution of samples over a large territory. Where a given district must be covered in a relatively short time, national advertisers generally resort to door-to-door distribution or distribution to special classes.

The Kolynos Company, which manufactures a dental cream and distributes thru the retail druggists, uses an effective method of sampling. Dentists, physicians, physical culture instructors and others who are interested in the public health are furnished with samples for distribution. In each package of dental

Land clearing fully explained

After you have read the chapter on "Better Stump Removing" in our book, "Better Farming with Atlas Farm Powder," you will know how easily and quickly you can clean up your fields. After you have blasted a few stumps you will feel like Harry A. Wright, Williamsburg, Mass., who writes:

"Now I know that land which I cleared by grubbing could have been cleared with Atlas Farm Powder more easily and at one-quarter the expense. I never dared tackle the stumps on part of my land before, but now I am getting the stumps out and planting it to trees."

"Better Farming with Atlas Farm Powder" also tells how to remove boulders, blast the subsoil and beds for trees, make ditches and do other farm jobs with Atlas Powder. A copy—sent free—will be a valuable addition to your library. The coupon at the right will bring the book.

ATLAS POWDER CO., Wilmington, Del.
Dealers everywhere. Magazine stocks near you.

**ATLAS POWDER CO.,
Wilmington, Del.**

Send me "Better Farming with Atlas Farm Powder." I am interested in explosives for the purpose before which I mark "X."

☐ Stump Blasting
☐ Boulder Blasting
☐ Subsoil Blasting
☐ Tree Planting
☐ Ditch Digging
☐ Road Making

Name_____

Address_____

Atlas Farm Powder
THE SAFEST EXPLOSIVE
The Original Farm Powder

The booklet offered is indicative of something interesting and helpful to the reader, rather than simply a catalog of explosives

cream is placed a postal having blanks for the listing of names of the customer's friends. The letter which accompanies the sample states by whom the request for the sample was made, thereby increasing the advertising value of the plan.

In addition to securing a volume of replies and creating immediate interest, "free" offers have an advantage in that they usually provide a list that is responsive to further sales effort.

12. *Follow-up after the sample.*—Once the sample is in the prospective buyer's possession and sufficient time has elapsed for noting its principal advantages, the question of follow-up arises. The follow-up must be worked out in such a way that the prospect is not prejudiced against the goods. The letter following the sampling may properly discuss some feature to which particular attention should be called.

If the product is being distributed by the retailer, a special inducement is usually made in the follow-up for the purpose of bringing the sampler actually into the dealer's store.

13. *Function of coupon.*—The coupon is to the advertising campaign what oil is to a machine. It makes action easy. Whether the action involves a request for a catalog or the sending in of a cash order, there is always some mental inertia to be overcome, and the coupon "sign, clip and mail" makes such action easy. It is estimated that a coupon increases returns fifty per cent, of which at least thirty per cent are good.

The uses of coupons vary. Ordinarily their use involves no more than the checking of some item desired and the signing of the inquirer's name and address. The coupon of the California Fruit Growers' Exchange on page 168 is a good sample of this type. Everything is made easy by providing checking spaces and sufficient room for writing the name and address. A more complex style of coupon contains a statement of certain conditions and when signed by the inquirer assumes the form of a contract. The trial-order coupon of the Baby Cariole advertisement on the next page is an example of the latter form.

Some coupons have real selling copy embodied in a few brief sentences. The Carnation Milk Products Company uses a direct suggestion when it says "Write Today." And since the coupon is to be used by women, it begins with a courteous introduction: "Gentlemen: Kindly send me . . ." Then instead of listing the names of the books to be sent and providing a check space, the coupon continues, " your free booklet, 'The Story of Carnation Milk,' which gives 100 practical and useful recipes for foods prepared with Carnation Milk."

The Northam Warren Company puts display as well as selling copy into its coupon. If a prospect is at all interested in keeping her nails manicured, a picture of the open box containing the sample manicure set offered is bound to inspire action. Other advertisers put in some good words for the product it-

Different types of coupons, the functions of which are discussed in this chapter

self. Note the wording of the Pennsylvania Textile Company's coupon and mark its selling quality:

FREE We will be glad to send you our authoritative style book FREE, together with some samples of MONEYBAK taffeta, so you can see and feel the crispy, puffy softness of this beautiful silk. Send for your copy today and be sure to mention your dealer's name.

Most of the appeals that make good advertising copy can also be used in an intensive way in coupon copy. A method frequently used is to ask the reader to solve riddles, puzzles and the like, the answers to

---

Gentlemen:
If the following names are correct, please send sample copies of your four publications to

Name..
Street..
City and State..

(1)..
(2)..
(3)..
(4)..

The Frank A. Munsey Company
8 West Fortieth Street, New York City

which are very easily found. An adaptation of this method to coupon copy is seen in a Frank A. Munsey Company advertisement. The coupon (see page 169) is surrounded with the pictures of four well-known tennis players. The problem of guessing their names is the incentive to induce readers to fill in the coupon.

The rebus, the puzzle and the riddle, will probably continue to be used in advertising. They constitute a challenge to the reader, to which the sending of the coupon is the response.

REVIEW

What is the purpose of "getting the inquiry" copy?

How do advertisers seek to eliminate the inquiries of persons who are merely curious?

When can samples be used effectively, and what methods are used for their distribution?

State the general character of booklet advertising.

Discuss the utility of coupons attached to advertisements.

From your experience name other advertisements which correspond to the types described in this chapter.

CHAPTER XI

"DIRECTING THE READER" COPY

1. *Purpose and scope.*—Copy intended to guide or direct the consumer in his purchasing is known as "directing the reader" copy. Many goods from their very nature are not adapted to mail-order selling. It is necessary to market these thru the various distributing agencies and to direct the public to the nearest dealer. Thus the two styles of copy known as "getting the inquiry" copy and "directing the reader" copy have developed.

Copy which directs the reader must be forcible enough first to overcome the reader's inertia toward change from one product to another, or his indisposition to spend money for some new product. Either of these obstacles may be met successfully by stimulating the enthusiasm of a prospect. But with this accomplished there remains the second barrier in the person of the dealer. He may be pushing a competitive product or he may desire to avoid trade-marked goods. The gratification of the wants of the customer may not always mean immediate profits for the dealer. The copy-writer who would overcome this difficulty must be capable of injecting the right degree of insistence into his prospects before they come under the influence of the retailer.

2. *Methods of directing the reader.*—There are seven kinds of copy designed to direct the reader. Most of them are characterized by some familiar trade slogan, as follows: (1) "Ask your dealer" copy; (2) "Ask your dealer or write us" copy; (3) "At all good stores"; (4) "For sale at Wanamaker's"; (5) "Sold nowhere else"; (6) Directing reader thru display; (7) "Take no other make."

3. *"Ask your dealer" copy.*—Men cannot be made enthusiastic about anything in this world if they distrust it, if they are ignorant of its effect upon themselves, or if they are not interested in it. This means that enthusiasm is a compound of confidence, knowledge, interest and emotion. The emphasis which is put upon each of these points will depend upon the conditions. A well-known company may possibly need nothing more than its name or trade-mark to inspire confidence. With an asset of this kind, the company can devote its advertising effort to stimulating interest and desire.

One of the best advertisements which was ever put out by the B. J. Johnson Soap Company, as tested by the comments of distributors, well illustrates the balancing of these motives.

Every one knows the Palmolive brand; therefore, the word alone prominently displayed establishes confidence. However, the picture at once piques the curiosity and serves as a strong attention factor; but

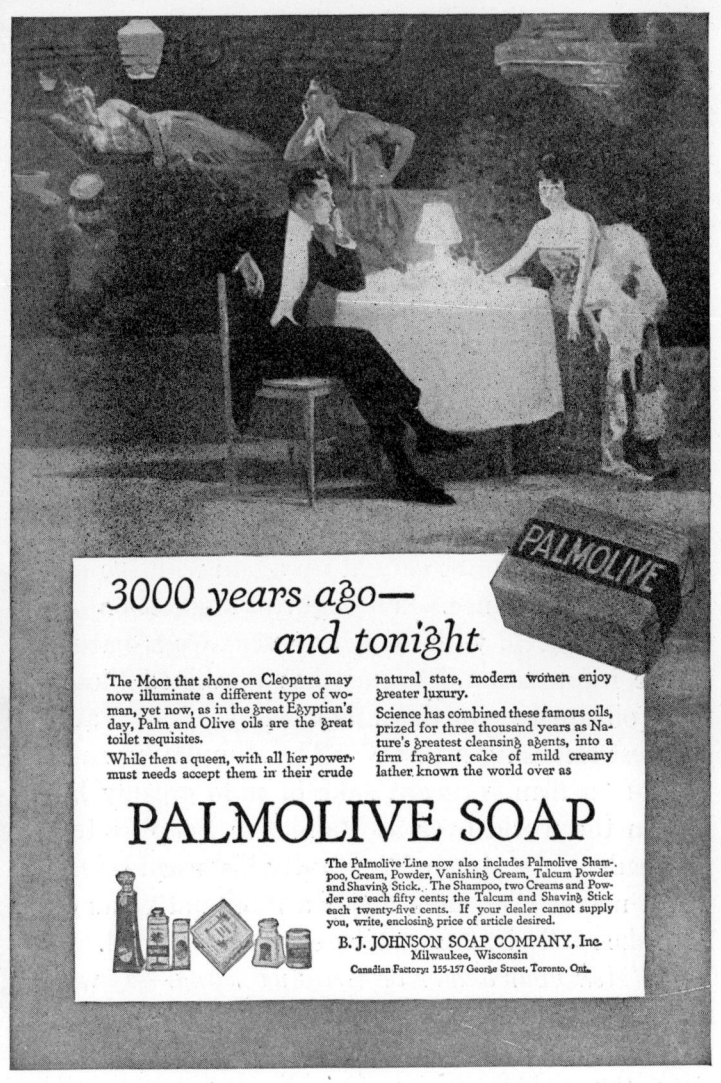

3000 years ago—
and tonight

The Moon that shone on Cleopatra may now illuminate a different type of woman, yet now, as in the great Egyptian's day, Palm and Olive oils are the great toilet requisites.

While then a queen, with all her power, must needs accept them in their crude natural state, modern women enjoy greater luxury.

Science has combined these famous oils, prized for three thousand years as Nature's greatest cleansing agents, into a firm fragrant cake of mild creamy lather known the world over as

PALMOLIVE SOAP

The Palmolive Line now also includes Palmolive Shampoo, Cream, Powder, Vanishing Cream, Talcum Powder and Shaving Stick. The Shampoo, two Creams and Powder are each fifty cents; the Talcum and Shaving Stick each twenty-five cents. If your dealer cannot supply you, write, enclosing price of article desired.

B. J. JOHNSON SOAP COMPANY, Inc.
Milwaukee, Wisconsin
Canadian Factory: 155-157 George Street, Toronto, Ont.

This advertisement directs what action the reader shall take if his dealer cannot supply him with Palmolive soap the name, Palmolive, and the picture of two attractive young people sitting at dinner with the dimly outlined figures of a reclining Cleopatra and a kneeling Antony as a "memory picture" in the background would not be sufficient to win the complete enthusiasm of the reader. The final touch is added by the copy. How naturally the words "3,000 years ago—and tonight" lead the attention which has been casually arrested by the picture, into a closer observation and a growing interest. "The moon that shone on Cleopatra," stimulates the interest of the reader, and before he is aware of it he has slipped over the prosaic statement—"palm and olive oils are the great toilet requisites" only to be caught up again with the promise of more romance. The indirect suggestion in the words "a queen, with all her power" leads naturally to the information, "science has combined these famous oils, prized for three thousand years as Nature's greatest cleansing agents." The stimulating suggestion of "a firm fragrant cake of mild creamy lather known the world over as Palmolive Soap" interests the reader. In spite of the faulty historical reference which makes Cleopatra about a thousand years older than she really is, the writer gets his story read.

4. *"Ask your dealer or write us" copy.*—It will be noticed that the direction of the reader to a dealer is not so important here as in the case of a new product, since the public expects a wide distribution of so well known a soap. If the manufacturer is not certain of the distribution of his goods, he fortifies him-

self by putting in the statement "if your dealer cannot supply you, write, inclosing price of article desired."

5. *"At all good stores."*—When an article has become so well known as to be on general sale it may be enough to say "At the best stores." Altho this style may be flattering to the stores that have the goods, it would not be well for a new concern putting out a breakfast food to advertise "Ask your grocer," when only a few hundred handle it. There are many examples of business failure due to using this form of directing the reader without first getting the dealer's cooperation in a general distribution. Except, therefore, in general advertising of goods which already have their required distribution, this type of "directing the reader" copy is being dropped.

6. *"For sale at Wanamaker's."*—The change from the general direction to the specific shows how vital it is to let the customer know where an article can be purchased. Substitution thrives on general advertising which says, "sold at all good stores." To announce, for example, that an article is for sale at Wanamaker's makes the offer more concrete while at the same time it ties to it a name well known in the locality, thus serving the further purpose of suggesting the article when the purchaser is on a shopping trip to that store.

The Columbia Graphophone Company has adopted the method of making monthly announcements of its new records.

For the metropolitan district of New York City, one hundred or more dealers are specified by name and address in the advertisements of the Columbia Company. Furthermore, the Manhattan dealers are classified according to location—"Below 14th Street," "14th Street to 43rd Street," "43rd Street to 96th Street" and so on.

7. *"Sold nowhere else."*—When the Holeproof Hosiery Company came to New York City, it got Brill Brothers to exploit its goods. The company might have taken another method and sold them thru twenty stores. To have done so, however, would have been to gain extensive at the sacrifice of intensive sales effort. When the firm could announce "Sold nowhere else" a premium was put upon the goods by means of the exclusiveness implied, and at the same time the dealers did not feel that they were advertising a competitor as strongly as they would advertise themselves.

One of the prime features of the advertising of the Coward Shoe on the opposite page is seen in the effect upon a reader who is forced to the conclusion that a firm which is able to say "Sold Nowhere Else—James S. Coward, 262–274 Greenwich Street, New York," surely must have a superior article or it would not last long in a business where competition is most keen. It might also be well to compare the general copy of this advertisement with the Douglas shoe advertisement on page 181. The Coward ad has no price, no general description, no bargain suggestion,

The Coward Shoe
"REG U S PAT OFF"

Good Shoe-Judgment Is Winning

The old improper forms of shoes have long shown their impracticability. Now modern standards insist upon sensible, natural shoes. Coward Shoes, designed on the foot lines as nature gave them, have been manufactured for 50 years. And for 50 years their comfort and good sense have brought unusual satisfaction to a patronage that has climbed steadily to many thousands.

The Coward Shoe still stands as a leader in the long battle for good shoe-judgment.

Sold Nowhere Else

JAMES S. COWARD
262-274 Greenwich St., N. Y.
(Near Warren Street)

Directing the reader to the only store where Coward shoes are sold, this advertisement gives the suggestion of a superior product but a simple, straightforward appeal to quality and then—"Sold Nowhere Else."

8. *Directing the reader thru display.*—Much successful advertising has been done by directing the reader thru tying up the appeal in the advertisement with display signs, and window displays. The Socony Oil copy urging the reader to purchase his oil and gasoline at the store or at the garage which displays the Socony sign is an illustration of this.

On the other hand, where the distribution of an article is centralized, much depends upon specific directions showing location and suggesting the ease with which the store can be reached. These elements are well illustrated in the Redfern Corset advertisement. The whole advertisement is based on the idea of directing the reader. From the familiar trademark and the number 510 over the door, down to the diagrammatic layout of the streets in the vicinity of the shop, everything points the way and suggests the ease with which a customer can reach the Redfern Corset Shop. Notice how this feeling is heightened by the use of the familiar landmarks of the Public Library and Grand Central Station.

9. *"Take no other make."*—A more common copy is that which uses the authoritative form of expression. "Beware of substitutes," "Take no other make," "Insist upon your dealer's supplying you," and similar phrases are used to warn the reader. These are likewise based upon the suspicious element which is particularly alert when a man thinks of

Emphasizing location

spending money. It startles a reader like the double challenge of a red light flashed in the dark, accompanied by "Halt! Who goes there?" There is nothing subtle in this type of copy except that the motive appealed to is carefully concealed by a strong bid for the reader's confidence in a straightforward type of copy and display. The use of such phrases by the Douglas Shoe Company may be seen in the accompanying advertisement.

10. *Establishing new trade connections.*—Where it is the house policy to sell thru the retailer, or where distribution thru the retailer is the most practical, the producer often advertises direct to the consumer. Such advertising takes into account the following objects:

(1) To get the consumer to call on the retailer, and either (a) buy the article advertised, (b) ask to be shown the line, or (c) ask for a free sample.

(2) To impress the trade-mark and special features of the product upon the consumer's mind, so that the advertised line will be preferred and selected over others.

(3) To further sales to the dealer by offering cooperative methods when soliciting sales to the trade.

(4) To obtain the general benefits of publicity advertising, even tho the advertisement is addressed specifically to the consumer.

It will be noted that there are two main objects in all advertising designed to sell the consumer thru the dealer. The advertiser aims to put the pressure of

Easter Styles

W. L. Douglas

FOR MEN — FOR WOMEN

"THE SHOE THAT HOLDS ITS SHAPE"

$4.00 $4.50 $5.00 $6.00 $7.00 & $8.00

IF you have been paying $10 to $12 for fine shoes, a trial will convince you that for style, comfort and service W.L.Douglas $7 and $8 shoes are equally as good and will give excellent satisfaction. The actual value is determined and the retail price fixed at the factory before W.L.Douglas name and the retail price is stamped on the bottom. The stamped price is W.L. Douglas personal guarantee that the shoes are always worth the price paid for them. The retail prices are the same everywhere. They cost no more in San Francisco than they do in New York.

Stamping the price on every pair of shoes as a protection against high prices and unreasonable profits is only one example of the constant endeavor of W.L.Douglas to protect his customers. The quality of W. L. Douglas product is guaranteed by more than 40 years experience in making fine shoes. The smart styles are the leaders in the fashion centers of America. They are made in a well-equipped factory at Brockton, Mass., by the highest paid, skilled shoemakers under the direction and supervision of experienced men, all working with an honest determination to make the best shoes for the price that money can buy.

For sale by 106 W. L. Douglas stores and over 9000 W. L. Douglas dealers, or can be ordered direct from factory by mail, Parcel Post charges prepaid. Write for Illustrated Catalog showing how to order by mail

W. L. Douglas, President W. L. Douglas Shoe Co., 210 Spark St., Brockton, Mass.

BOYS' SHOES
Best in the World
$3.00 $3.50 $4.00

CAUTION
Before you buy be sure W. L. Douglas name and the retail price is stamped on the bottom and the inside top facing. If the stamped price has been mutilated,
BEWARE OF FRAUD

W.L.DOUGLAS STORE: 428 Wabasha Street, cor. 7th, ST. PAUL

This advertisement features the warning to "Beware of Fraud"

demand upon the dealer and plans to identify his product with his brand. The one helps to place the line with the dealer; the other tends to tie the business created to the advertiser.

One of the most effective bits of this sort of advertising is done by the Aluminum Cooking Utensil Company. Reference to the accompanying advertisement shows that the appeal focuses on getting a sample into the hands of the consumer, either thru a call upon the dealer or by mail. Substitution is guarded against by devoting approximately one-quarter of the advertisement to particulars telling why " Wear-Ever " is the best aluminum ware.

The principles to which "Wear-Ever" advertisements conform can be observed to advantage in practically all consumer advertising where the product is sold at retail. First, get a sample of the product into the hands of the consumer so as to arouse interest and create a demand. Second, divert the resulting trade to the advertiser's retailer. Third, feature the brand, emphasizing its points of supremacy to such a degree that substitution will be difficult, if not impossible.

11. *Dealer cooperation.*—The products of many large concerns have become so well known that the advertising has reduced itself to little more than a display of the trade-mark. Under such conditions dealers generally carry the line as a matter of course; their cooperation consists merely in selling what is asked for.

A new form of dealer cooperation is found in

Recipe for Filling—Juice and grated rind of one Lemon, 1 Cup Sugar, Yolks of 2 Eggs, 1 Cup Hot Water, 1 Heaping Tablespoon Corn Starch. Cream together the juice of the lemon, sugar and yolk of eggs. Add cup of hot water and let all come to a boil. Add corn starch (previously dissolved in cold water). Let cool. Bake crust before putting in filling.

Recipe for Pie Crust—1½ Cups Flour, ¼ Cup Lard, ¼ Cup Butter, ½ Teaspoon Salt, Cold Water. Add salt to flour and work in lard with finger tips. Moisten to dough with cold water. Toss on board sprinkled lightly with flour, pat and roll out. Fold in butter, pat and roll out. Line a "Wear-Ever" Pie Pan with paste and build up a fluted rim.

Recipe for Meringue—Beat the whites of 2 Eggs to a stiff froth with 2 tablespoons powdered sugar. Spread over top and brown in oven.

Bake this One-Lemon Pie in a
"Wear-Ever"
Aluminum Pie Pan

IF YOU want pies with light, flaky crusts—cooked evenly all the way through—use "Wear-Ever" Aluminum Pie Pans and don't grease them. They take the heat quickly and distribute it evenly so that every part of the pie bakes thoroughly at the same time.

The enormous pressure of rolling mills and stamping machines makes the thick, sheet metal in "Wear-Ever" utensils dense and smooth, hard and rigid. They are made without joints or seams—no place for food to lodge—no coating to chip off—are pure and safe. Their wonderful durability saves the expense and annoyance of continually buying new cooking utensils.

Replace utensils that wear out with utensils that "Wear-Ever"

Sold by leading Department, Housefurnishing and Hardware Stores. If you do not yet know why so many women prefer "Wear-Ever" to other kinds of aluminum and enameled utensils, get a one-quart Stewpan for only **25c** at store or from us, postage paid. Offer good only until November 30, 1916. Address

The Aluminum Cooking Utensil Co., Dept. 87, New Kensington, Pa.

This advertisement puts the pressure of demand on the dealer thru a direct appeal to the consumer

"national newspaper window display week" during which time dealers all over the United States display in their windows the products that are nationally advertised thru the medium of the daily newspaper. This is a tremendous feature and the newspapers give it a considerable amount of space.

But a new product is usually compelled to fight its way to the dealer's shelves thru the insistence of the consumer. Growers of fruit, makers of breakfast foods and similar products, attempt to increase consumption by constant suggestion, appetite appeals and educational copy, and then induce the readers to ask their dealer for the specific brand advertised. The value of the trade-mark, slogan or catch phrase is very great in this connection in aiding the memory of the prospect.

The advertisement of the Florence Oil Cook Stoves illustrates copy which combines the trade-mark and a direct suggestion of more heat with less care, with educational copy and specific directions by which the reader can supply himself. The suggestion, "Call at your dealer's today" gives added emphasis for a class of prospective customers—women—who often prefer following that suggestion to writing for information.

12. *Substitution.*—Substitution ranges all the way from a legitimate sales talk down to outright cheating, and the advertiser must meet this obstacle from the beginning to the end of his business career. The branch store, the sole agency, the distribution of samples, the store demonstration, canvassing, the pre-

FLORENCE
OIL COOK STOVES

MORE HEAT

The Quick Breakfast—Start the coffee. Put on the cereal. Have the oven heating while you whisk up some johnny-cake. With a four-burner Florence Oil Stove all this is done easily and quickly.

The Easy Ironing Day—One burner of a Florence Oil Stove is ample to keep your irons hot, because the heat goes right up under the irons, not out into the room. Your kitchen is cool and comfortable.

The Busy Baking Day—Perfect lever control gives you just the right degree of heat. Intense heat for pop-overs; medium heat for bread; slow, steady heat for sponge cake. The glass panel in the door enables you to watch the baking without opening the door.

LESS CARE

Summer Canning—All four burners busy. Every one will burn as long as you need it, giving you the strong, even heat which is vital to successful canning. No wicks to trim; the asbestos kindlers replace them.

Whatever the stove task, the Florence Oil Stove is easy to use and easy to keep clean. Complete directions accompany each stove. The Florence Tank Water Heater, burning kerosene oil, will supply hot water for kitchen and bathroom.

Call at your dealer's today and see how this Florence kitchen equipment will make your work much happier.

Send for the Home Canning and Drying edition of the Household Helper, which tells you how to can by the cold packed method and how to dry fruits and vegetables using a Florence Oil Stove equipment. It is gladly mailed free upon request.

CENTRAL OIL & GAS STOVE COMPANY, 156 School Street, Gardner, Massachusetts

Manufacturers of Florence Oil Cooking Stoves, Florence Tank Water Heaters, Florence Portable Baking Ovens, Florence Gas Room Heaters and Florence Oil Heaters
Made and sold in Canada by McClary's, London, Canada

Impressing the name and trade-mark, "Florence Oil Cook Stoves," and giving the positive suggestion, "Call at your dealer's"

mium offer—all bear more or less directly upon the question of substitution. The necessity for controlling substitution enters into many of the business policies connected with marketing; no business can rely solely upon its advertising to overcome substitution.

If the advertisements of various companies are studied, it will be noticed that they vary much in the relative amount of space given to picture and other display and to copy. As a rule, the older houses with well-established brands use a preponderance of display and make little effort to direct the reader to a dealer. An example of this is seen in the Palmolive advertisement on page 173. The somewhat newer houses or those pushing a new product are prone to allow educational copy to predominate and to make the copy for directing the reader moderately conspicuous, as in the case of the Cleveland Foundry Company's "Perfection Heater." But a third class of advertisers, because of the newness of their product or the unfamiliarity of their trade-mark, must meet substitution face to face. They must send their readers to the dealer with a prejudice in favor of their wares, strong enough to "demand the goods asked for." Firms of this class do much advertising based on educational copy, but they often force the question of substitution into the foreground.

The consumer usually depends upon the retailer's judgment. However, there has arisen a tendency to resent any attempt on the part of retailers to put a customer off with "something just as good." The general confidence of the public in trade-marked goods gives the advertiser a strong weapon even tho he must use it at long range. An evangelist, a labor agitator, a political orator, an ad writer or any person whose business it is to lead a crowd, can measure his success by the ability first to arouse the enthusiasm which leads to action, and second, firmly to fix that determination by an appeal to prejudice. If the suggestion that one is being tricked, whether it is in religious belief, in labor adjustments or in buying goods, is put in a man's mind, there is little hope for the cause, or its supporters, toward which this suspicion is directed.

It may take time to arouse enthusiasm, but suspicion lies ever ready to crop up. The advertiser who constantly exhorts the reader to ask for such and such a brand and to take no other, appeals to a general prejudice, which looks upon trade as a trial of wits where *caveat emptor* plays a ruling part. This warning directing a buyer to beware starts him to a store with his prejudice aroused by a suspicion that he may be tricked; and as a consequence, the moment that the dealer attempts to explain the merits of another brand, he is met with indignation which hardens into stubborn opposition as the dealer's argument progresses.

There are various shades of suggestion by which prejudice may be aroused. The character of the firm, the nature of the business, the extent of the selling campaign, etc., all bear upon the nature of appeal to be used.

REVIEW

What conditions make it necessary for many business houses to use copy which sends readers to the dealer?

Why should copy intended to direct the reader need to be particularly strong in stimulating enthusiasm and creating a strong prejudice for the product, firm or for a standard price principle?

How may the dealer's cooperation be forced thru advertising?

Under what condition is a dealer justified in trying to substitute a brand of goods for the one asked for?

What advantage is gained by using such specific directions in the copy as "For sale at Dayton's"?

How can display be used to advantage in connection with the principle of directing the reader?

How may the style of copy be used to influence the manufacturer as well as the dealer?

CHAPTER XII

"MOLDING PUBLIC OPINION" COPY

1. *Purpose and scope.*—Advertising is intended to do three things—to make people do something, buy something or think something. Copy that is intended to make people "think something" is termed "molding public opinion" copy. It is used for pure publicity—to direct public sentiment for political or legislative purposes, and frequently to advertise an industry. Another style of copy is designed to create good-will toward a product. An advertisement which aims to induce a general impression favorable to some policy, act or product, obviously employs copy designed to influence public opinion.

2. *Styles of copy.*—The first problem of the advertiser in determining the style of copy to adopt is to discover the existing state of public opinion. If the company is an old one, there may be old grudges, wrong impressions and the claims of competitors to combat. Second, there may be a question of just what part of the public it is desirable to reach. A national advertiser whose product appeals to men alone, at once cuts to one-half his possible audience of 100,000,000 Americans. Considerations of race, employment, territory or politics will, for most articles, re-

duce the public interested in any matter advertised to perhaps 6,000,000 families.

When the right attitude and the right people have been found, a third problem presents itself. How is the appeal to be framed so as to make the public interested in the company's affairs, policies or product? To decide upon the specific appeal to be used is a problem which will depend upon the special conditions prevalent at the time, but a general method may be adopted dependent upon the social mood or habit of accepting opinions or arguments. A few years ago real estate promoters drew thousands of settlers from the Middle West into sections of the Far West by means of pictures with a little explanatory matter. The public responded to the sentimental appeal, perhaps because the spirit of the people was strongly influenced by the restlessness characteristic of a frontier community.

Contrast that method with the advertising put out by the Union Pacific Railroad which spent one and a half million dollars in one year in educating the public to the opportunities existing along its lines. Of course, for such an extensive campaign there were no styles left entirely unused, yet educational copy predominated. This same style is prevalent in other lines of advertising as well, showing that public opinion is reached most readily today thru educational copy.

There are four closely related types of "molding public opinion" copy. The simplest type consists of the name or trade-mark alone. Another type closely allied to the first is the advertisement which uses a picture or other display with little or no reading matter other than the trade name. A somewhat more complex type is that which depends entirely upon the reading matter without display in any form, while the most complex of all is the advertisement which combines copy and display in about equal space proportion.

Styles of "molding public opinion" copy may be grouped under the following headings: (1) repetition of name; (2) repetition of name and picture of product; (3) setting forth a policy; (4) cooperation copy; (5) creating atmosphere copy; (6) educational copy.

3. *Repetition of name.*—Many occasions arise when it may be desirable to keep the name or brand of an article in the public mind without attempting to endow the advertisement with a further degree of selling quality. Hence an advertiser may print the name of his product day after day in the papers or post it in the street cars during the intervals between intensive campaigns. The well-known Clysmic advertisement shown on page 192 appeared for many weeks in the New York papers.

The advertisement served at least two purposes by its strong attention-attracting features of brevity and distinctiveness. First, to those persons who are well acquainted with this table water, the name stands out as a continual reminder of its virtues. At luncheon time the suggestion is particularly strong, since the advertiser by putting the name on several pages of newspapers, makes of this medium a supplement to the bill of fare in every hotel and café in the city. Secondly, such an advertisement serves to create curiosity where the goods themselves are not known. The word "Clysmic" is unique and easily remembered. To satisfy new readers whose curiosity has been aroused, advertisements are run which explain the uses and virtues of the product.

4. *Repetition of name and picture of product.*—A type of advertising somewhat similar in purpose to the table water advertisement is one which depends upon the use of a picture to attract attention. Many of the same conditions are behind the use of this style of copy as in the case of the simple name or trademark. Either the people must have their curiosity aroused in a new product or their memories stimulated by coming upon the name of a well-known brand as they ride in street cars, glance thru magazines or enter stores. The Coca-Cola advertisement on the opposite page, is an illustration of this style. It shows the power that can be exerted over public opinion thru the use of a pleasing picture and a name, after a product has become well known and its virtues are generally accepted. Illustrated advertising of this kind cannot be said to have displaced display, but

MOLDING PUBLIC OPINION 193

rather to have reached a high degree of success in the art of "picture writing."

Showing effective use of the "pretty girl" illustration type of display advertising

The two styles of copy just discussed are the kind used purely for publicity.

5. *Setting forth a policy.*—Every progressive business expends some part of its outgo in the purchase

of good-will. Advertising is now recognized as not only one of the surest means of producing good-will, but one of the most economical. Many of the great organizations, dependent largely upon the favorable consideration of the public, now take the direct route and show why they are entitled to such good-will. Managers no longer consider silence a defense either against attack or against insidious growth of adverse sentiment. Corporation directors now frequently foresee adverse opinion, and advertise to head it off.

When the price of milk was increased one cent per quart in New York City one of the first companies to raise the price immediately began advertising. The copy used is plainly and frankly of the good-will class. One of the series is as follows:

Borden's

MILK

Is Honest Milk

It is delivered to you just as it comes from a healthy cow, plus the added safety of thoro pasteurization.

There is no juggling, no tricks, no "standardizing" to skimp a penny here and there. You get pure, honest milk, just as tho you took it from your own pet "bossy" in your own barn.

This is no more nor no less than what you have a right to expect, but you didn't get milk of this kind until Borden's came and the Borden Quality having set the pace for the milk trade years ago is still the leader today.

Use Borden's Milk

Public service corporations, particularly, are utilizing the good-will style of advertising. A part of one of the advertisements of the Chicago surface lines reads as follows:

RETURNED—INTACT

Every day several score of street car patrons leave their purses or other belongings in the cars and get them back later by calling at the depots and furnishing satisfactory evidence of ownership.

In a year more than 30,000 articles of value are reported found by trainmen and handed to the owners. Some days the total money recovered runs into hundreds of dollars. Bags containing jewelry and other things of worth frequently are returned to patrons. Seldom are losses reported which are not recovered immediately.

6. *Cooperation copy.*—Since good-will is intangible, it often is insufficient in itself for an advertiser's requirements. In many cases, he must have active cooperation. This cooperation is based on good-will.

Cooperation copy is found at its best as one of the comparatively late developments of advertising. Copy of this class does not aim to sell anything; it aims to make sales of commodities or service easier.

The public is singularly short-sighted and selfish, but often needs only a reminder to improve. The "Do your Christmas shopping early" slogan of the department store advertisers is a case in point. Street car passengers invariably crowd on the first car, choosing to stand, tho comfortable seats are to be found in the next car. Hence such cooperative copy as the following:

TAKE THE NEXT CAR—AND SAVE TIME

A broken wagon, open bridge or other traffic blockade sometimes brings together two or more street cars of the same line.

When these cars pull up to load nearly all who are waiting to get on try to crowd into the first car.

Do not overload the first car. Save time by boarding the second or third car instead. A heavily loaded car gets along more slowly.

It has to stop oftener and people have to take more time in getting on and off.

When one car has to do all the work it holds up a whole string of cars.

They all get thru sooner if you get on the second or third car—so that the load is distributed.

Think of this when you start to board one of a bunch of cars.

Take the one which has most seats—and save time.

CHICAGO SURFACE LINES

7. *"Creating atmosphere" copy.*—Another class of advertising devotes itself to the building up of goodwill for some particular quality of its product. The types of this style of copy vary from a bare announcement accompanied perhaps with appropriate display, to the advertisement which contains a combination of every form of copy. The Pierce-Arrow advertisement, opposite, features style and endeavors to create an atmosphere of public approval. Its efforts are

LUXURY

Luxury is something more than comfort, something more than beauty and something more than style. It is even something more than a combination of all three. It lies not only in making a cushion soft; it includes arranging that cushion at angles and heights to suit the position of the body. It means more than an engine which ceaselessly propels the car; it conceives an engine which starts and stops with so little friction that one glides from motion to rest, or from rest to motion. Luxury is sensuousness, softness, silence.

The numerous refinements in the Pierce-Arrow Car give it an effect of opulence, a justifiable opulence built upon and around a dependable and hard-headed piece of machinery.

THE PIERCE-ARROW MOTOR CAR CO · BUFFALO N Y

PIERCE-ARROW

An example of "creating atmosphere" copy by means of a dignified presentation of a high quality product based on the desire of most persons to own something which is superior to other members of its class. This advertisement has none of the elements of mail-order copy—neither is there any attempt to direct the reader to the dealer nor any direct effort to induce him to send in an order or even an inquiry. Thus the copy is in perfect harmony with the attitude of the class of people to which it wishes to appeal. A man who will spend $6,000 for an article usually goes to see it himself. The way does not have to be made easy for him by the use of a coupon.

8. *Educational copy.*—Advertising thrives in a democracy and democracy is fostered by education. To demand facts in connection with any attempt to mold public opinion has become a habit in America. In comparing the "best advertisement" of fifty or more representative American firms in the year 1915 with those of 1916, it will be seen that while 70 per cent in the first period used educational copy, over 90 per cent used educational copy in the second period. There may be various purposes for general publicity copy, but when the main purpose is to make an impression for or against some proposition, the reader demands the information necessary to form an opinion upon the subject.

9. *Political purpose.*—The adoption of an administrative policy by a city, state or federal government may not become effective until the party is actually in power. In this case the party which goes before the public in an advertisement and frankly explains the

situation just as would a business concern, stands the best chance of molding public opinion to its point of view.

In its highest form, an advertisement of this kind rises to the plane of the political pamphlets of the early days of the republic into which went some of the best thought and writing power of the day. To be sure, the modern advertisement must differ in form, method and expression, but the same judgment and knowledge of facts and conditions must be employed in preparing the copy.

It is indeed a significant sign to see political parties using the business man's methods of stimulating interest, holding attention, creating confidence and getting support of the public. Such methods will have as beneficial an effect upon political parties, their programs and methods as it has had upon the manufacturer of trade-marked articles and upon corporation policies. Publicity tends to make men, parties, and corporations live up to their best intentions and keep up the quality of their output. The many advertisements that appeared during the presidential campaign of 1916 in the national advertising mediums, as well as in the local papers, explaining the platform on which candidates for office were taking their stand is sufficient evidence of the high place which this method has attained in the mind of the public.

The political advertisement is destined to supplant the spellbinder, the stump speaker, and the soap-box orator. But aside from the election of candidates, the public is going to be called upon to decide many questions of moment within the coming years as they did the suffrage question in New York State in 1917.

A New Yorker of national reputation who was mentioned for food controller of the State of New York found much opposition to his appointment. He challenged his opponents to a public discussion of the merits of the case in the advertising columns of the newspapers. When they complained they had no funds for the purpose he offered to supply the money. And he did.

Advertising is giving the discussion of such fundamental issues as war and peace, democracy and the relations of capital and labor, new and larger audiences than ever before considered these questions from all sides. Editorials express at best the opinions of a small circle of men whose ideas exert an influence upon their news columns. The newspaper reader saw only one viewpoint presented to him—his editor's—until advertising showed him that there is frequently another side to the question.

10. *Legislative purpose.*—One of the best illustrations of advertising to mold public opinion is seen in the advertisement of the Youngstown Sheet and Tube Company, opposite, which appeared previous to our entrance into the war. There is not the slightest reference to the company's product. No attempt is made to make sales. The advertisement ties the headline to the public interest of the moment. Its

The Call to Duty

IN THE crisis now confronting this country, the spontaneous and universal tenders of assistance made to our government form one of the most inspiring incidents in our history. The melting pot of American citizenship has done its work well.

It is worthy of note that in the front rank of those who have tendered unreserved support to the nation in a time of possible need are to be found the great industrial organizations of the country. Many months ago this company furnished to the War Department a detailed statement of its equipment and resources, pledging these without reservation to the national defense. Many others followed the same course.

These pledges still stand, awaiting only the call of the country for their redemption. The industrial organizations of America hold their patriotic obligations above all others—to be fulfilled first at any cost. This policy reflects the spirit and, in the highest sense, protects the interests, of both stockholders and customers, whose most solemn obligations and most fundamental welfare are served by the perpetuation of our national safety and our national ideals.

In the voluntary enlistment of our great industries for national defense, even before the people had been heard from, may be found a lesson for those who have been unwilling to concede to corporations the civic virtues they claim for themselves. These large aggregations of capital, necessary to efficiently carry on the business of the country, have demonstrated that they are owned and directed by men who represent the highest type of citizenship, are animated by deepest concern for the national welfare, and are willing to make for that end sacrifices that represent the supreme limit of patriotic devotion.

It is not unreasonable to hope that, out of the universal manifestation of these virtues brought about by the present situation, may come a better understanding among all our people, rich and poor, employer and employed. This would prove some compensation should peace, so ardently desired by all Americans, eventually become impossible.

THE YOUNGSTOWN SHEET & TUBE CO.
YOUNGSTOWN, OHIO

This appeal is designed to mold public opinion by creating good-will toward corporations by frankly stating their policy toward questions of national importance

Spies and Lies

German agents are everywhere, eager to gather scraps of news about our men, our ships, our munitions. It is still possible to get such information through to Germany, where thousands of these fragments—often individually harmless—are patiently pieced together into a whole which spells death to American soldiers and danger to American homes.

But while the enemy is most industrious in trying to collect information, and his systems elaborate, he is *not* superhuman—indeed he is often very stupid, and would fail to get what he wants were it not deliberately handed to him by the carelessness of loyal Americans.

Do not discuss in public, or with strangers, any news of troop and transport movements, of bits of gossip as to our military preparations, which come into your possession.

Do not permit your friends in service to tell you—or write you—"inside" facts about where they are, what they are doing and seeing.

Do not become a tool of the Hun by passing on the malicious, disheartening rumors which he so eagerly sows. Remember he asks no better service than to have you spread his lies of disasters to our soldiers and sailors, gross scandals in the Red Cross, cruelties, neglect and wholesale executions in our camps, drunkenness and vice in the Expeditionary Force, and other tales certain to disturb American patriots and to bring anxiety and grief to American parents.

And do not wait until you catch someone putting a bomb under a factory. Report the man who spreads pessimistic stories, divulges—or seeks—confidential military information, cries for peace, or belittles our efforts to win the war.

Send the names of such persons, even if they are in uniform, to the Department of Justice, Washington. Give all the details you can, with names of witnesses if possible—show the Hun that we can beat him at his own game of collecting scattered information and putting it to work. The fact that you made the report will not become public.

You are in contact with the enemy *today*, just as truly as if you faced him across No Man's Land. In your hands are two powerful weapons with which to meet him—discretion and vigilance. *Use them.*

COMMITTEE ON PUBLIC INFORMATION
8 JACKSON PLACE, WASHINGTON, D. C.

George Creel, Chairman
The Secretary of State
The Secretary of War
The Secretary of the Navy

Contributed through Division of Advertising — United States Gov't Comm. on Public Information

This space contributed for the Winning of the War by

The Publisher of

An advertisement written in the endeavor to prevent careless persons from furnishing German agents with news for propaganda purposes

argument progresses logically, its statements are concise, and important ideas are emphasized. The company never in a single word suggests any ulterior motive in its advertisement. It is quite evident that this company took into consideration the first principle of writing copy of this kind, the existing state of the public mind toward corporations, and their relations to politics. The American public today wants more publicity in connection with company policies.

The Committee on Public Information used an effective method to prevent the spread of German propaganda. This organization employed a number of advertisements, one of which is here shown.

11. *Directing public sentiment.*—A slightly different application of the same principle is frequently used by concerns which find themselves in a business situation so extraordinary that their policy for the future, while based on sound practice, might turn public sentiment against them.

An illustration of the use of advertising for the purpose of directing public sentiment may be found in the announcements of the anthracite coal operators in the early part of 1916. It was decided to acquaint anthracite coal users with the vital conditions of the industry, as well as with the social and working conditions of the army of employes engaged in the operation of the mines. That the operators deemed it wise advertising to give the full facts in the situation is shown by the following:

The operation of the anthracite mines of Pennsylvania represents an investment of upwards of $275,000,000 in plant and equipment, in addition to the value of the coal lands leased by the operators. . . .

The average returns are entirely too small to meet the increased cost of additional compensation to miners, or substantial changes in conditions of employment, without a consequent *increase* in the *price* of coal to the consumer. . . . We believe that the users of anthracite coal are vitally interested in the readjustment on April 1, 1916, of the relations between the operators and the miners.

We have conceived it to be our duty to inform the users of anthracite coal of the state of affairs, in order that an enlightened public sentiment may operate to fairly adjust the conditions which will arise, and which must be discussed and determined within the next few weeks.

If, after such presentation, the *users of anthracite coal say it is our duty to make a large advance in the income of the miners and others employed in the industry, and are prepared to meet the advanced cost by paying a higher price for coal, now is the time to say so, and we can meet the issue on that basis,* but if the anthracite coal using public is opposed to such concessions *its voice should be plainly heard.*

The coal operators desire to *deal justly with their employes, granting every fair request*, but they also *deem it their duty to protect the coal consuming public* and to conserve its interest, just as they propose to protect, so far as possible, their own interests.

12. *Advertising an industry.*—A few years ago a company which manufactured coal-tar products de-

cided to advertise. Coal-tar pitch is used in laying tar and gravel roofs. These roofs must be put on by a local builder or roofer. On this account, it was desirable to advertise, and, at the same time, advertising was rendered difficult. Among the people engaged in the business there was no generally accepted standard for the use of this kind of roofing material. Some of them found it easy to save a little money, as a badly put on roof did not show until after the weather had had a chance at it. As a result, manufacturers suffered from not selling as much material as they should, and the public suffered thru not knowing how to get the best results from the materials. This, then, was a problem which advertising was expected to solve.

The firm finally conceived the plan of a standard method for laying tar and gravel roofs. The company consulted engineers and architects, and the best method and the proper proportions of materials were specified. The specifications sent out by this concern did not call for materials made by themselves. There were other materials on the market, but this company handled so large a proportion of the coal tar that it could afford to promote the entire industry. Further, the fact that the name of the company was put on the specifications would naturally suggest their products. Under this plan advertising was begun, not of any particular product, but of a *method,* calculated to result in a job. Architects and builders were quick to see the value of such a plan and to adopt it. A great improvement in the condition of the coal-tar roofing industry was brought about and an increase in the consumption of this kind of roofing material was immediately noticeable.

A recent tendency shows that some industries thru their national associations are beginning to advertise nationally. They wish to create public opinion in favor of a certain type of product or service and thus enable the local distributers or stations to push for direct sales.

The Society for Electrical Development, for example, carries on a national campaign known as "America's Electrical Week." Each association prepares a suitable slogan and poster to be used thruout the country, while at the same time a national advertising campaign is carried on thru the magazines and newspapers. A typical advertisement is that shown in the Electricity's 1916 poster. Over 200,000,000 reproductions of this poster were used to advertise "America's Electrical Week" thru newspapers, magazines, lithographs, cards and stamps. By this means the whole industry as well as the public generally have their attention drawn to the service of electricity. An excellent opportunity is offered for the local companies and appliance dealers to push for business thru "celebrations," window displays, and selling campaigns.

Another example of this kind of publicity may be found in the advertising of the California Fruit Growers' Association and of the National Dairy Council.

MOLDING PUBLIC OPINION

The latter, shown on page 208, is a recent convert to this form of advertising and is of special interest since the products in question are used universally.

13. *Change in the public's attitude.*—It is to be noted that the tendency to influence public opinion thru the columns of paid advertising is increasing.

Creating public opinion in favor of electric industries and giving local companies an opportunity for interior sales campaigns

It is supplanting the more indirect way, noticeable a few years ago, of influencing readers thru the "news item" or "feature article" which have their origin in a bureau of publicity or in the publicity office of a business corporation.

The business man by his high-grade advertising has not only created an open mind toward merchandise

VIM DEPENDS ON VICTUALS

MILK
Both Food and Drink

Milk is not merely a delicious beverage. It's a food.

Nature combines in milk all the food elements your body needs. Some produce bone and muscle. Some rebuild it. And some create energy. And they are carefully balanced. So that you get the right proportions.

Amongst foods none can compare with delicious, stimulating milk. None are so easy to obtain. None so economical.

Prof. Rosenau of Harvard says you would have to buy and prepare ¼ pound of beef, or 8 eggs, or 2 pounds of chicken or codfish to get the nourishment contained in a single quart of milk.

Milk is a concentrated food, you see.

Eat Less—Drink More Milk

Fresh milk is the ideal food for men and women who work with muscle or with brain—people who are doers. Milk drinkers are always temperate. They know that what one eats and drinks today is thinking and working tomorrow.

Milk drinkers seldom over-eat. They keep their bodies in fine physical trim. Their efficiency is 100 per cent every day. They are ready for emergencies.

Then heed the advice of great food specialists. Dr. J. H. Kellogg says: "Most people will find that they can reduce their daily rations by one-third, sometimes one-half, without any inconvenience whatever."

For Young and Old Alike

Nature first gives the infant milk. Why ever stop it? Why defy Nature? For the growing child, for the young man and woman, and for the maturer years milk is a needed food.

Drink it slowly—eat it. That insures complete digestion. Consider milk in the place of the heavier, slowly digestible foods. Use milk as a substantial part of your meal. Begin today to drink more milk. Teach every member of the family to know its value. Stop overeating. Excess calls the doctor.

When you come to drink more milk for every meal you'll know the real joy of living. Brain fag will be rarer. Bodily fatigue will disappear. Remember, good health is the foundation of all success.

Milk points the way.

BUTTER
The 98% Food

Pure, golden butter, fresh and crisp, is the chief energy food.

Unfortunately, too many people think of butter as merely a spread for bread. They forget that butter is one of the foremost energy foods 80 to 85 per cent of butter is pure fuel-fat in the rarest form. Then there is mineral matter, for bone building. And some protein for muscle making and repairing.

Butter comes from cream alone, with salt ordinarily added. It takes the cream of 8 to 10 quarts of milk to make a pound of butter.

Practically No Waste

The stomach quickly absorbs butter—98 per cent of it. And it is the digested portion of what you eat that counts. Foods with excess waste in them are luxuries. But certainly not butter. You pay for a pound of butter. Your body gets that pound. And uses it.

Butter is everybody's food. Food for the delicate and robust child. Food for the man who wields the sledge or produces by brain work, for the sick and the well, for the rich and the poor.

Old fashioned, plain bread and butter has always been and always will be the Staff of Life. The combination is unmatchable.

Use Butter in Cooking

More butter in soups. Meat and fish broiled in butter. Vegetables heavily buttered. Such are the practices of famous chefs.

Consult cook-books, and you will find that the foremost cooks recommend butter in dough-making. Better pie-crust, better bread, better cake comes from using more butter.

You do more than create more palatable dishes. The butter is absorbed into the foods. That increases their nutritive values. So there is no waste here.

Commence now to eat more butter. Give the children all the bread and butter they want. Force it on them, if necessary.

For remember, butter is concentrated energy. The body needs it.

And since butter is a concentrated food, it is most economical.

CHEESE
Compared with Meat

"So far as its composition is concerned, cheese is entitled to be considered as directly comparable with meat," says Dr. C. F. Langworthy, of the U. S. Dept. of Agriculture.

Then compare cheese with the 15 principal foods. You will find that cheese is first in food value per pound. It precedes meat, eggs, bread, potatoes and eleven others.

Cheese costs less than meat and these other foods. So there is no easier way to cut your food bill than by using more cheese. Old-world nations know its economy. They know its value as one of the most palatable, nourishing and delicious foods.

Highly Nutritious

Cheese is a highly concentrated food. It saves us from over-indulgence. It takes the place of bulky, diluted food.

The sturdiest people in the world come from nations where cheese is a basic food—eaten three times a day.

Cheese has been one of the world's Staples since the beginning of civilization. But in these days of sky-high prices it takes on a new meaning

Nothing to Throw Away

You use it as it comes from the market. You squander no money for bone, gristle, skin or seeds.

Cheese is made from milk. When you read about milk in the first column you noted its food value. Then think of the food value of cheese. Compare its cost with other foods. To every pound of cheese you get the food value of about 3 quarts of milk.

Your cook book is full of recipes for delicious cheese dishes. They stimulate digestion. They add a zest to any meal. They help you add variety to your family table. They give your family more nourishment at less cost and trouble.

Commence to use cheese in place of heavier, less digestible dishes.

Remember that a diet is a better cure than medicine and the lancet.

Give cheese its rightful place. *For cheese is a real food.*

ICE CREAM
The Dessert Food

Ice cream contains more real nourishment than many of the dishes which you think essential and necessary. A quart of ice cream has the full food-value of one and a half pounds of round steak, or four pounds of potatoes, or eighteen eggs.

Delicious—Nutritious

Mothers now realize that ice cream is fine for growing children. And as a prominent part of a grown-up's meal, there are unmatchable food values in this combination of cream and sugar.

Dr. Woods Hutchinson, one of the world's greatest food experts, says: "A high place in the summer diet should be given to ice cream, ice puddings and frozen custards. Their combination of sugar and fat gives them high nutritive value, and they are readily digested by healthy stomachs, especially when eaten slowly, with plenty of good cake, home made cookies or salted crackers."

So it is well to eat ice cream at lunch and at supper. It's just the thing, too, to eat between meals and before going to bed.

The Handy Food

You can get good ice cream at your nearest drug store. It is ready to eat, requiring no preparation. And as in other dairy products, there is no waste. Your body gets every ounce of nourishment you pay for.

Ice cream should not be *added to* the meal. *It should be a part of the meal.* Less bulky foods during the meal and a big, heaping dish of ice cream at the end is a sensible plan.

Ice cream is easily digested. It keeps the stomach in good order. It is so safe that it is often the first food allowed to convalescents.

As people come to know ice cream better and its real value as a food, more will insist on it.

Begin eating more ice cream now. Substitute it for other foods. You will live better and longer, feel happier and stronger, earn more and spend less.

Send for the Dairy Menu Book. It's free, postpaid.

NATIONAL DAIRY COUNCIL — GENERAL OFFICES CHICAGO, ILL.

"This Council is composed of 280,000 dairymen, dairy cattle-breeders and representatives of all allied dairy interests. Its purpose are to build a greater and better American dairy agriculture — resulting in improved soil-fertility and better farm life—to encourage every American consumer to have a keener appreciation (like European nations) of the high food value of dairy products. The Council believes its mission is patriotic.

A wider use of dairy products on the tables and in the kitchens of our American homes will mean a healthier and cheaper fed nation. Our slogans are: "Drink and use more milk." "Eat and cook with more butter." "Ice cream is not alone an excellent dessert but a real food." "Cheese is the stuff of life of many nations; why not in U. S. A.?" "Dairy products—palatable, nourishing, economical—are Nature's best foods."

Another example of advertising to create increased demand for nationally used products

on the part of consumers and dealers as such, but he has established advertising as the standard method of influencing public opinion in general. That educational copy predominates in all the different uses to which publicity copy is put, is significant of the present attitude of the public. The people desire to learn, and ask only that a good article, an enlightened policy, a sound platform, or worthy motive be honestly represented before they decide to buy or express their opinion.

REVIEW

For what general purpose is "molding public opinion" copy used?

What styles of copy are useful for this purpose and why?

Cite instances in your experience where advertising to mold public opinion could be of value to the advertiser.

What is cooperation advertising and how does it benefit the public and the advertiser?

What is the value of advertising like that of the anthracite coal operators before raising the price of the coal?

CHAPTER XIII

PREPARING THE ADVERTISEMENT

1. *Three parts of the advertisement.*—The first step in the preparation of an advertisement is to block out the idea. The heading for the copy is the first consideration; the second is the body; the third is the close.

2. *The heading.*—"What will most surely attract the attention?" is the first question that arises. The copy writer will need to divide this general question into a number of specific questions.

When it is decided whether the heading or "attention-attractor" shall be general or specific, the space it is to occupy is fixed by this decision. Usually the more general the heading the greater the space, compared with the body and close, which it should occupy. This is illustrated in the Pierce-Arrow advertisement on page 197, the heading used being the one word, "Luxury."

When the wording or illustration to be used as a heading is remarkably specific or striking, comparatively small space may be allotted to it. In the earlier history of advertising, the single word, "STOP!" in bold-face type was enough to attract the attention. This, however, has become hackneyed. News events are sometimes made to furnish a heading, tho these must be used with caution. They may attract attention to the heading only, but the function of the heading is to attract attention to the rest of the message as well.

After the advertiser has decided whether the heading is to be pictorial or text, or both, whether it is to be general or specific, and what proportion of the advertisement it is to occupy, he is free to take up the details of the body of the advertisement.

3. *The body.*—The principles laid down as governing the heading apply in many respects to the body of the advertisement, but they are modified by the difference in the purpose of the work to be done. The body is designed to *hold* the interest rather than to induce it; to tell the story rather than to set the reader to speculating on what the story is. But the same general questions must be considered: the space, the methods of display designed to retain attention, and the form in which the material is to appear.

Two tendencies are found regarding the amount of space to be allotted to the body of the advertisement. The first recognizes the competition of other advertising matter as of extreme importance and throws the emphasis on getting attention. The other tendency is to tell a complete story, even at the expense of the attention-attracting matter. These tendencies may be noted in advertising today by observing so-called publicity advertising that is de-

The Comfort Car

Hupmobile

In this advertisement the attention is secured solely thru the illustration —a form of publicity advertising which compels attention

signed to interest as many readers as possible, in contrast with mail-order advertising. The publicity advertisements of Kellogg's Toasted Corn Flakes, brands of clothing such as Kirschbaum or Kuppenheimer, Ivory Soap and Kodak—all are devoted to attracting the attention, while the messages may vary from a few words to a few terse paragraphs. The advertisement of the Hupmobile, opposite, is a good example of this type. In mail-order advertising and in advertisements of both specialties and staples which have new features or uses, the stress is placed on the message.

4. *The close.*—When the advertisement has a direct close, present practices show uniformity. The tendency is to make the close of the advertisement exceedingly brief. Perhaps the phrase, "At dealers," is about as condensed as the directing message can be made. Even corner coupons are models of terseness. It is hardly possible to find a superfluous word in the following coupon, yet it forms a climax to the story told by the advertisement:

―――――― QUICK ACTION COUPON ――――――
HALLET & DAVIS PIANO CO.,
145 Boyleston St., Boston, Mass.

Please mail me at once full information about the Virtuolo and address of nearest Virtuolo dealer.

Name ――――――――――――――――――――
Address ――――――――――――――――――――

5. *Importance of display.*—The importance of display in connection with an advertisement may be

Illustrating the effect in appearance of proper display

shown by noting what display does. Note as a contrast in display, the advertisements for Premium Bacon shown above.

In each case the reading matter is the same. Each occupies the same amount of space. Yet one presents an attractive appearance, while the other does not. One stands out because of its arrangement and pleasing form, while the other is hazy in its effect. One draws attention to itself; the other makes no definite impression.

The quality which makes the difference is termed display, by which is meant the form and general appearance of an advertisement. On the quality of the display depends much of the success of the advertisement.

There has been much discussion as to the relative value of form and subject matter. There must be subject matter, both to make the sale and for display.

All things considered, the advertising writer who thoroly understands display will write to conform to its requirements. Many writers find it possible to lay out an advertisement and then "think to fit the space." Others focus their thoughts on the subject matter first and then derive the display, a snappy headline, a novel arrangement, or a striking illustration.

6. *The inclosing shape.*—The first question to solve in determining the display is the form that it shall take. Commonly, some form of rectangle is the most practical and convenient. It is safe to say that there is scarcely a geometrical form which has not been used to define the boundaries of an advertisement. The circle, square, triangle, polygon, all have been used both singly and in many combinations. Shields, keystones, crosses and other symbolic forms are occasionally to be seen, tho now less frequently than in times past.

Usually the shape of the column or page to which the advertisement must conform gives the advertisement the form of a rectangle. The most pleasing rectangle is one whose proportions are 3 to 5, termed the "golden section" because of its artistic proportions. The Locomobile advertisement on the next page is a practical example of the "golden section."

LOCOMOBILE

1917

Unhampered by cost, convention, or conditions, the builders of the Locomobile have developed the fine motor vehicle to its highest plane for 1917.

For superb engineering and luxurious coach work, the Locomobile excels. Such progress can obtain only in an ideal plant where quality instead of quantity is the practice as well as the policy.

Six Cylinder Models, $4600. upwards.

THE LOCOMOBILE COMPANY OF AMERICA

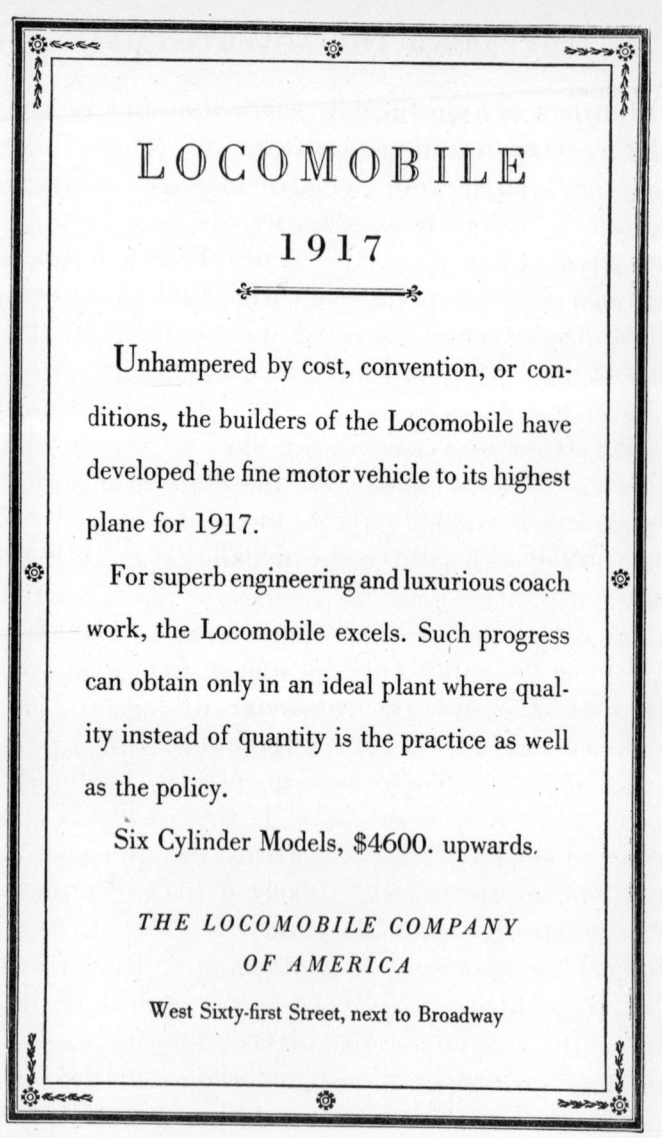

West Sixty-first Street, next to Broadway

This border presents a pleasing and dignified appearance, conforming well with the copy of the advertisement and the page on which it appears.

Borders or rules usually mark the limit of the inclosing shape of the advertisement. Marked exceptions are seen, however, in advertisements whose illustration is left without a border, the text only being bordered. This is a step out of ordinary usage, and its unusualness may prove an attraction, tho care must always be exercised in using such methods to attract attention.

7. *Size.*—It is a truism that "the appropriation, rather than art, governs the size" of an advertisement. Once the amount of the appropriation to be expended is known and the mediums decided upon, the problem of size is principally a mathematical one.

Small advertisements are usually measured in width by the single column, and in length by inches or lines. Larger advertisements are figured down to fourths or eighths on a page basis.

8. *Margins.*—The rules governing white space seem to be fairly well fixed. If the subject is one in which inherent interest is great, the advertisement may be "crowded," particularly if the appropriation be limited. If artistic quality is desired, a wide margin for text and illustrations is well-nigh essential. One-fifth white space is considered desirable to produce a well-balanced advertisement.

Page margins have been reduced to mathematical exactness from which it is not desirable to depart. When pages face, the order of greatest width for a left-hand page is, bottom, left side, top, right side.

For a right-hand page the order is, bottom, right side, top, left side. When pages are single, the order is commonly, bottom, right and left margins, top. In other cases, the custom of "sinkage" is observed. The extra margin at the head of a chapter, as in a book, is termed "sinkage." In some cases, a single page advertisement on a single sheet is sunk at the top to correspond with the book custom.

A page advertisement has, of necessity, the same margins as the periodical in which it is published. When the advertisement forms a part of a page—perhaps a quarter page in one of the standard magazines—the margin is important if a coupon is used. The coupon should always be in the outside corner of the page so as to be easily detached. If the advertisement is to appear in the lower right-hand corner of the right-hand page, the bottom and right side will adjoin white space. If it appears on the left-hand page, the coupon should be on the left.

9. *Selection and arrangement of material.*—Great care should be exercised both in the selection and the arrangement of the material comprising the advertisement. Violence in contrast, ugliness in shape and size, mark many badly constructed advertisements.

The other extreme is stilted preciseness of form, so that the advertisement has the effect of being mathematically correct rather than humanly and ar-

PREPARING THE ADVERTISEMENT

tistically appealing; such advertisements are often divided into sections exactly equal in area. Checkerboard arrangement, once so common, lacks artistic appeal. Shapes and sizes should bear proper relation to each other; unequal masses are to be preferred to equal and, in general, arrangement should conform to universal principles of design.

10. *Appropriateness of illustration.*—Harmony is nowhere more desirable than between illustration and text. Pictures not only have high attention-attracting power, but they speak a universal language. If there is no harmony between the illustration and the text, the emphasis is thrown upon the illustration rather than upon the thing advertised.

The illustration, after having attracted the interest and held the attention, should divert that attention to the text. Close harmony between illustration and text, in fact, is the only assurance that interest in the thing advertised will not be diluted to an unfavorable degree, unless the text is more forcible than the illustration, which is not commonly the case.

The advertisement on page 220, "The Eternal Feminine of Tecla Pearls," shows a well-harmonized combination of the two factors, illustration and copy. Even the general layout, the artistic yet simple border, and the styles of type used, all lend an impression of refinement and elegance. Note how closely in the following statement the copy is made to tie up with the picture:

The Eternal Feminine of Tecla Pearls

Tecla Pearls may be termed the feminine for jewels—in French it is, in fact, a grammatical distinction: the jewel is masculine, but the pearl is feminine, superimposing its soft and subtle beauty on the French Academy—and what is there in the whole gamut of gems that looks so essentially feminine, so part of the woman who wears them, as a Necklace of Tecla Pearls, suspended from the throat like a mist of tears.

*Tecla Pearl Necklaces with
Diamond Clasp $75 to $350.*

T E C L A

398 Fifth Avenue   New York

10 Rue de la Paix, Paris

This advertisement shows perfect harmony between the illustration and copy. The picture is attractive and compels attention, while the text supplements the theme of the picture.

—and what is there in the whole gamut of gems that looks so essentially feminine, so part of the woman who wears them, as a necklace of Tecla Pearls, suspended from the throat like a mist of tears.

Appropriateness may be evident in mechanical treatment as well as in correlation of ideas. Daintiness of treatment in the illustration normally indicates a similar daintiness in the product advertised. Slapdash or cartoon illustration best advertises goods appealing to men, such as tobacco, liquors and sporting goods. If the illustration has more intimate connection with some part of the text than with another, the use of connecting lines, arrows or darts is often favored. In some cases, loops are used with good practical effect.

11. *Importance of headlines.*—Whether or not an illustration is used to attract attention, the headline is of primary importance. If used in connection with an illustration, it must both attract attention to itself and divert the attention aroused to the body of the advertisement.

The headline resembles, in many respects, the title to an article or story. To meet the requirements of a good title it should have a point of contact, it should be the keynote of the story, arouse curiosity, and produce a vivid mental picture.

An example of a good title is given in the advertisement of Columbia Batteries on the following page. The illustration pictures both the batteries and their

The Mighty Thunder Cloud and the Fiery little Columbia are first cousins

THE mighty thunder cloud often generates and wastes 150 thousand horsepower, when it hurls its terrific bolt flashing and crashing through the sky.

The fiery little Columbia generates a fraction of this volume, but sends its power on a specific errand, through wires, under control, without waste.

It is electricity in both cases. But the mighty thunder cloud works at the command of Nature for an unknown purpose. The fiery little Columbia works at your command for a definite use.

THE DRY BATTERY

THE Columbia Dry Battery is the handyman of the world. It ignites stationary engines, autos, trucks, tractors, and motorboats, rings bells and buzzes buzzers; lights lanterns and makes telephones talk; runs toys for the youngsters.

Motorists the world over know the wisdom of carrying the extra set of vigorous Columbias—to be connected in a jiffy when the regular ignition begins to loaf.

THE STORAGE BATTERY

THE Columbia Storage Battery is so hale and hearty it is guaranteed to do definite work for a definite time. Its health certificate even stipulates that another battery will be put to work for you without additional cost if the original should fail within the guarantee period.

A unique plan is back of this Columbia Storage Battery Service. Any Columbia Service Dealer will test, charge, or water your battery. But if surgery is necessary, he will pass it along—with its seal unbroken—to a nearby Columbia Service Station, where only competent experts will open it and remedy it. This plan heads off tinkering—which, as you motorists know, is responsible for half your battery troubles.

Columbia Service Dealers or Service Stations anywhere will be glad to demonstrate why and how you—like legions of other automobile owners—will prosper with Columbia Quality and Service.

Columbia
Storage and Dry Batteries

An example of a good headline

"first cousin," the thunder cloud, and the title stating that "the Mighty Thunder Cloud and the Fiery Little Columbia are first cousins," arouses the curiosity of the reader, leading him on to read the copy to find out how they are related.

In advertising, the "teasing" headline is favored, expressed plainly in the clearest wording. Commonly it should be specific—applying to and designating *the,* not any *similar* product. "You pay nothing to try this razor," might be made specific by saying, "You pay nothing to try the Auto Strop." "Her House in Order," suggesting a telling scene in "The Second Generation" to the literary reader, or the work of a skilled maid to the housewife, becomes more specific thus: "Your House Kept Clean the *Clean* Way." "Columbia Orchestral Records— A Triumph" phrases specifically and tersely what is to follow, and is one of the best illustrations of relevancy of headline as it stands. "Take Elevator— Save $10," advertising a clothing shop on the third floor is attractive since it has terseness and appeal and furnishes the right amount of information.

The characteristic that can least be spared in the headline is *point of contact.* The headline which has the power to recreate in the reader's mind some past experience and to insinuate that this past experience, if pleasant, may be renewed, or if unpleasant need never be repeated, is commonly the most telling.

12. *Proper phraseology.*—To every line of goods

or products certain more or less definite terms which make for economy in expression can be adapted. A cash register, for example, can be described either as to construction or use by specific expressions arranged with almost as much precision as a formula. Tabular or outlined information, in fact, may be the basis of the points used in such an advertisement.

On the other hand, altho the product is a definite quantity, the reader is not. He may range from the ignorant man to the scholar; from the rich to the poor; from a low motive in life to a high social position. In general, the style best suited to the greatest number of readers is that which employs simple Anglo-Saxon words, comparatively short sentences, short paragraphs, and definite, concrete expressions.

13. *The key.*—The purpose of keying an advertisement is to determine its pulling power. Most general publicity advertising is not keyed, while nearly all "get the order" and "get the inquiry" copy is keyed.

One method of keying is based on some variation of the offer, this being particularly applicable to advertising in periodicals. The seedman may offer a free sample of alfalfa seed in one journal, a sample of clover seed in another. Comparison of returns gives approximately the pulling power of each medium. For general use, nothing has been found more practical than to vary numbers, letters, or names. Where a firm occupies a building with several street numbers, a different number may be given in each medium. Frequently, wide range is permitted in the use of such numbering; some firms even use those outside the limits of their own frontage. Various letters of the alphabet, either singly or in combination, as "60B Grove Street," may be made to serve as keys. "Desk A," is a favored variant. "Address our Mr. Nye, personally," also serves as a key. Reference to a specific department may serve a similar purpose especially where coupons are used. One method followed is to use the word "Department" preceded by a descriptive name or followed by a number or letter.

14. *The coupon.*—In order to assure a large number of replies, a part of the advertisement may be devoted to making an "easy request." Analysis of several thousand coupons, several of which are given on page 168, Chapter X, brings out the following facts:

(a) An imperative sentence or phrase, or one strongly suggestive, usually displayed prominently, separates the coupon from the advertisement proper. "Mail Coupon Today." "Mail This Coupon," "Mail for Trial Box," and the like, are among the imperative forms. "Better Protection Coupons," "The Way to Opportunity," "I Will Save You Money," are strongly suggestive.

(b) Simplicity is obtained by the use of a "boiled-down" request. "Please send me full information about ——," "Send me without charge Moore's Modern Methods," "Send me book of 100 coupons for which I inclose $2.50"—these requests are made as terse as possible.

(c) Obligation on the part of the inquirer is often waived. "Without cost or obligation," "Without obligation on my part," are telling phrases.

(d) Blank lines for name and address are more commonly provided than is the request made to "Write name and address in the margin."

(e) The lower outside corner of the advertisement is the preferred position. The ease with which the coupon can be clipped is the test of the place to be used.

15. *Grouping the elements.*—The three factors that make up the advertisement—heading, body and close—should be given prominence commensurate with the work each is to perform, and should blend so as to produce a proper effect.

In preparing an advertisement the question arises, "What shall carry the main idea?" While each part should be subordinate to the general plan, one phase of the advertisement should present itself to the mind as a dominating factor. Obviously the most essential consideration is to get a working plan for the main idea, trusting that the remaining factors may be brought parallel to it in strength, thus preserving the unity of the whole.

16. *Fitting the advertisement to the medium.*—One of the difficulties of preparing advertisements is the necessity for producing copy that can be reconstructed. Give even an ordinary writer his choice of

mediums and all the numerous advertising points of a proposition, and he may produce, with comparative ease, an advertisement which will be successful in the right medium. This, however, may be far from the ideal advertisement for all mediums. For instance, slang in a *Scribner's Magazine* advertisement would be inappropriate, while this form of expression might prove very effective next to the sporting page of a newspaper.

The ideal advertisement, judged by the environment in which it must appear, should stand condensation, expansion, and modification to suit the demands of various mediums. A well-prepared advertisement on a subject of ordinary interest should be of moderate length, but at the same time it should be capable of being condensed to suit the requirements of a street-car card or capable of being expanded to the limits of a small booklet.

A further requirement demands that the advertisement be adaptable to mediums either general or technical in character. A well-written advertisement of aluminum ware, for example, should admit of changes that will make it appeal to any one of various special readers. Such elasticity is possible only when the advertisement is prepared according to correct principles.

REVIEW

In preparing an advertisement what three parts are of prime consideration?

What is the difference in meaning between the terms "display" and "copy"?

Of what importance are headlines?

What are the different methods of keying ads?

Why are coupons used? What are the main elements to be considered in preparing coupon copy?

What is meant by "grouping the elements"?

What principles should be kept in mind in the preparation of an advertisement?

CHAPTER XIV

LAYOUT OF ADVERTISEMENTS

1. *Object of layout.*—By means of the layout, the ideas in the mind of the person preparing the advertisement are given form. "Setting them down in the rough" shows the comparative worth of his ideas so that a clearer notion of their probable effect may be gained. In fact, the layout furnishes the first of many tests which an advertisement must undergo.

Layouts vary both in extent and in detail. In some cases, a few rough lines may constitute the "map" for the ideas; in other cases a particular worker may convey, by a detailed sketch, an exact representation of his finished advertisement. Such a layout may resemble the specification for a complicated machine. In ordinary practice, however, the layout merely covers the leading points of illustration, typedress and stock.

The layout is designed to act as a guide for the mechanical preparation of the advertisement. It determines the appearance and, to a great extent, the effectiveness of the finished advertisement.

While the ultimate object of the layout is to provide the printer with specifications from which he can work with economy of time and labor, it is also valu-

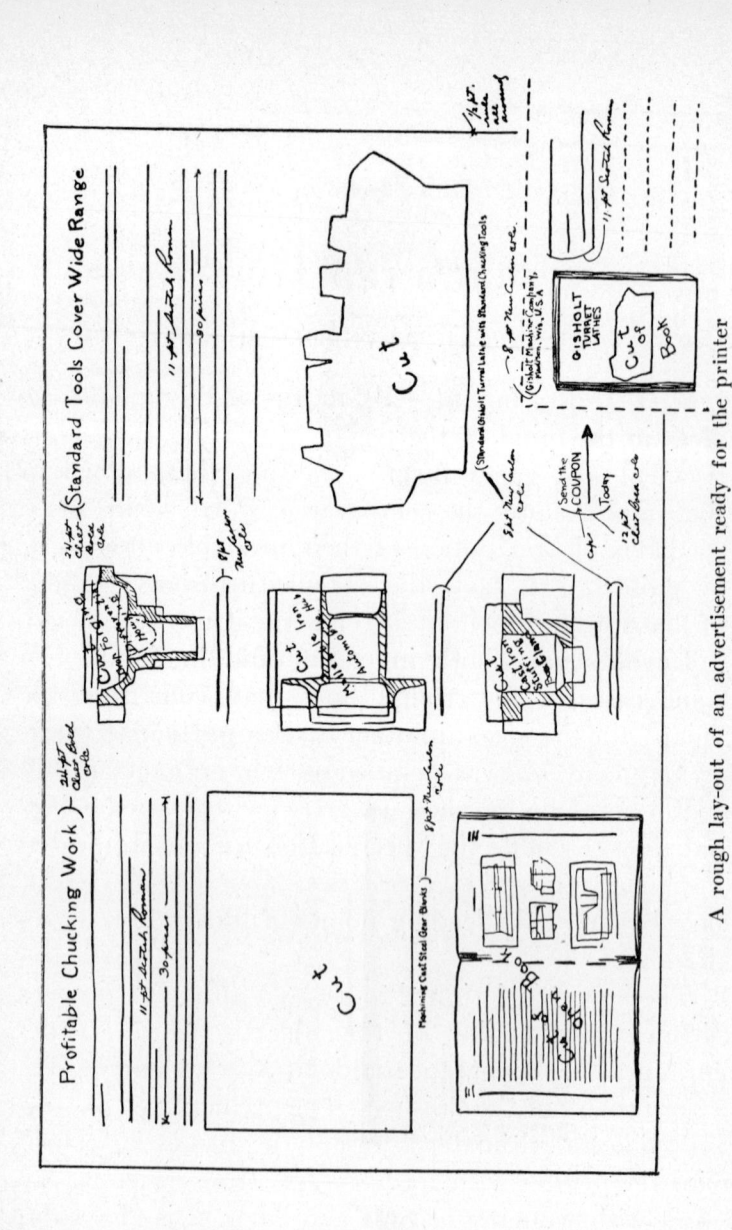

A rough lay-out of an advertisement ready for the printer

Profitable Chucking Work

Each of the pieces shown was finished as indicated by the drawings in the time named.

In each case the only tool equipment used was the set of Standard Chucking Tools shown on pages 66 and 67 in the Turret Lathe book.

Note the amount of work performed and compare this production with your time on similar parts.

You can gain the same advantages on your work as these machines are made in sizes from 13" to 41" swing, to cover a vast range of requirements.

Machining Cast Steel Gear Blanks

Drop Forging Differential Housing
Finished as indicated in 40 MINUTES

Malleable from Automobile Hub
Finished as indicated in 9 MINUTES

Cast Iron C. I. Stuffing Box Gland
Finished as indicated in 11 MINUTES

Standard Tools Cover Wide Range

Many pieces of work can be finished with this lathe and the Standard Chucking Tools shown on the machine by changing the cutting tools to fit the dimensions of bore in part to be finished.

The Universal Facing Heads and the Adjustable Cutter Boring Bars will finish work covering a wide range of sizes.

Some of the many advantages obtained by the use of the Gisholt Standard Turret Lathes are given on the back page of this folder.

The new turret lathe book will show you how this machine will cut your manufacturing cost, help you keep your delivery promises and increase your profits.

Send the coupon today for your copy.

Standard Gisholt Turret Lathe with Standard Chucking Tools

Send the
COUPON
Today

Gisholt Machine Company,
Madison, Wis., U. S. A.

................................191

Gentlemen:

Please send me copy of the new
Gisholt Turret Lathe Book.

....

....

TLA

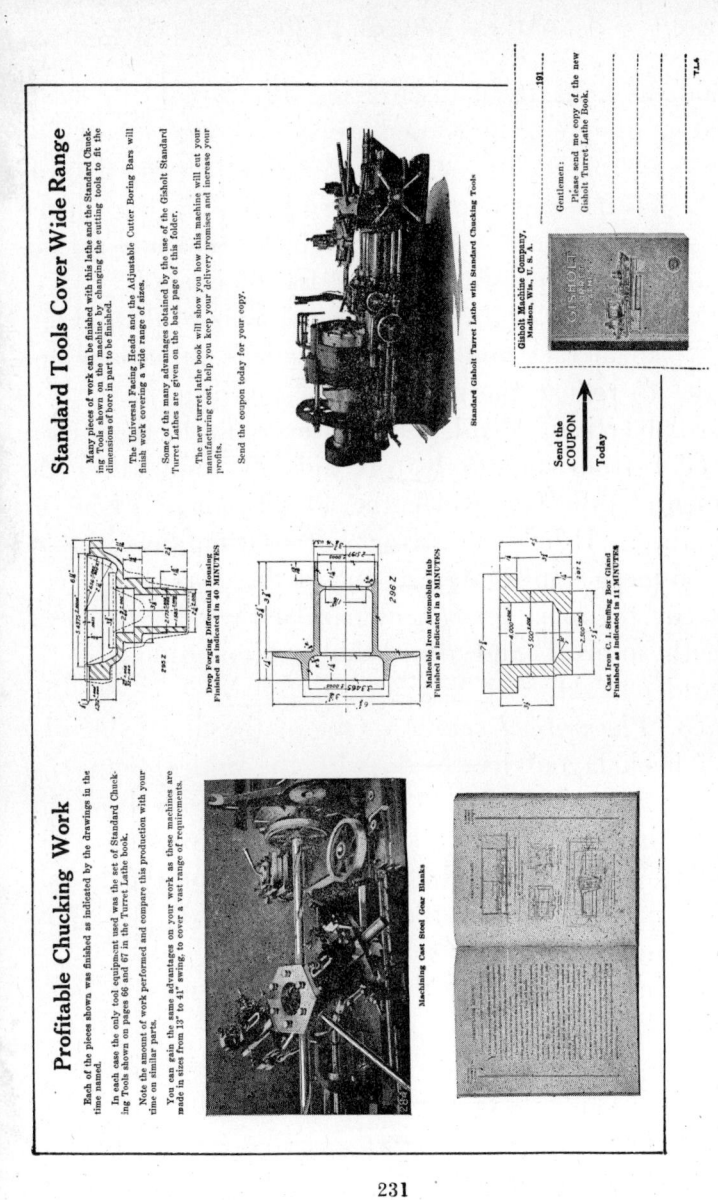

231

The printed advertisement from the preceding lay-out

able as a means of discovering any faults of conception, design or proposed dress. If the advertising writer, the client, the artist and the printer all study the advertisement carefully while it is in the formative stage, there is little probability that any serious mistake will persist after the layout is made.

2. *Objects of display.*—The objects of display are (a) to attract and hold the reader's attention, and (b) to relieve the monotony of uniformity.

Advertising display is, however, more than mere relief from monotony. It aids in stimulating the mental processes which the advertisement wishes to induce. It helps to attract initial attention. Attention merges into interest, and as the display is necessarily the most prominent part of the advertisement, both indirect and direct suggestion stimulate the reader to act.

3. *The optical center.*—One of the first principles of book layout has to do with the optical center of the page. Usually, at the beginning of a book the title is displayed in a single line running across the page. This is the first consideration of the layout. For ease in reading, the title is placed slightly above the mathematical center of the page.

The point at which the title is placed may be called the optical line. Its center is the optical center of the page. This point has not only the highest attention value, but from it as a center the question of balance must be determined.

4. *Balance in the layout.*—Frank Alvah Parsons,

in "The Principles of Advertising Arrangement," has the following to say about balance:

> There are two types of balance recognized: first, the bi-symmetric balance, or the balance in which there is the same degree of attraction on either side of a vertical line thru the center; and, second, what is known as the occult balance, or a "felt" balance. Occult balance is that balance which is rather sensed than mathematically worked out. The bi-symmetric balance is simple, dignified, strong; the occult is interesting, more involved and more difficult to perceive and control.

In laying out advertisements, it is advisable to conform to recognized principles. The proper relation of cuts, type, type-masses and ornaments to the optical center should be determined. Equal masses should be caused to balance at equal distances from this center; unequal masses at unequal distances.

The proper division of the space in the vertical direction is the most important matter in securing balance. Advertisements should not be divided in the geometrical center but on the optical line. Balance on this line is more important than balance on the horizontal axis.

5. *Securing emphasis.*—Lack of balance gives a form of emphasis, but it is not always to be commended. The fact that variation from the ordinary is reasonably sure to attract attention often leads advertisers to depart from standard customs as a means of securing emphasis. The advertiser who has his advertisement set so as to read from the bottom up, employs difference to secure emphasis, but he soon dis-

covers that few will puzzle out what he has to say. Emphasis is properly secured by varying the following elements:

(a) Position. The advertisement itself or thru its parts may secure emphasis by means of position.

(b) Size. If the advertisement is of large size compared with its surroundings, it not only attracts attention to itself but it also has an opportunity to emphasize its message by completeness of copy and display. The internal elements of greatest importance, too, will receive the emphasis that comes from size.

(c) Shape. Either the whole advertisement or any of its parts may be emphasized by novelty of shape. Eccentricity in this respect, however, is usually purchased at the expense of sales value.

(d) Color. Strength or beauty of color emphasizes both the advertisement as a whole and its various elements.

(e) Motion. The entire advertisement may actually be in motion, as in certain electric signs or in moving displays, or motion may be indicated and the attention directed toward the element that it is desired to emphasize.

6. *Value of movement.*—So accustomed has the eye become to obey certain directions that it will obey those directions even if the command be made only in the form of suggestion. In reading, the eye is accustomed to move from left to right and downward, hence it habitually follows a straight or dotted line,

if the line runs in a direction corresponding to that of print. If emphasis be put upon the line, the eye will follow it no matter what its direction.

Another common tendency which the advertiser makes use of is to follow the gaze of a person looking in a certain direction. It is a matter of common observation that if one person in a crowd looks intently at an object or in a certain direction others will do the same. Thus the direction of the gaze as indicated by the way a person in an illustration is looking has the same effect.

In advertising language, this tendency of the eye to follow an indicated course from one point to another is called movement. It is induced by (1) direction of lines or dots; (2) direction of gaze; (3) direction of action.

Slanting lines suggest motion, while rest is suggested by horizontal and vertical lines. No matter how motion is suggested, the gaze should be directed toward some essential element in the copy. If the old, familiar "fist" is used, its forefinger should point to an essential part.

7. *Display type.*—The face of display type selected should be in harmony with the product or service to be advertised. It should be striking, without violating any of the laws of good taste. It should be legible. It should meet all the requirements of emphasis; both large and small lines should compel attention while retaining attractiveness and legibility.

When the display type has been selected its position may be penciled suggesting the size of the type to be used, as shown in the illustration on page 230.

It is often desirable to pencil the entire headline in outlines that indicate the style of type to be used. If the headline consists of two lines of type, the second is usually made shorter, as this leads the eye toward the body of an advertisement and not away from it.

8. *Body type.*—The selection of body type is largely governed by the principles that govern display type. However, since body type is used to convey the greater part of the message, it must be of a style that will bear repetition. It must be so open and legible as to permit the eye to take in a mass of detail without growing tired.

The choice of experienced advertisement designers has led to the use of four general type faces which, in different sizes or modfications, have practically been accepted as standards in body type. These are Caslon, Scotch Roman, Cheltenham and Bookman.

9. *Illustrations.*—The mechanical treatment of illustrations in the layout depends, to some extent, on what is available for the purpose. Where drawings have been made in advance or are held over from previous advertising, it is possible to determine how they will appear in smaller sizes by means of a reducing glass. Where no illustrations are available, rough sketches may be made, either of the size in which they are to appear or larger. If a standard trade-mark is to be used, this is commonly available

in various sizes, so that a proof may be attached to the layout in approximately the same size as will appear in the advertisement.

10. *Borders and rules.*—When a border is to be used, the required effect may be obtained in the layout by roughly sketching it in or by cutting out pieces of a printed border and pasting them to the layout sheet. At times it is possible to have the border harmonize with the product, as, for example, a rope in a cordage advertisement.

11. *White space.*—It is generally admitted that an advertisement with plenty of white space attracts by its openness and that its message is easily read. Because some white-space advertisements take the form of paragraphs it is assumed by some that this type of advertising is easy to write. It takes as much time and skill to prepare a white-space advertisement as it does to prepare well-balanced display copy, because the copy writer is developing brevity as well as clarity in order that the reader may grasp the idea at a glance. The white space attracts the eye, and a person reads the advertisement before he realizes it. The advertiser who insists on returns from every advertisement and who keys his advertisements carefully, will want to make certain that white space enhances the value of the space that he buys. If he is a mail-order man, it is probable that the only white space he will favor is that which comes at the end of paragraphs where the lines are not complete. It will usually be found that for advertising in the mail-

order style, white space will be cut down to a minmum; for advertising in publicity style, white space will be largely used.

REVIEW

Explain the various purposes of the layout of an advertisement.

Describe the practical work of preparing a series of advertisements for a magazine.

How is balance obtained in an advertisement?

What are the means of obtaining emphasis?

Explain the value of movement and how the advertising man secures this advantage.

How and when is white space effectively used?

CHAPTER XV

BOOKLETS, CATALOGS AND FOLDERS

1. *Aim of booklets, catalogs and folders.*—The object of booklets, catalogs and folders is to present a complete description of advertised goods. They serve to answer the questions suggested in the limited space of the advertisement. They are less personal than the letter, which is usually unable to sustain the reader's interest for more than a few pages.

The extent to which this literature is employed depends largely upon the amount of supplementary advertising that is necessary. When the prospect has responded to the advertisement, it may be that a small four-page folder will fully answer his inquiries. In other cases a catalog of several hundred pages or a series of booklets and folders may be needed to make the sales offer clear and to connect the buyer's needs with the seller's goods.

Booklets, catalogs and folders aim to present in as concise form as possible, the various selling points of the goods or service offered, so as to make it easy for the customer to order. Prices may or may not be given in the body of these pieces of advertising matter; sometimes they are reserved for a special sheet or for a contract blank.

2. *Purposes of each form.*—The booklet is intended to give information and to inspire a desire for the goods; the folder is a modified form of booklet which serves practically the same purpose; the catalog informs and quotes prices. There is a definite and relatively restricted field for each. Yet each piece of advertising literature whether booklet or catalog should, as far as possible, be a complete presentation—a full sales talk in itself.

The booklet is capable of greatest variety, not only with regard to the subjects that may be covered, but also with regard to the method of presentation. It may touch upon the quality of the goods or service; it may treat of some related subject not necessarily allied with selling.

The "inspirational" style is peculiarly fitted to the booklet. The booklet, catalog or folder is usually demanded by market conditions. A new machine may have been added to the line manufactured, and a folder probably will serve to arouse interest in the work which the new machine performs.

The catalog is restricted normally to descriptions, brief explanations, prices and associated matter. The catalog calls for conciseness of description and for price quotations. It aims to give highly specialized information. It is the general salesman.

The folder, like the booklet, may be used to fill in any niche in the advertising. Its greatest value lies in focusing interest on the special product. It employs what may be termed the selling style—skilled argumentation in the vernacular of business. It is, primarily, intensified selling talk. It is the specialty salesman.

3. *Color and typography.*—Booklets and folders permit the use of a wider range of colors for stock than do catalogs. Few catalogs may depart to advantage from the customary whites and creams. For the covers of booklets and catalogs, on the other hand, a fairly wide range in colors is permissible. Brown, tho relatively unattractive, has the merit of enduring much handling. A booklet in a dark brown cover does not show dust, while one in light gray will become soiled in a short time. In the selection of cover stocks, the sample books issued by paper manufacturers and jobbers, showing the stock in blank and as printed by the different processes, are valuable guides.

The typography of the booklet, catalog or folder should be of the simplest. People may not be anxious to read the message that the type conveys, therefore it should be presented in the most legible type faces. Caslon and Scotch Roman for light face and Bookman for a somewhat heavier face, are standards. Bodoni Book, resembling Scotch Roman, is a favorite. Kennerley has merit and is particularly suitable to booklets.[1]

4. *Need for simplicity.*—The variety in form afforded by the printer's art has led to much that is bizarre and unattractive. The chief aim of advertise-

---

[1] For specimens of these types see Chapter XVII.

ing literature—to effect sales—is sometimes overshadowed by less important considerations of elaborate display. The skilled advertiser will hold to simplicity, because he knows that simplicity is most effective; the unskilled cannot hope for success if he violates this rule.

5. *Booklets.*—The make-up of booklets varies with the purposes for which they are used. Thus, a new company which seeks subscriptions to its stock, needs to place a great deal of information in the hands of those to whom the appeal is made. What is commonly taken for granted in connection with a successful company—financial soundness, reputation, general quality of goods or service offered—must be clearly demonstrated to the prospective customer.

The established company which has long marketed an extensive line of products is confronted by a different problem. A booklet of this sort may devote its subject matter concretely to a "trip thru the factory," as does the Enterprise Manufacturing Company's booklet, "Who Paid the Freight on Perfection?" It may take up a phase of a subject only remotely related to the product, as in the Waltham booklet, "Mental Nuts," a book of 100 tricks and problems. The tricks appear on the right-hand page while the watch ads appear on the left.

Booklets similar to catalogs are often issued on the unit plan. A nationally known manufacturer may wish to feature an improvement in watches. His regular catalogs are already in the hands of his deal-

BOOKLETS, CATALOGS AND FOLDERS

ers. Quick action is necessary to get the new article on the market. Since he markets thru the dealer, is a national advertiser and has many direct inquiries, his booklet must inform both the customer-inquirer and the dealer. In the next issue of the catalog, pages already used in the booklet may be incorporated.

To send a full catalog is often a waste of costly printed material and of postage. It may serve to confuse the customer, instead of focusing his attention upon the item in which he has expressed an interest. A booklet made up of pages from the catalog is usually better. If the direct plan of selling is employed, prices are always quoted; if the product is sold thru dealers, prices may or may not be quoted, but the reader is directed to call upon the local dealer.

6. *Catalogs.*—The preparation of a catalog requires definite knowledge not only of the goods, but also of book-making. If the business is a new one or the catalog is the first to be issued, even a simple matter like the determination of the size of the catalog page is of importance. Shall the finished book be built large so as to afford an opportunity for display or shall the page be small enough to let the book fit the pocket?

Since illustration is employed in nearly every catalog, the problem of making the text fit both the illustration and the page calls for careful preparation and measurement of copy. Consequently, catalog-building has become a skilled trade—in some respects even an art—based upon a knowledge of both advertising and printing requirements and limitations. The importance of such knowledge can be surmised when it is realized that the catalogs of the big mail-order houses run well over a thousand pages each and as many as eight million copies a year of some of them are distributed. The first step in catalog-building is the preparation of a typical or "style" page. The copy is prepared, laid out, the type set and proofs taken. Details are studied and costs are figured. If satisfactory, the "style" page may be taken as a standard; if unsatisfactory, other pages may be prepared until one is found that meets the various requirements.

7. *Layout.*—The illustration on the next page shows one of the modern methods of laying out a catalog. On page 246 is shown the final form. The position that the printed matter and illustrations are to occupy on the page is important, and must be indicated as early in the preparation as possible. To aid in the planning of the catalog and particularly to indicate where various sections of copy are to appear on the printed page, a key or master page is used to indicate the schedule. For example, when four pieces of copy make up the catalog page, these are numbered from 1 to 4. Corresponding numbers are placed on the key or layout page, indicating the exact place the copy is to occupy. This makes it possible for the pages to be made up as fast as the type composition is finished.

When a catalog is built on the unit plan, special

The rough lay-out of a catalog page

LIBRARY SUPPLIES

Automatic numbering machine

For registering the accession number in books or on cards; for numbering papers, reports, letters, etc. The figures shift automatically, and can be changed from consecutive to duplicate or continuous numbering by moving the pointer on the dial. The 5-wheel style E figure stamp is most used, and this style will be shipped unless otherwise specified.

Cat. no.
1310 4-wheel, 1–9,999
1311 5-wheel, 1–99,999
1312 6-wheel, 1–999,999
1313 7-wheel, 1–9,999,999

STYLE A   STYLE E

12345   **12345**

STYLE F   STYLE G

12345   **12345**

Actual size of type

Embossing stamp

For marking the name of the library on the pages of the book, on plates, maps, and inserts not printed on the regular forms and therefore liable to be removed. It is impossible to iron out its impression. We recommend plain gothic letters for name and location of library.

Cat. no.
1320 Stamp with straight line lettering or circular die
Prices for special design (note illustration) on request.

Perforating stamp

Makes an absolutely indelible mark by perforating the leaf and avoids increasing the thickness of the book or marring the surface of a plate or drawing.

Cat. no.
1321 Stamp with 26 or less, straight line letters

Actual size of perforation

Ink and ink pads

Excelsior ink and stamp pads are furnished in six colors: red, blue, green, carmine, purple, and black. When ordering specify color desired. Special ink for metal letters is furnished in black, red, green, purple, and blue.

Cat. no.
1325 Excelsior ink stamp pad (2½ x 4½ in.)
1328 Stamp ink, for rubber stamps. One oz. bottle
1329 Special ink for metal letters for numbering stamp.
1338 Higgins' black India ink.
1337 Thaddeus Davids' gold letterine.
1339 Thaddeus Davids' white letterine.

Shellac

Cat. no.
1390 White transparent shellac for varnishing labels on backs of books. Half pint cans.

[35]

The finished page, a complete unit that can readily be shifted to any part of the booklet

care is taken to make each page complete, i. e., a "unit" so that it is possible to shift the pages at will, merely changing their folios. In this manner, a special catalog may be made up on short notice from selected pages and with no extra expense for layout or composition. It is even possible, in technical catalogs, to make the pages loose leaf, so that old pages may be discarded and new ones added, thus keeping the catalog up to date at comparatively small expense.

8. *Size.*—The size of the catalog page is governed largely by custom within the particular field in which the catalog is to circulate and by the need for "spreads" in order to show the line. The National Veneer Products Company issues a 16-page catalog with fly leaves and cover. The size of the catalog page is 9 x 12 inches, with a center double-fold "spread" 12 x 36 inches. The Willys-Overland Company requires a page 8½ x 11 inches to display suitably the Overland line of motor cars. Stove catalogs are usually no smaller than the 7 x 10-inch page of the Kalamazoo Stove Company.

The use of a smaller page is sometimes made possible by combining the folder idea with the catalog. The Coldwell Lawn Mower uses a catalog 7½ x 4 inches, but obtains the benefit of a 7½ x 12-inch "spread" by making two folds. The E. A. Strout Farm Agency secures a wide display by folding the 9 x 12-inch pages so as to take a 6 x 9 cover. This makes a book that fits easily into the pocket, yet retains its impressive size and affords room for display.

9. *Quoting the price.*—Some catalogs quote price immediately after the description; others have a price list as a separate and distinct feature of the catalog; while still others use the catalog purely for description and quote prices in the accompanying letter or separate literature.

A modern method which is coming into general use where large catalogs are used is that employed by the Kalamazoo Stove Company and other companies which "pay the freight." The catalog is prepared, giving a full description of each article carried. Price quotations are placed in a supplementary price list in the back of the book, and these make it possible for the customer to see immediately what his expenditure will be for both goods and freight. Different price sheets are printed, so an inquirer from any locality can be quoted prices on the entire line.

This method of having a separate price list permits the catalog to be used longer than when prices are given after each article. No matter how prices vary, the descriptions are not affected; a new price list will cover the changes that occur.

10. *Folders.*—Because they may be prepared quickly and printed rapidly, folders are frequently used to advantage.

Advertising literature, other than folders, must conform to certain more or less definite standards in size. Folders have no such restriction. Occasionally some advertiser asserts his freedom from conventionality by putting out a circular—oval, round or irregular in shape; but the majority of folders of all sizes are rectangular.

The "big display" of the folder is usually made by the "spread." Whenever space from facing pages is available, the use of the "spread" is made possible. Folders make the "spread" available wherever desired. One entire side of the sheet may, if desired, be used for a single display.

Their relative freedom from restrictions, their adjustable size and the ease with which they permit striking displays to be made, account for the increased use of the folder, particularly in direct advertising.

11. *The dummy.*—The catalog frequently calls for a dummy covering practically every detail. The skilled catalog preparer thoroly realizes that it is much cheaper to work with pencil and paste than with types. This being the case, he uses every available "short cut" to make as many of the necessary changes as possible in the dummy and as few as possible in the type-form.

In laying out a folder, the form of the fold and the succession of the type-forms leading up to the spread, when there is one, must be considered. Hence the dummy also becomes an important aid in the preparation of folders. The layouts shown on pages 231 and 245 illustrate the method used in preparing any layout.

If a return card is to be used, this may be attached

to the folder by inserting the corners in slits cut for the purpose or it may be a perforated part of the folder.

In preparing a dummy for a booklet, sheets of the stock selected are folded to the proper size. The folded sheets are pinned, stapled or stitched together approximately as in the case of the printed booklet. If headings are to be used, these are indicated thruout the pages. The illustrations are indicated either by rough drawings or by "tipping" or pasting proofs of cuts on the pages to be illustrated. The cover, cut from the stock to be used, is added. The completed dummy gives an exact idea of how the booklet will look when finished, and furnishes, when specifications are added, a simple guide to the printer and binder.

In the catalog, the page is the dummy unit. Illustrations are carefully indicated on each page. The space, in terms of the number of words, is exactly figured so that the type will neither fall short of nor exceed the space allotted. By the use of style pages, the most complicated layouts may be indicated with clearness and precision. If desired, the entire book may thus be assembled in blank page form.

REVIEW

Make a list of the relative advantages of the booklet, catalog and folder. What is the purpose of each?

What considerations should govern the size of advertising literature?

Which of the three forms lends itself most easily to variety in the presentation of subject matter?

What things must be kept in mind when preparing the catalog?

What is the best way to specify prices in a catalog? Is the matter of size of importance considered from the point of view of selling quality?

What consideration should govern the preparation of a folder to advertise a new electrical device? How would you go about preparing a dummy for a folder of this sort?

CHAPTER XVI

DRAWINGS AND REPRODUCTIONS

1. *Value of illustrations.*—According to an old Japanese proverb, "a picture is worth a thousand words." In the early days of advertising illustration, an untrained person could produce a picture which, tho of slight artistic value, had attention and interest value because of its novelty. Today, however, art as well as copy demands greater technical skill and more care in expressing an idea in order that it may carry a definite message.

The rapid multiplication of illustrations and copy would be impossible without the aid of modern duplicating methods. Obviously, the advertiser who understands how his illustrations can be reproduced to the utmost advantage is best able to judge the power of his copy.

Because of the great importance of art in modern advertising, advertisers often go to great expense in obtaining suitable work. Art filing systems as well as art reference libraries are being introduced. The American Lithograph Company has been twenty-five years in collecting its reference data. One advertising agency has files of about 7,000 clippings under such headings as babies, automobiles, city scenes, and more than one hundred other subjects. It has samples of the work of more than six hundred artists, whose names are filed and cross-filed under various headings to show the kind of work they do, together with price quotations and time requirements.

2. *Tendencies in advertising art.*—There is a strong tendency among modern advertisers to employ artists of note to do the illustrating. This began when Sir John Millais' picture "Bubbles" was sold to the proprietors of Pears' Soap for £2,200. Artists of reputation had always refused to do advertising work before this initial consideration of commercial art in a more favorable light. Many advertisers demand that the artist "sign" the picture while others feel that this detracts from its advertising value and prefer to omit the artist's signature.

3. *Styles of art.*—In the matter of illustration, favorable effect is the advertiser's ultimate aim. The means of pictorial representation are the line, the dot, the tone, the mass, the drawing, the painting, and the photograph.

4. *The line.*—A satisfactory effect is most simply and easily secured by the use of the line. The line-drawn illustration is easily reproduced, and generally retains its individuality and charm in print.

John W. Harland, in *The Printing Art,* says:

First, line is able to give the proper weight and force of expression necessary in depicting the exact shade developed by Nature in her balance of light and darkness.

Second, line is capable of expressing the perspective of all

"Bubbles"

The celebrated painting by
Sir John Millais, R. A.
President of the Royal Academy.

In the possession of
A. & F. Pears, Ltd.

All Rights Reserved.

Good Morning, Have You Used Pears' Soap?

Whenever you hear that old familiar hail, think *why* Pears' is the perfect toilet soap.

It is because Pears' is the result of more than a century of experience in soap making. The purest materials are skilfully and carefully blended into an exquisite soap—matchless for the complexion.

And then Pears' is *aged a year* before it is sold. This improves the quality and removes all moisture. That is why Pears' is so economical.

Millions of people prefer Pears' Soap. They will have no other kind.

AT YOUR DEALER'S—15c a cake for the unscented; ($1.50 a box of one dozen). 20c a cake for the Glycerine Scented; (51c for a box of 3 cakes).

4c in stamps brings you a Test Cake of Pears'

Walter Janvier, U. S. Agent, 419 Canal Street, New York City

In this advertisement a masterpiece costing £2,200 is used for an illustration, adapting the subject to the product, "Pears' Soap"

DRAWINGS AND REPRODUCTIONS

surfaces, and of producing on paper the effect of atmosphere, often called chiaroscuro, or aerial perspective.

Third, line affords the best possible means of representing "texture," i.e., the substance of the surface itself.

5. *Stipple, tones and masses.*—When dots instead of lines are used, the process as well as the effect is called "stipple." Stipple effects are much used in clothing and furniture advertisements. The tintograph or "Ben Day" process has given stipple a prominent part in the production of tints in advertising.

The use of tones of varying intensity is a third means employed by the artist. The brush is obviously a more difficult tool to use than the pen.

The use of mass is seen in the silhouette and in the half-silhouette.

6. *Pen drawings.*—In the hands of a skilled commercial artist, the pen is a most effective instrument. With it, the entire advertisement may be produced.

Pen drawings are usually well adapted for all advertising purposes. The mechanical processes favor the pen-drawn line. Lines can be reproduced exactly, and the contrasts and shadings of the drawing are truthfully reproduced in the zinc etching.

Pen drawings are not successful in reproducing intricate patterns or pictures with a great amount of detail. Where detail rather than mass is desired in the illustration, photographic illustration is usually preferable. The alternating black and color pages of the mail-order catalog illustrate this point. Carpet sundries, stair rods and the like are pen-drawn, whereas rugs are photographed from the originals and reproduced in color.

7. *Wash drawings.*—When a photographic effect is desired a wash drawing is usually best, since it reproduces not only blacks and whites, but intermediate tones. Wash drawings are in some respects superior to photographs. Details which have selling quality may be given the right degree of emphasis, perspective may be rightly represented, and backgrounds may be added or taken away. The texture of a filing case, a piano or a chair having massive lines may call for this form of reproduction. The wash drawing is often preferred as a matter of economy, since the desired effect may be secured more easily in wash than in a retouched photograph.

8. *Oil paintings.*—Recent developments in color-printing have created a growing demand for "copy in color." The direct color-photograph is sometimes too faithful a likeness of the object. The oil painting, when correctly executed, makes ideal color copy. The cost of good oil paintings and the time required for successful execution necessarily restrict their use.

The Liggett and Myers Tobacco Company, in its reproductions of paintings in Fatima cigarette advertising, employs paintings of distinct artistic value.

9. *Retouched photographs.*—The camera makes no allowance for poor or unequal lighting. Some color values it fails to bring out; others it indicates wrongly. A commercial photograph as received from the pho-

FATIMA may never become the only cigarette smoked by keen, substantial men of this type. But you will find that Fatima has already become more popular with such men than almost any other cigarette. This is because men who choose wisely want a SENSIBLE cigarette—a cigarette that is cool and comfortable to the tongue and throat and that leaves a man feeling "fit" and clear-headed even though he may smoke more often than usual.

Liggett & Myers Tobacco Co.

FATIMA
A Sensible Cigarette

Effective use of the oil painting gives a dignified appearance to this advertisement, and lends a sense of distinction to the Fatima cigarette

tographer nearly always needs to be retouched. Such retouching brings out contrasts and adds details.

10. *Sources of art supply.*—The advertiser may procure his illustrations from several sources. These include the art department of an advertising agency; an art organization; a "free lance" artist who is trained in the business requirements of art work; the art departments of photo-engravers; the art departments of some periodicals and newspapers; and the stock-cut organizations that supply ready-made cuts.

11. *Kinds of engraving.*—There are three general methods of engraving. The first employs raised characters, in the second the characters are sunken, while the third makes use of surface characters. All engraving is done by one of these three general processes or a modification.

Printing from raised characters is the oldest method. The parts that are not to appear are cut away or kept below the printing surface. Surface printing is used mainly in one process—lithography. A plain surface may be made to "take ink" in one place and "refuse ink" in another, by special treatment. When paper is impressed upon the surface, that part which is inked prints, the remainder leaves the sheet blank.

The advertiser is necessarily concerned with the relative advantages of the various methods of engraving. On a catalog run he may use zinc etchings, photo-engravings, wood cuts or lithographs thruout. For the covers of the book he may use any of these

DRAWINGS AND REPRODUCTIONS 259

mediums or he may use one of the embossing processes, either wholly or in part. Each process has its merits and its limitations.

12. *Wood cuts.*—Wood cuts were made when printing was first invented. Playing cards and religious pictures were cut on wood as early as 1400, and advertisers used wood cuts up to about 1880. Altho later engraving processes have largely supplanted this method, wood engraving is sometimes employed for illustrations of machinery and similar subjects. The cost of the engraving is relatively high, but the printing costs no more than letter press work.

The accompanying reproduction of a wood engraving, used in the Millers Falls Company's advertisement, shows the present-day use of the wood cut process. The varying textures and surfaces are

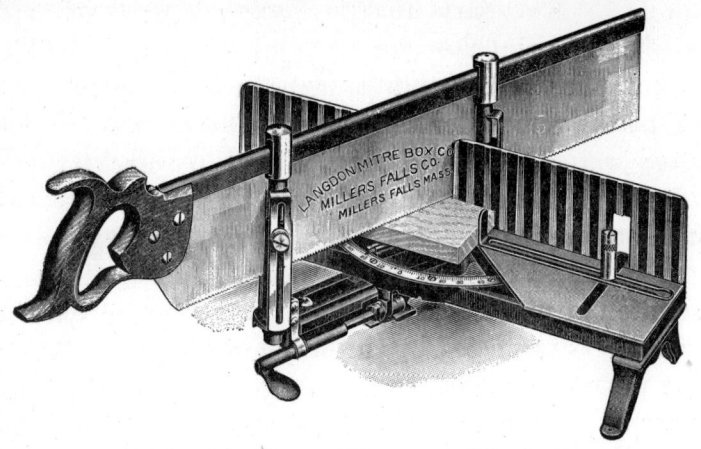

An example of present-day usage of wood cuts

brought out by differing methods of lining and dotting.

13. *Zinc etchings.*—In the process of zinc etching, the copy is photographed and the negative is made on glass. The developed film is toughened, removed from the glass and remounted in reversed position on another glass. A zinc plate, having one surface highly sensitized, is clamped to the glass negative. Light, either from the sun or from an electric arc, is

A good type of zinc etching

applied to print the photographed copy on the zinc. Ink applied to the plate adheres only to the exposed parts, the remainder coming off after a bath in running water. After drying, a red powder termed "dragon's blood" is dusted over the plate; this adheres to the inked portion and is brazed on it.

The actual etching is now done. Immersion in a solution of nitric acid and water cuts the zinc, except where it is protected by the "dragon's blood." After the plate has been subjected to the mechanical processes of "routing," and mounting to type height, it is ready for use.

Zinc etchings may be prepared from any copy made up of solid lines, points or contrasting surfaces. Wash drawings, photographs or copy containing color tints cannot usually be reproduced by the zinc etching process. Pen drawings in black india ink on white paper furnish the best copy. Comparatively cheap stock may be used in printing zinc etchings, particularly if the artist has been instructed to make the drawing "open," so that the cut will not blur on long runs on cheap paper. The cost is lower than for half-tones.

14. *Half-tones.*—Half-tones stand at the head of engravings for most purposes—for catalogs, booklets, circulars and advertisements in mediums of the better class. The half-tone can be made to print on any stock which has a fairly smooth surface and can be used for color-work. The cost is reasonable. A relief-plate, photographically made on metal, in which the printing surface is made up of a regular series of small dots, or a grating of fine lines in white, is called a half-tone.

Half-tone plates are produced as follows: The copy is photographed thru a screen or glass, marked by cross-lines meeting at right angles. The lines are opaque; the squares transparent. The photograph, therefore, is taken thru the transparent squares. An enameled copper plate is printed as in the zinc etching process. The plate is placed in a bath of perchloride of iron which eats away the coating of the plate that is unaffected by the lines and dots produced by the screen. A proof is then taken, and further etching may be done on parts of the plate by using the perchloride again. Hand-work, somewhat after the manner of wood engraving, may be done if a particularly fine plate is desired. Mounting, commonly on a wood base, completes the process.

Most half-tones are made from retouched photographs. Wash drawings, pen, pencil, crayon or charcoal drawings as well as paintings in color are reproduced accurately by this method, as has been done in a number of instances for this volume.

15. *Importance of the screen.*—The screen is a clear plate of glass ruled accurately in two directions with lines at right angles. The light cannot pass thru the lines of the screen, but filters freely between them and registers on the plate. The result is a series of light and heavy dots, bringing out in detail the shading in the photograph. Screens are named according to their number of lines per inch. The coarser the screen the lower the grade of stock that may be used in printing. If a half-tone is to be printed in newspapers or on a similar grade of stock, 65-line to 85-line screen may be used. If the paper is of a better grade, 100-line screen; for the ordinary fiction magazine, 120-line screen; for booklet work on fairly good, coated paper, 133-line screen; while for the best results on very fine grades of paper, 150 or even 175-line screen is employed.

The following plate shows different screens from

120 Line

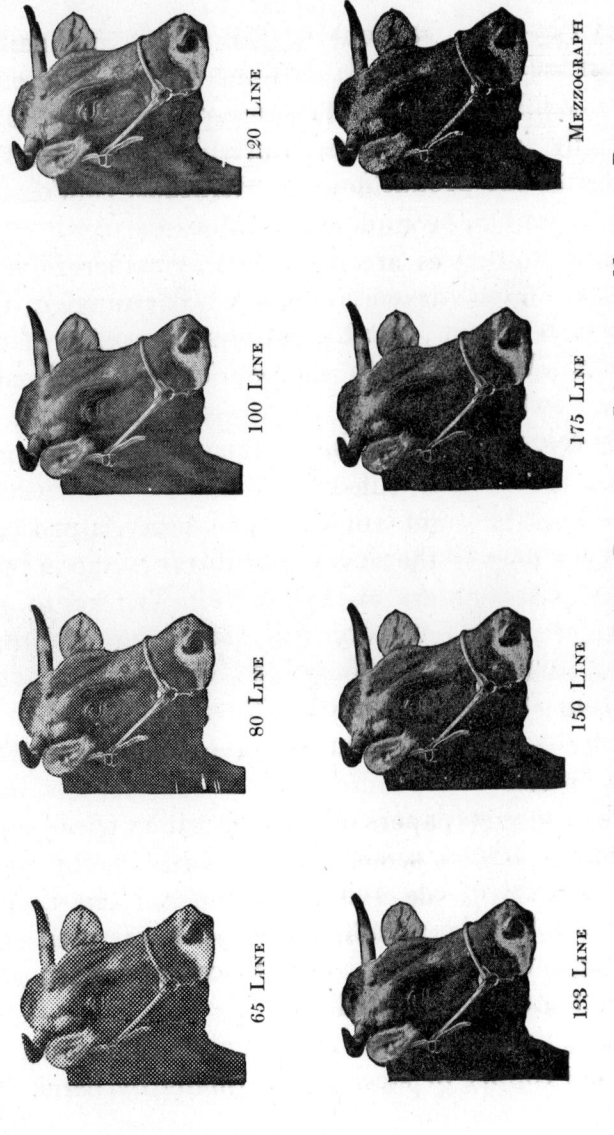

Mezzograph

100 Line

175 Line

80 Line

150 Line

65 Line

133 Line

The Selection of the Proper Halftone Screen Prepared by Gatchel and Manning, Philadelphia

65 to 175-line. It should be noted that the finer the screen the greater the detail which may be secured.

16. *Lithography.*—Lithography, printing from specially prepared stones, is useful to the advertiser chiefly in the production of letterheads, catalog and booklet covers, and in reproductions of pictures and designs in color. The unit cost is rather high on short runs, but low on long ones. The range of usefulness is narrow, but the process is capable of fine results. It comes into competition, in single-color work, with engraving and embossing, and in multi-color work with the other and later color processes.

Lithographic stone of the best quality is procured from Bavaria, tho the United States furnishes a large part of the supply. A grained stone is used to give a stipple effect; the ordinary sharp line of lithography requires a perfectly smooth surface. The printing surface is washed with a solution of nitric acid and water, which roughens the stone where there is no design.

17. *Hand-made engravings.*—To the experimental work of Finiguerra, an Italian goldsmith, the world owes the art of engraving on copper. The process was invented about 1460, and copper was used until the beginning of the nineteenth century when steel was generally substituted.

The printing is made from sunken characters, cut into the copper or steel plate, usually by hand. In some cases, machines are used for cutting or tracing the characters; in others, chemical processes are used. In printing, ink is applied to the face of the plate. The sunken parts become filled with ink, and retain enough to bring the characters level with the surface of the plate. Any ink adhering to the smooth surface of the plate is carefully removed. The plate and the stock on which it is to print are forced between two rollers, one solid, the other covered with woolen cloth or a rubber blanket. The stock-paper or cardboard is forced into the depressions of the plate under the pressure of the meeting rollers and comes from the press printed and embossed. In the best work the embossing is plainly marked, owing to the depth of the incisions and to the heavy pressure applied. In cheaper grades of work, the embossing is comparatively slight, but the ink has a peculiar raised effect which distinguishes it as "engraved." Steel and copper plate engravings are of limited utility. The latter are employed chiefly for conventional announcements and cards. Copper plate is frequently used to announce an offering of millinery, furs, jewelry or other high-grade goods. Stationery of high grade is printed from steel engravings.

18. *Ben Day process.*—By the use of a sheet of celluloid having a raised design, known as a Ben Day screen, it is possible to introduce the pattern of the screen into any part of the engraving. The parts of the negative that are not to take the pattern are protected by being treated with a liquid resistant to the ink. By this means artistic designs may be intro-

duced on a printing plate; light colors or shadings may similarly be shown. This process makes zinc etchings available for a wide range of color work.

Many Ben Day plates closely resemble hand stippling or line work. In the Moon motor car advertisement, the illustration is made by the Ben Day process.

19. *Electrotyping.*—Where forms cannot be printed as soon as made up, or where permanent plates are wanted, any form, cut or plate may be duplicated as many times as needed. By means of the electrotype, an advertisement may be reproduced and distributed to all the periodicals in which it is to appear, thus insuring uniformity of display and clear printing.

The ordinary electrotype is wax-molded, the mold being dusted with graphite and submitted to electrolysis. The resulting film of copper is backed with lead. So-called nickel types, or nickel-plated electrotypes, are used on long runs and in some color printing. They may be used with any colored ink without disintegrating, thus preventing the color change that takes place in some inks when the printing is done from a copper electrotype.

20. *Stereotypes and matrices.*—Stereotyping is the process employed in many newspaper offices to duplicate forms. Advertisements in the larger newspapers must conform mechanically to the restrictions of the stereotyping process. In general, body-type smaller than six point should be of an open face; cuts should be free from minute detail, and no half-

The Season's Smart Cars

Whatever the price may be, a car so *convincingly* attractive as the new 1917 Moon hasn't yet "come along"

Here is beauty of the kind that is deeper than mere nickel or brass and fresh enamel. The Moon—with its sweeping, unbroken lines; long, double-cowled Delaunay-Belleville body and rakish slant of windshield—is obviously the season's smart car.

Within, the new Moon is *Moon* straight through—powerful—staunch—on the *qui vive* to do your bidding—generous of elbow and leg room—upholstered (both models) in genuine tan Spanish leather.

Six-66
(66 Horsepower Actual Brake Test)
Seven passenger fully equipped $1650

Six-43
(43 Horsepower Actual Brake Test)
Five passenger fully equipped $1295

Write for literature, illustrating and describing these and other models

MOON MOTOR CAR COMPANY   ST. LOUIS, U. S. A.

Showing the effective use of the Ben Day process in illustration

tones of finer screen than 80 to 100-line are adaptable.

The method of stereotyping is simple. A sheet of prepared paper is beaten into the face of the form or pressed into it by means of a brush or roller. The impressed sheet, called the "matrix," is placed in a mold and molten type metal is poured in. If the plate is to run on a rotary press, the mold is curved to conform to the curvature of the press cylinder.

When an advertisement is to be run in a number of newspapers that have stereotype foundries, it is more economical to forward the papier-maché matrix than the plate itself. Even a large matrix can be mailed at first-class postage for a few cents.

21. *Mechanical processes.*—In the various modern methods of reproduction, certain mechanical processes are constantly employed.

"Stripping" enables the operator to join parts of different photographs or drawings into one cut or to combine photo-engraved and etched surfaces. In stripping, the film is removed from the glass plate to which it was originally attached. The stripped film can then be trimmed and placed where desired.

An engraving or other picture having a background that shades off gradually into the surrounding white space is termed a "vignette." Vignetted half-tones are difficult to print, especially on a platen press, as the shading tends to cloud under heavy impression, while a light impression gives only a shadowy effect. This difficulty is overcome by using the silhouetted half-tone, made possible by the "routing" process.

Routing consists in cutting away those parts of an engraving that are to be below type height. Often it is necessary to rout blank spaces deeper so that they will not smudge the paper in printing.

Reverse cuts are those in which the impression is exactly the reverse of that in the drawings. "Reverses" are made by reversing the negative. The term is also applied to plates in which the blacks and whites are reversed.

REVIEW

Describe the different forms of originals from which reproductions can be made and explain the advantages of each for special purposes.

Distinguish between zinc etchings and half-tones and describe the methods by which each is produced.

What is the Ben Day process?

How is the reproduction affected by the processes of electrotyping and stereotyping? By the kind of paper used?

CHAPTER XVII

PRINTING ART IN ADVERTISING

1. *Relation of printing to advertising.*—Except for a small amount of word-of-mouth advertising, printing must be relied upon to deliver the advertiser's message. Without some mechanical means of multiplying the written message, extensive advertising would of course be impossible.

In view of the practical importance of the subject, the advertiser should possess a fair knowledge of the work that can be performed by printing processes.

2. *Standard flat-press bed.*—Inasmuch as the printing art, as applied to advertising, embraces a variety of processes, it is well to note the number and sequence of the steps which an idea may take before becoming permanently embodied in print.

Many presses now in use retain the flat bed. Platen presses bring the type against a flat bed; cylinder presses rotate a cylinder against a flat form. The rotary press commonly used in newspaper offices departs from the use of a flat bed by employing a curved form that rotates with and against the impression cylinder.

3. *Offset process.*—The tendency of ink to transfer under pressure is the basis of the so-called "offset" process—one of the later developments of the print-

ing art. The plate with the form to be printed does not meet the paper directly. The impression is made on a rubber roller and transferred from this to the paper.

By means of the offset process, rough papers, such as those with "antique" finish, may be used as readily as smooth papers. This is of particular advantage in the printing of half-tones. Reproduction of delicate shades of color is also made possible by this process. Admirers of the offset process claim for it superiority over lithography in the production of soft yet distinct color effects.

Since offset work requires special plates, entailing a high cost, it is not practical for short runs. For large runs, the rapidity with which the work can be turned out greatly reduces the unit cost.

4. *Multicolor process.*—The multicolor process is based on the theory that any color may be produced from the three primary colors—red, yellow and blue—singly or in combination. Three plates, each carrying one of these colors, are used, one after the other; the resulting picture will contain nearly every variation in colors.

It was found that the three-color process could be improved by the addition of a fourth plate carrying black. This is especially advantageous on long runs, since it permits more rapid printing and imperfect register is less apparent than when but three plates are used. The paper is fed from rolls thru the cylinders; inks of the desired colors are fed from different fountains and distributed by individual sets of rollers, each color going to its appropriate form.

The colored sections of the Sunday newspapers are familiar examples of multicolor presswork. Many catalogs, printed in one and two colors, carry inserts in multicolor.

5. *Lithographic printing.*—Lithography in colors calls for great exactness in execution. Not only must the presswork be accurately done, but the colors must be chosen with the eye of the skilled artist. In lithography a satisfactory effect is seldom obtained with three or four colors, as is the case in other color processes. In the finer grades of lithographic work, ten or more impressions are necessary.

Lithographic printing is commonly done on a press similar to those on which printing in colors by other processes is done. The stones holding the impressions are first dampened and then inked. The ink-rollers have a calf-skin surface instead of one of glue composition. For each color desired a separate stone is used.

6. *Photogravure.*—Work of distinctly artistic value can be done in photogravure. In this process, an intaglio printing plate is used. This plate carries no sharply incised lines, but is marked by many minute depressions. In printing, these depressions produce the shadows, the high parts of the plate showing white.

To produce a plate in photogravure, the photographic sensitive film upon which the picture has been taken is imposed upon a metal plate. The plate is then developed and the picture bitten into the metal with mordant. From the resulting plate, impressions may be taken in substantially the same manner as from a copper plate.

Of late years this process has been adapted to a cheaper grade of printing, called rotogravure from the fact that the printing is done on rotary presses. Rotogravure is much used for pictorial supplements of newspapers.

7. *Copperplate printing.*—Formerly, copperplate printing was done entirely by hand. The plate was carefully wiped by hand before the stock was fed to the press. Power was also applied by hand. The cost of production was necessarily high. The use of power presses has now reduced the printing cost of plate-printed matter to little more than that of letter-press printing.

8. *The make-ready.*—When the printing form is placed upon the press bed, it is not yet ready for printing. Some words and lines tend to print heavy. Cuts, especially if mounted on wood, may not be exactly type-high. They may come out gray unless the pressure is exceedingly strong. All such inequalities must be adjusted. This adjustment is called the make-ready. When the make-ready is rightly done, the printed side of the paper shows an even color and the reverse side shows an even impression thruout.

9. *Correcting the proof.*—The first impression

taken of type matter often contains a number of errors. When the proof is "pulled," the copy is usually read aloud by a copy-holder and the errors corrected on the proof by the proofreader. A skilled proofreader not only corrects typographical errors, but calls attention to errors in style and suggests improvements generally.

For indicating changes to be made in the proof, a kind of shorthand is used. The characters with their meanings are tabulated herewith:

¶	Paragraph.
No ¶	No paragraph.
Rom.	Change from italics to Roman.
Ital.	Change from Roman to italics.
l. c.	Put in lower case, or small letters.
s. c.	Put in small capitals.
Caps.	Put in capitals.
ꭤ	(Dele), take out the type or matter with a line drawn through it.
ꮖ	Reverse the type.
∧	Left out; insert the matter which is written in the margin.
tr.	Transpose the order of letters, lines, or words which are underlined.
w. f.	Change the incorrect type or a wrong font or style.
Stet.	Let the matter stand as it was originally set. Stet is written in the margin.
.....	These are put below a crossed word. Let it stand.
⌒	Close up.
#	Insert more space where caret is marked.
V	Correct uneven spacing between letters and words. The mark is placed in the type and "even" is written in the nearest margin.
⌊	Bring line to this point.
×	Change faulty letter.
⊙	Insert period.
,/	Insert comma.
;/	Insert semicolon.
⌣	Push down space, which blackens the proof, into correct position.
◻	Indent line an em.
/—/	One-em dash. Insert dashes of this length.
/——/	Two-em dash.
✓	Less space.

Out, see copy. Something omitted. See copy.
== Straighten lines.
Qu. or ? Is this correct? See to it.

Proof corrections should be made in the margin directly to the left or right of the error. If a line is used to connect the error and the correcting mark, this should run between the lines to the nearer margin.

10. *Styles of type.*—The variations in type faces are today almost as numerous as the variations in handwriting. Some characteristic forms in twelve-point type are here shown.

This line is set in Priory Text

This line is set in CASLON OLD STYLE

This line is set in ITALIC

This line is set in SCOTCH ROMAN

This line is set in GOTHIC

This line is set in French Script

This line is set in BODONI

This line is set in BODONI BOOK

This line is set in KENNERLY

This line is set in OLD STYLE ANTIQUE

This line is set in CHELTENHAM BOLD

This line is set in CHELTENHAM ITALIC

This line is set in CHELTENHAM BOLD CONDENSED

This line is set in Chelt. Bold Extended

This line is set in CASLON BOLD

This line is set in PABST

This line is set in HANCOCK

This line is set in PLYMOUTH

This line is set in HEARST

This line is set in Bookman

The rapid improvements on the typesetting machines render it possible to cast almost any size and face of the standard types which were formerly confined to the hand-set types.

Linotype matter is cast in continuous lines or slugs in a linotype machine.

Monotype matter is cast in individual letters, each character separate, thus affording facility in correcting.

11. *Type families.*—While the printer of a generation ago crowded his jobs with type faces as diverse as his equipment permitted, it is considered better nowadays to do good printing with but two or three type faces. Gradually, printers began asking for types in "series" or "families," so that a job might

be set entirely in one face. Eventually the type family was evolved, in which different modifications of a single face are made in a wider range of sizes. Thus the Cheltenham family, which is the largest, embraces the following: Cheltenham (with Italic), Cheltenham Bold (with Italic), Bold Condensed (with Italic), Bold Extended, Bold Extra Condensed, Bold Extra Condensed Title, Bold Outline, Extra Bold, Inline, Inline Extended, Inline Extra Condensed, Medium (with Italic), Oldstyle, Oldstyle Condensed, Wide.

Modern advertisements are in most cases displayed in relatively few faces of the same series or family.

12. *The point system.*—Until comparatively recent years, type manufactured by different founders, tho bearing the same name, differed more or less in size. In 1878, Marder, Luce and Company undertook to remedy this defect. They divided an inch into 72 equal parts and called each 1/72 a point. They took a Pica body which measured 1/6 of an inch in length, as a standard. As this measured 12/72 of an inch in length, they named this type "twelve-point," and renamed all the other type according to the point system as follows: Nonpareil, which measured 1/12 of an inch in length, was renamed six-point; Brevier, which measured 8/72 of an inch, was renamed eight-point, and so on down the list. This point system was generally adopted in 1887.

The "standard line" was introduced by the Inland

Type Foundry in 1894. Previous to that time there had been no uniformity in the placing of type-faces on the body; as a result, the alignments from different faces of type, even tho they were on bodies of the same size, might be imperfect. This is shown in the following line:

$$hSd\&mTcNmPD.hC7Uaa$$

Types are now cast accurately on interchangeable point bodies and, with the exception of scripts and certain title faces, align perfectly, as seen in the following arrangement of the same letters:

$$hSd\&mTcNmPD.hC7Uaa$$

13. *Type bodies.*—The standard of type measurement is the "em." Since M takes more space than any other letter of the alphabet, a square which will just contain this letter in any type face is called an "em" of this type face and serves as the unit of measurement.

The relative width of the individual letters necessarily determines the number that can be set in a given line. Faces vary in width, as seen in the following illustration where the first line is set in "extended" type, and the second in "condensed."

Alexander Hamilton Institute

Alexander Hamilton Institute

Varying widths of the same face—Cheltenham Bold—are shown in the following:

M Extended

M Standard

M Extra condensed

14. *Practical type arrangement.*—Much that pertains to type arrangement is treated elsewhere in this volume under appropriate chapter headings.

For effective arrangement select a display type that is striking in appearance, one that conforms to the general tone of the advertisement, is legible and, except in certain cases, of the present vogue.

Set introductory headings in 12-point if the body type is 10-point. This difference of two points for headings and bodies can be followed generally. The size of the headings should be in harmony with the style and size of the body.

Use 6-point or a larger size for the body of an advertisement. Type smaller than 6-point is not advisable unless much matter must be crowded into a limited space and the paper is of a high printing quality.

Among the appropriate headings one may employ 8-point for single column sub-heads. 10-point for two or three column sub-heads, and 12-point if a greater width than three columns is desired.

For display heads it is appropriate to use

from 12 to 18-point, single column
" 18 to 30-point, two columns
" 24 to 36-point, three columns
" 36 to 60-point, four columns

In computing the space that a headline will occupy, allowance should be made for:

a. Space between words, which counts as one letter.
b. Difference in the widths of type letters.

A table showing the average number of letters in a line 2⅛ inches wide may be constructed.

AVERAGE NUMBER OF LETTERS PER LINE

Type size	All caps	Caps and lower case
12-point	18	22
14 "	15	19
16 "	13	17
18 "	11	15
24 "	9	11
30 "	7	9
36 "	6	8
48 "	4	5

If it is desired to use a type size larger than 60-point, which will be but seldom, wood and not metal type must be ordinarily relied upon. Few shops carry the larger metal type. The wood type is made in multiples of 12-point or pica and its different sizes are designated as 8-line pica, 10-line pica and so on.

15. *Estimating space for copy.*—The modern newspaper and magazine practice of running a large amount of display in various sizes of type makes it difficult to estimate the number of words that will go

into a definite space. In planning matter that takes several pages, the following table arranged from data in the "Advertiser's Handbook," will be found useful:

	Words Per Square Inch Solid	Leaded	Words Per 14 agate lines, one column wide, 2⅙ inches Solid	Leaded
6-point	47	33	106	87
7 "	38	27	85	60
8 "	30	21	72	51
9 "	26	20	63	47
10 "	21	16	47	36
11 "	17	14	38	31
12 "	14	11	31	25

16. *Figuring stock.*—Suppose it is desired to produce ten thousand booklets consisting of 32 pages, self covered, size 6 x 9, and that the advertiser wishes to know how much stock will be required to produce the edition.

The usual method the printer would employ is to print the 32 pages in one form. He would impose the form 8 pages from left to right and four pages from top to bottom, as illustrated on page 282. There must always be added to the page size one-eighth of an inch for trimming on the front and one-eighth of an inch on the top and bottom; the size, therefore, to be considered is 6⅛ x 9¼, thus the size of the paper should be 37 x 49 inches. After printing one side of the sheet, the printer reverses the paper and prints the other side, which is technically known as "backing up," so that out of every sheet 37x49 inches two complete copies of the booklet are obtained, and for ten thousand booklets there would be required five thousand sheets plus waste. The usual method and the best method is for the advertiser to consult with the printer on all subjects pertaining to the production of booklets for the obvious reason that different printing plants employ different machinery, and where one method of imposing would be satisfactory

15	18	23	10	9	24	17	16
2	31	26	7	8	25	32	1
3	30	27	6	5	28	29	4
14	19	22	11	12	21	20	13

How a printer imposes a thirty-two page type form

in one plant, it may not be convenient or practical in another. It would also be wise for the manufacturer to familiarize himself with the stock sizes of paper so that he could make his book conform in size so that it would cut economically and without waste out of the sheet.

17. *Selection of material.*—Every advertiser should know how to apply simple tests for determining the fitness of papers for specific jobs. Mr. George French in his book, "The Art and Science of Adver-

tising," gives the following suggestions on the testing of papers:

Usually, printing paper requires a surface adapted to receive the impression of the type, rather than great strength or much sizing. It is important that the paper shall be free of acid, alkali and chlorine; that it has no uncooked wood or ligneous matter; that the sheet be opaque.

To test paper for durability, tear a sheet in halves. Put one half in a dark drawer and the other in sunlight. After two weeks compare the color, and test for strength on the Mullen tester. (The Mullen tester is an apparatus for testing the strength of paper.)

To test the sizing, touch the paper to the tongue and note if the moisture is quickly absorbed or remains on the surface; or make a wide line on the paper with pen and ink, and when the ink is dry examine the edges of the line and the reverse side of the paper, to note if the edges of the line are sharp or if the ink soaks thru.

To detect clay in paper, burn a piece and rub the ashes in the fingers. What happens?

To detect dirt, hold the sheet before a light and mark each spot; count the spots and compare with a standard sample of same grade and size.

To judge of the formation of a sheet, hold it to the light and look thru it, or tear it in different places and both ways of the sheet. If properly made, the sheet will tear evenly and will not look cloudy.

To judge if a sheet will "fuzz" in printing, rub it with the coat sleeve and look across it toward the light. If it is "fuzzy" the fibres will be plainly seen standing on edge on the surface. (This test is not infallible. There are papers that are difficult to print on, on account of the "fuzz," but which endure this test successfully.)

To determine the way the "grain" runs, cut two strips one-half an inch wide by eight inches long; cut one lengthwise the sheet and one crosswise. Lay one on the other and hold by one end between the thumb and finger, and note if the top strip supports its own weight or rests on the under strip. Reverse them. The strip cut with the grain will show itself stronger; that cut across the grain will sag more. Another method is to take the sheet of paper and fold it one way and then the other. If you fold it with the grain there will be no cracks. When you fold it the other way the sheet will break and crack.

Strength of paper may be judged by tearing it, but it can only be satisfactorily determined by using a tester such as Mullen's.

To judge the opacity of paper, lay two sheets over printed matter and note thru which the type can be more plainly seen.

To judge of the finish look across a sheet held level with the eyes.

To find the thickness of a sheet, and to estimate its "bulking" quality, fold it twice and measure it in the micrometer gauge.

REVIEW

How were the earliest printing presses operated?

In what way is the offset process an improvement over the earlier methods?

What is the difference in the effects produced by means of the multicolor press and lithography?

What is the importance of the "make-ready"?

What styles of type do you think would look most effective in an advertisement of silver tableware? A trick automobile? A fountain pen? A canoe? A business correspondence course?

What considerations should govern the size of the type for these articles?

How con you prevent waste in cutting when preparing a booklet?

CHAPTER XVIII

TRADE-MARKS, SLOGANS AND CATCH PHRASES

1. *Origin of trade-marks.*—The trade-mark appears to have been originally an ownership mark. Before trade was known, the savage placed some identifying mark upon the weapons he made. In hunting, the arrow identified the game. The ownership mark identified the arrow. Hence the importance of the individual mark in the entire scheme of property. When the arrow-maker developed skill in his craft, his mark was a guarantee of quality—genuineness—and it was, incidentally, an advertisement.

The oldest trade-mark of which there is any knowledge is said to be a triangle with one apex missing. This marks a piece of Egyptian pottery estimated to be of the era 2000 B. C. Chinese pottery of great age bears a trade-mark. Bricks found in excavations in Asia Minor and Egypt bear marks supposed to possess trade value as well as to indicate some form of government license. The manufacturers of Greece and Rome used trade-marks, many of them strikingly like certain ones in use thruout the world today. In the ruins of Pompeii small jars of fish sauce were found. One jar is inscribed: "Scaurus' tunny jelly.

Blossom Brand, put up by Eutyches, slave of Scaurus."

2. *Purpose of trade-marks.*—Primarily, the trade-mark exists for the purpose of establishing the identity of an article. It is the definite emblem of quality or service and is therefore an asset to the advertiser. The trade-mark establishes trade relations with the buying public; it enables the marketing firm to build up tangible good-will. It establishes the quality of an article; it stabilizes prices; it creates sentiment in favor of goods and builds markets.

The term trade-mark has several shades of meaning. Originally, it identified the article which was "traded." Now the "trade-mark" has been extended to cover any characteristic distinction in nature, color, or shape, container and the like, which is associated with the product.

As legal restrictions have come to surround the use of the trade-mark, a comprehensive definition would read as follows: "Any symbol, mark, name or other characteristic or arbitrary identification, secured to the user by legal restriction; adopted and used by a manufacturer or merchant, to designate the goods he manufactures or sells, and to distinguish them from the goods of competitors."

3. *Early restrictions.*—As early as 1512, the Council of Nuremberg restrained an impostor from selling paintings bearing the forged signature of Albrecht Dürer. In 1544, by an edict of Charles V, infringers of laws affecting tapestry trade-marks were punished

by having their right hand cut off. Charles IX of France, by royal edict, made trade-mark forgers subject to capital punishment. England began the protection of trade-marks in 1783. The States of Connecticut and Pennsylvania were the first governments in the United States to regulate the use of marks on goods. The national law was enacted in 1870.

4. *Creating a trade-mark.*—Usually the maker of a product wishes the mark by which the product is to be known to bear something of his individuality. Hence the "face" trade-mark. Patent medicine men have overdone this to such an extent that unless the face used as a trade-mark is that of a notably great man, the mark lacks distinction. That the face and signature of Thomas A. Edison on phonograph products, or of Luther Burbank on a seed package has selling quality as well as distinction is obvious, but the fact offers no assurance to the obscure advertiser who follows these examples.

Glen Buck, in "Trade-Mark Power," has given twelve directions showing what is to be avoided in devising trade-marks. They are as follows:

First—Common and familiar forms do not usually make good trade-marks, for they lack distinction. The circle, the square, the crescent, the star, the diamond, the heart, the oval, the shield, the cross, all have long ago been usurped and are burdened with significance.

Second—If one is anxious to acquire legal title to a trademark, he will not have it resemble any other trade-mark, nor will he put in it any descriptive phrase or name.

Third—Flags and emblems of all nations, the established devices of societies, associations and institutions should be avoided as not legally usuable or protectable.

Fourth—Complicated or confused pictures or devices do not make good trade-marks, because they cannot be seen and comprehended at a glance. As they lack simplicity they lack strength.

Fifth—A good trade-mark will not depend upon any color arrangement for its effect, as it will undoubtedly be necessary to reproduce it in many places where color cannot be used.

Sixth—It is advisable to avoid designs that are higher than they are wide. A tall trade-mark is often difficult to fit into attractive and harmonious layouts.

Seventh—A trade-mark should be capable of reproduction by all engraving processes, by zincs, half-tones, and the different offset and lithographing methods, that it may be well printed on all kinds of paper and other printable materials.

Eighth—If the trade-mark is not as simple as it can be made, and carefully proportioned in all its parts, it may be found impossible to reduce it to small sizes without losing the design, or to increase it to large sizes without rendering it ugly.

Ninth—Care should be taken to evolve a design that will not print too black or too light, for undoubtedly it will be used with many styles of lettering and kinds of type faces.

Tenth—Designs that have only a temporary significance should be discarded. They may be meaningless, absurd or quite impossible of use tomorrow.

Eleventh—That which is vulgar, repulsive or ugly will never make a good trade-mark. Also, one should be extremely cautious in the use of comic motives.

Twelfth—It will save expense and trouble, and perhaps prevent disappointment, if the work of designing the trade-mark is put into trained and understanding hands. It is work that can't be hurriedly done in an idle moment by one who has no conception of the importance of the task.

TRADE-MARKS, SLOGANS, CATCH PHRASES 289

5. *Trade-mark individuality.*—One of the essentials of a trade-mark is that it shall distinguish the product from others. To do this it must possess individuality. Not only is individuality necessary to prevent infringement on other similar marks, and to fulfil the legal requisite for registration, but to give *selling quality*.

Selling quality in a trade-mark means not only that the mark "stands out" so as to be remembered, but that it is readily adaptable to all advertising requirements. The Dutch girl "chasing dirt," with her swinging stick, as depicted by the flashing light in the electric sign, not only impresses the trade-mark on the memory, but suggests to the housewife that the help of this efficient dirt-chaser will be worth while. Dirt vanishes like magic and everything becomes spick and span. This trade-mark has great selling quality.

The Old Dutch Cleanser trade-mark is impressive, suggestive and has great selling value.

If the mark can show distinguishing features, selling quality is secured in high degree. An illustration of selling quality is found in the trade-mark of "Conklin's Self-Filling Fountain Pen." There are other self-filling pens, but none which fills in the same manner as the Conklin. Therefore the trade-mark showing the working of the pen while it is being filled, the simple manner in which it may be made to "drink," has the high individuality that confers the necessary selling quality.

The trade-mark is fundamentally an advertisement, hence it is subject to the same principles which govern all advertising. The various elements are practically the same in a trade-mark as in an advertisement, but *the relative value of the elements differs in each case.*

The trade-marks identifying Dutch Cleanser and Conklin's Self-Filling Fountain Pen have a marked strength of appeal. Each can be easily understood; each is concrete; each has human interest; each embodies the spirit of doing something easily that has heretofore been difficult; and each is capable of retaining its full value under the demands of the various mediums and mechanical processes of printing.

There are special requirements other than making an appeal. The Yale Lock trade-mark is particularly well suited for locks, as it is easily read and suggests strength and simplicity, altho it carries no "human" appeal.

The Gold Dust Twins furnish an excellent illustration of flexibility, in the use of a trade-mark. The twins are taken off the package label and used to illustrate vividly the slogan, "Let the Gold Dust Twins do your work."

The trade-mark of Armour and Company, page 292, permits a series of products—Armour's Veribest Bacon, Ham, Selected Eggs, Tomatoes, and other foods to be featured under similar marks. Their advertisement features the oval label trademark and explains that their mark on *any* product is a guarantee of quality, for the oval label is "not only a trade-mark but a grade-mark." It was pointed out in other advertisements in an advertising campaign that the ability of Armour and Company to hold down prices lies in the fact that "Instead of marketing a *single* commodity, the same manufacturing organization and the same selling force market over *three hundred* food products at practically the same *fixed overhead charges.*

Another application of the same idea is the Na-

Learn What the Armour Oval Label Means to YOU

SUPPOSE you could have the best from the orchards, fisheries, dairies and farms of *all* America brought *to your own door* How carefully you would select the *choicest*! How sure you would be of choosing the best!

Yet, this is precisely what the *Armour Oval Label* offers you—the best foods from *everywhere* —delivered to you in packages—*perfect in condition*—*just as if you lived alongside the farm!* For Armour is the American farmer's largest customer.

What you buy under the Armour Oval Label is always satisfactory. More, it is always *top* grade, for the Armour Oval Label is *more* than merely a *trade*-mark; it is unique among trade-marks in that it is also a *grade*-mark— the design reserved exclusively to identify the BEST in *each* of Armour's pure food products. Back of it is the Armour responsibility, *reinforced by a hundred million dollars invested and a half century of experience* — your assurance of UNVARYING QUALITY!

The Armour Oval Label is the outward sign of *the Armour Ideal of Service to the Consumer.* Under it the best that Armour produces may be bought from dealers, no matter where you live.

Look for the Armour Oval on dealers' store fronts, and on the packages in their windows and on their shelves. It identifies Star Stockinet Ham, Star Bacon, "Simon Pure" Leaf Lard, *Veribest* Package Foods, Cloverbloom Butter, Armour's Grape Juice and Armour's Oleomargarine — Glendale (natural color), Silver Churn (white) — and many others.

Our Domestic Science Department is under the direction of Mrs. Jean Prescott Adams, food adviser Write her, care Armour and Company, Dept. 142, Chicago, for information, menus, recipes and booklets.

ARMOUR AND COMPANY

The Armour trade-mark can readily be adapted to feature each one of their many products

Identifying the Best Biscuit

Whenever you see the famous In-er-seal Trade Mark on a package of National Biscuit Company products, you may know that inside are the best crackers or cookies, wafers or snaps.

You will find the In-er-seal Trade Mark on packages of Uneeda Biscuit, N. B. C. Graham Crackers, Zu Zu Ginger Snaps, Baronet Biscuit, Social Tea Biscuit, Tokens, N. B. C. Zwieback and a host of other delightful varieties of these delightful biscuit.

No matter where you buy packages of National Biscuit Company products, you may rest assured that the contents are made of very choicest materials. Their preparation and baking are according to most scientific methods. They are clean, fresh and wholesome, and uniformly good.

NATIONAL BISCUIT COMPANY

The In-er-seal is used in exactly the same form on every National Biscuit Company product

tional Biscuit Company's "In-er-seal" mark. The difference between the use of these two trade-marks is that the "In-er-seal" mark remains the same on all packages, while the Armour mark retains only its general form and is applied to different products.

Allegorical figures are losing the strong appeal they once had. A figure of Mars as a trade-mark lacks appeal to the ordinary purchaser of revolvers, while, on the other hand, the representation of "hammering the hammer" on an Iver-Johnson firearm appeals in a quite forcible manner to every buyer of a revolver.

6. *Appropriate trade-marks.*—A trade-mark which suggests some feature of the goods that it identifies is likely to be more forceful and consequently to have greater selling value than any arbitrarily chosen device. It may be simply descriptive as "Swans Down" cake flour, the winged foot of the Goodyear Company for tires, "Rub-dry" towels, "Come-Packt" furniture, "Slidewell" collars, "Simon Pure" leaf lard, "Holeproof" hosiery, and others.

Reg. Trade Mark

The spinning wheel, the trade-mark of James McCutcheon's linens, is an illustration of appropriateness in marks.

The name "Prophylactic" means "tending to prevent disease" and goes well with the slogan "a clean tooth never decays." "Kiddie-Koop" is relevant in its suggestion of making the "kiddie" safe in his crib. "Wear-Ever" suggests durability and serviceableness in aluminum kitchen utensils.

7. *Trade-marking perishable eatables.*—One of the latest tendencies in advertising is to put a trade-mark upon perishable eatables, especially fruits.

One of the most fitting trade-marks of this sort is the term "Sunkist" for oranges. As used in the advertising pages of magazines, the color of the orange with the suggestion that it is "sun-kissed," ripened by the sun, is most appealing. The appetite needs little further stimulus to want a Sunkist orange.

The trade-mark "Seatag" for oysters is excellent. There is a suggestion of freshness in the word sea, and the suggestion of being tagged in the sea, tagged while at the height of freshness, is stimulating to the appetite.

8. *Trade-mark as a reminder.*—The value of the trade-mark as a reminder is particularly high in those fields where competitive products—all approaching the same degree of quality—are numerous. Suppose a city man finds that he has use for a saw He makes a note to call at a hardware store to buy *a* saw. So far, he is concerned only with his need for any good saw at a fair price. Before calling at the store, he remembers that, ten years before, his father had several saws which gave good service. He has a hazy recollection that those saws were marked with a keystone of some sort.

When he gets to the store he looks over a number of saws. One of them bears the "Keystone Mark." Then the customer remembers that that good saw of his father's was a Disston. So he buys a Disston; the trade-mark, acting as a reminder, makes the selection for him.

9. *Preventing substitution.*—The manufacturers of Lea & Perrins Sauce are constantly called upon to prevent the use of substitutes, which are offered for consumption in a Lea & Perrins bottle bearing the genuine label. The restaurant keeper buys a number of bottles of the genuine sauce, carefully preserves the labels intact on the bottles and refills them with a cheap mixture. This involves considerable labor, affords but little extra profit, and may drive away trade, but it is often done, and shows to what lengths substitution will be carried. The non-refillable bottle and the pasting of a genuine label over the cork are precautions against this kind of substitution.

If a purveyor will go to such extreme measures to substitute, what chance has a firm to build up a reputation on a product which is not protected by a trade-mark? While some lines of trade-marked goods are, from the nature of their use, subject to piracy even when trade-marked, ordinarily a distinctive trade-mark insures reasonable protection against substitution.

The refilling of an original package is held to be substantially the same as giving out a brand of goods when another brand has been requested; yet this con-

DISSTON
SAWS AND TOOLS

"I've never sawed with anything but a Disston"

Sixty-three years ago, this veteran carpenter bought his first Disston saw. He is still sawing with it.

His name is Charles H. Fields. He lives in Brooklyn. He was born seventy-nine years ago — one year before Henry Disston manufactured the first Disston saw.

In his sixteenth year, young Fields finished his apprenticeship in Rye, New York. By that time the foreign make of saw, which had been popular with American carpenters, had practically disappeared before the successful competition of Disston saws.

The young carpenter promptly added both a Disston rip-saw and a Disston cross-cut saw to his equipment. In those days he had to go into the woods, fell his own trees, square them off, cut them into lengths, and finish them into lumber.

Thirty years ago, he added a new Disston hand saw to his collection. It's a "76." He still calls it his "new Disston."

But he has never abandoned his sixty-three-year-old Disston. It is his "baby."

The saw that has stood faithfully by old carpenters through thick and thin for generation after generation is a good saw for you to buy.

You will find Disston saws in the hands of three out of every four carpenters everywhere. The great edge-holding Disston blade, made of fully tempered Disston crucible steel, has made thousands of Disston saws last a lifetime in the hands of thousands of industrious members of the carpenter's trade.

Talk to nearly any white-haired carpenter in your neighborhood and have him tell you the interesting history of his Disston saws.

Disston saws and tools are sold by all progressive hardware dealers in your vicinity.

Send for the free Disston Handbook of Saws. It contains many valuable suggestions on the care of Disston saws and tools.

Henry Disston & Sons, Incorporated
Philadelphia, U. S. A.
Canadian Works: Toronto, Canada

Chicago Cincinnati Boston San Francisco
New Orleans Memphis Seattle
Portland, Ore. Bangor, Me.
Vancouver, B. C.
Sydney, Australia

In this advertisement the importance of a trade-mark is emphasized by reproducing it in the text and in the illustration

stitutes but a small part of the substitution methods of dishonest dealers. If the customer has but a hazy idea of what brand is wanted, and should ask for "the cleaner with the twins on it," or "the chocolate with the girl on the label," there is a chance to substitute. To prevent just that, some firms which have been particularly subject to this form of commercial piracy lay special emphasis in their advertising on the trade-mark. The Coca-Cola Company says: "Demand the genuine by full name—nicknames encourage substitution." The B. V. D. Company in the advertisement on the opposite page, for example, features its trade-marked label at the top of the advertisement and says: "If it *hasn't* the Red Woven Label shown above, it *isn't* B. V. D. underwear." If the product has a distinctive form which identifies it, as the shape of the "Cascarets" package or the container for "Log Cabin Syrup," the trade-mark becomes a bulwark against substitution.

10. *Registration of a trade-mark*. Registration is evidence of a public nature, that the one registering the trade-mark claims a right in it. Registration creates no rights; it merely makes public the claim to ownership. Once owner of the design, the use and the right to advertise a distinctive mark has been acquired; registration then provides an additional safeguard against infringement.

11. *The slogan.*—Attached to the trade-mark is often found a phrase that helps to fix the trade-mark in the memory. This slogan is more than a catch

MADE FOR THE
B.V.D.
BEST RETAIL TRADE

(Trade Mark Reg. U. S. Pat. Off. and Foreign Countries)

This world-known label on Summer Underwear is the Sign-Post on the Road to Comfort that guides you straight to Money's Most.

If it hasn't the Red Woven Label shown above, it isn't B.V.D. Underwear.

"B.V.D. Closed Crotch Union Suits (Pat. U. S. A.) B. V. D. Coat Cut Undershirts and Knee Length Drawers."

The
B. V. D. Company,
New York.

The advertiser in this advertisement aims to prevent substitution by featuring his trade-mark

phrase; it has greater significance and is often an evidence of service.

The following expressions may be properly classified as slogans:

"One Policy, One System, Universal Service."—American Telephone and Telegraph Company.

"Ask the Man Who Owns One."—Packard Motor Car Company.

"The Linen Store of America."—James McCutcheon and Company.

"There's a Reason."—Postum Cereal.

"His Master's Voice."—Victrola.

"Velvet Grip."—Boston garters.

"No Metal Can Touch You."—Paris garters.

"57 Varieties."—Heinz Company.

"Not the Name of a Thing, but the Mark of a Service."—Mazda lamp of General Electric Company.

"A Clean Tooth Never Decays."—Prophylactic tooth brush.

"A Sensible Cigarette."—Fatima.

"It Floats—$99^{44}/_{100}\%$ pure."—Ivory Soap.

"Has the Strength of Gibraltar."—Prudential Insurance Company.

"Silver Plate That Wears."—Rogers Bros., 1847.

"Hasn't Scratched Yet."—Bon Ami powder.

"Let the Gold Dust Twins do your Work."—Gold Dust washing powder.

"The Watch that made the Dollar Famous."—Ingersoll watch.

TRADE-MARKS, SLOGANS, CATCH PHRASES   301

"If it isn't an Eastman, it isn't a Kodak."—Eastman Kodak.

"Have you a little Fairy in your Home?"—Fairy Soap.

12. *Catch words and phrases.*—Closely allied to the slogan is the catch phrase, which stands second to the picture in attraction value. A striking word or phrase will remain long in the memory.

The identification mark, catch word and slogan used by Simmons Hardware Company is a good illustration of the comparative use of these different elements. The identification mark, in this case, consists of the triangular blade cutting cleanly thru the rectangular bar. The trade name, which is a catch

**Be guided by
This Trade-Mark**

E. C. SIMMONS
KEEN KUTTER
CUTLERY AND TOOLS

"The recollection of QUALITY remains long after the PRICE is forgotten."
—*E. C. SIMMONS.*
Trade Mark Registered.

The KEEN KUTTER trade-mark will never fail you. When you see it on tools and cutlery you can absolutely depend on their high quality. For years, its dependability has been universally recognized.

SIMMONS HARDWARE COMPANY

word lettered in characters with sharp edges, is "KEEN KUTTER." The slogan is "The Recollection of QUALITY Remains Long After the PRICE is Forgotten."

There are two tendencies in the use of catch phrases: the short and rhythmic phrase, not necessarily a complete sentence, and the phrase in the form of a complete sentence. "Taste the Taste" (Underwood Devilled Ham), "The Nation's Spread" (Karo), are phrases exemplifying the first tendency. "Don't buy a pig in a poke," used by the Majestic Manufacturing Company, and "Buy insurance when you buy your spoons," used by the Holmes and Edwards Silver Company, are illustrations of the completed thought form.

Of special appeal to the thrifty farmer is the question, "WHY PAY FOR GASOLINE WHEN WIND IS FREE?" (to advertise the Samson windmill). This phrase not only has selling quality, but savors so strongly of country store philosophy as to make it stand at the top for appropriateness. "Hook 'er to the biler" (Ridgeway Elevators) illustrates the colloquial catch phrase in the imperative form.

There has always been a strong tendency toward the use of rhymed catch phrases. "A Kalamazoo direct to you," of the Kalamazoo Stove Company and "The ham what am" being typical of the Armour Company; "All the taste—none of the waste" (G. Washington Coffee), "Bring them back with Jap-alac," "An apple a day keeps the doctor away" (Skookum), "The Proven Best by Government Test" (Colt's Patent Fire Arms Manufacturing Company), are good examples of phrases that are "catchy."

13. *Other tendencies in trade-marking.*—Along with trade-marking perishable eatables there are other recent tendencies that are rather ingenious. Music is being trade-marked by the Victor and Columbia Phonograph Companies. Parasols have a trade-name inserted on the inside of the ribs. In Chicago, the City Fuel Company uses the representation of a coalman, entirely made of coal, in all its advertising. Cartoons are marked with the insignia of the artist. The London Feather Company uses a tiny label of celluloid as a mark, which is sewed inside the stem of each ostrich plume.

Because of this tendency to trade-mark everything that is advertised, it becomes more and more necessary that the trade-mark be simple, distinctive, appropriate, striking, suggestive and imbued with real appeal and selling value. Furthermore, every trademark should be formally registered, so that it may have the full protection of the law.

REVIEW

In what did trade-marks have their origin?
How is a trade-mark an asset of the advertiser?
What is the value of an appropriate name as a trade-mark?
What is the value of a trade-mark to the public?
How does registration of a mark protect the advertiser?

CHAPTER XIX

LEGAL LIMITS AND RESTRICTIONS ON ADVERTISING

1. *Restrictions of the Federal Government.*—Advertising is relatively too new a branch of business to have become directly subject to Federal control. Altho Congress has the power to regulate interstate commerce and has complete control of the mails and of trade-marks, like the Dominion Parliament, it has used this power only for the following purposes: (1) to prevent lotteries; (2) to insure the sale of pure foods and drugs; (3) to prevent the mails from being used to perpetrate frauds. In the regulation of all these matters, however, restraint on advertising is incidental.

The Federal pure-food law limits the advertiser in making representations concerning the materials composing the food and drug products sold by him.

The Food and Drugs Act of 1906 reads as follows:

The term "Misbranded," as used herein, shall apply to all drugs, or articles of food, or articles which enter into the composition of food, the package or label of which shall bear any statement, design or device regarding such article, or the ingredients or substances contained therein which shall be false or misleading in any particular, and to any food or drug product which is falsely branded as to the state, territory or country in which it is manufactured or produced.

LEGAL LIMITS AND RESTRICTIONS

The Canadian Adulterations Act provides heavy penalties in similar circumstances.

The term "lottery" has been broadly defined as "a scheme for the distribution of prizes by lot or chance; a game or hazard in which small sums of money are ventured for the chance of obtaining a larger value, in money or other articles."

Congress has passed statutes forbidding the use of the mails for sending a letter, postal card or circular "concerning any lottery." Advertising of any kind pertaining to lotteries is forbidden and penalties are prescribed for sending lottery advertisements into the United States or from one state to another. In Canada, the laws against lotteries are enacted by the Dominion Parliament as of right, and are very stringent.

The mere fact that all the purchasers of chances are, in any event, to receive a full return for their money will not make the plan legal. If it is likely that some purchasers may receive more than others, the scheme will be a lottery. When the distribution of prize offers is determined solely by skill or judgment, there will be no lottery; but this rule is violated if skill is apt to be thwarted by chance. There is no lottery when no consideration is paid; but a consideration may consist in the rendering of services. Whether the filling in of a form on the part of the purchaser is a sufficient consideration is doubtful, but to furnish the names of other prospects would probably be indefensible.

One of the most effective means of conveying the idea of authenticity, or reliability, is to show a reproduction of an addressed envelop bearing the stamp and post mark, or the reproduction of the money that is to be paid out in a prize offer. Such reproductions of stamps or money are considered illegal in the United States.

Altho the Federal law prohibiting representations of either United States money or postage stamps is supposed to be known by advertisers, in many instances advertising matter has been held up because of the non-observance of this law. In one case the entire edition of a magazine was kept from transmission by mail until the representation of a postage stamp could be blotted out.

2. *State regulations.*—The states generally have passed laws governing the sale of foods and drugs. Those laws may be summarized as follows:

(a) The label must describe the contents accurately.

(b) It must contain a statement of the quantity or proportion of morphine, opium, etc.

Negative provisions:

(a) The label must not contain anything which is false or misleading in any particular regarding the ingredients or contents.

(b) It must not bear the distinctive name of another article.

(c) It must not have an incorrect or obscure statement of weight or measure.

LEGAL LIMITS AND RESTRICTIONS 307

Many of the states prohibit lotteries by constitutional provision, and, with one exception, they have enacted statutes that prohibit lotteries and the various transactions connected with lotteries.

3. *Postal regulations.*—The postal authorities enforce rates for the different classes of mail which the advertiser sends out, and regulate the use to which inquiry coupons may be put.

The third-class rate is of great interest to the advertising man, altho attempts have frequently been made by advertisers to get the benefits of second-class rates. Printed engravings, printed circulars (or circulars made by the mimeograph and similar processes), other matter in print (except books), proof sheets, etc., are included in third-class mail matter.

Upon matter of the third class, or on wrappers, envelops or tags, inclosed or attached to it the sender may write his name, occupation, business and address.

Other miscellaneous postal regulations may be summarized as follows:

Typewriting and carbon letter press copies of typewriting are classed as handwriting. Matter reproduced by photographic process (including blueprints) is printed matter; matter printed on material other than paper is fourth class.

A circular which is defined as a printed letter, sent in identical terms to several persons, may bear a date and the name and address of the sender and the person addressed. When a name or date, other than those of the sender or addressee, is typewritten in the body of the circular except to correct a genuine typographical error, the circular is subject to postage at the first-class (letter) rate, whether sealed or unsealed.

Reproduction or imitations of handwriting and typewriting done by means of the printing press, multigraph and similar mechanical devices are treated as third-class mail, provided they are mailed at a post-office in a minimum number of twenty, identical, unsealed copies; if mailed elsewhere, or in smaller quantities, they take the first-class rate.

The Curtis Publishing Company restricts the acceptance of coupons as advertising matter as follows:

No copy is acceptable bearing a coupon, the redemption value of which equals or exceeds the news-stand value of the publication in which it appears.

Third-class mail in Canada includes bona fide samples, printed pamphlets, printed circulars, maps, photographs, drawings, engravings, book jackets, manuscripts of books or newspapers, calendars, printed or written music, proofs of printing, with or without the manuscript. The rate is one cent for two ounces or a fraction thereof. Third-class matter must be put up so as to admit of easy inspection. The limit of weight is five pounds, and ten pounds for a single book. Third-class matter may also be mailed at parcel-post rate, in which case the limit of weight is eleven pounds.

Circulars typewritten are subject to the letter rate.

Circulars produced in imitation of typewriting are allowed to pass at the one cent per two ounces rate when at least twenty copies in exactly identical terms are handed in to the post-office at one time.

The rate for second-class matter—newspapers and periodicals—is one cent for four ounces.

The Postal Laws and Regulations of the United States, section 462, paragraph 7, on the subject of coupons, reads as follows:

> Coupons, order forms and other matter intended for detachment and subsequent use may be included in permanently attached advertisements, or elsewhere, in newspapers, and periodicals, provided they constitute only an incidental feature of such publications and are not of such character or used to such extent as to destroy the statutory characteristics of second-class publications, or to bring them within the prohibition of the statutes denying the second-class rate postage to publications "designed primarily for advertising purposes," or to give them the characteristics of books or other third-class matter.

4. *Municipal regulations.*—Questions of local interest are usually regulated by state laws or by municipal ordinances. With reference to overhanging signs, municipal regulations in general concern one or more of the following restrictions:

Area shown, or projection upon the street, height above street, or degree of obstruction of public travel.

Material of which signs are made.

Attachment to building or other support.

A typical law in force in the District of Columbia reads as follows:

Signs must be authorized by the inspector of buildings and no such sign can project more than three feet six inches beyond the building line, or be lower than eight feet above the surface, if projecting over an alley.

Where restrictions affecting the size of billboards are in force they are usually based upon possible danger from windstorms. As these restrictions are more necessary in thickly populated districts than in the country, they are, in many states, given over to the municipal authorities.

Among the ordinances passed by the city of Chicago for the regulation of billboards is the following:

All signs or billboards other than those painted or erected upon any building, shall be limited in their superficial area to one hundred (100) square feet. . . . No such sign or billboard shall be constructed at a greater height than ten (10) feet above the level of the adjoining streets; in case the grade of the adjoining streets has not been established, no sign or billboard shall be constructed at a greater height than ten (10) feet above the surface of the ground.

In many states, billboards of any size may be erected on private property, provided that they are erected in a safe manner. Frequently, flagstaffs, weathercocks and solid signs of any sort are not allowed to rise more than a specified number of feet above the roof.

5. *Constitutionality of billboard restrictions.*—The fight against the billboard is one of long standing. A number of states and several of the Canadian provinces have passed laws regulating roadside billboards,

while the municipalities have sought thru taxation, licensing or direct prohibition to restrain the use of the billboard when attached to buildings. More frequently the Canadian statutes, where these exist, are directed against indecent advertisements. In most cities and towns there are municipal ordinances regulating and licensing advertisements with a view to restricting and regulating them.

The decisions in most of the state cases have been made on the ground that while the city can regulate the construction of billboards to protect the health and safety of the citizen, it cannot for esthetic reasons restrict the use of private property.

6. *Distribution of circulars and dodgers.*—Dodgers and handbills distributed carelessly in streets and areas are classified under the head of "public nuisances"; city and state regulations in this regard vary widely.

The Pittsburgh ordinance reads as follows:

Be it ordained and enacted by the City of Pittsburgh . . . that hereafter it shall not be lawful for any person or persons to distribute by throwing from wagons or other vehicles, any handbills, dodgers or other advertising device.

The distribution of handbills and other printed advertising matter is forbidden by Section 41 of Chapter 47 of the Revised Ordinances of the city of Boston, as follows:

No person . . . shall distribute to persons on a street handbills, cards, circulars, or papers of any kind except newspapers.

In New York, New Jersey, and Pennsylvania, the insertion of circulars between the leaves of a newspaper has been made a criminal offense.

Many national concerns as a part of their sales campaigns have included a wholesale distribution of samples and descriptive literature. Their activity in this respect has been greatly curtailed by ordinances similar to the above.

The constitutionality of these ordinances raises interesting legal questions. On the part of the municipalities, they are claimed to be a valid exercise of the police power in the interest of residents to prevent the streets from being littered with advertising matter and the like. Cases are cited of children or pet animals having been poisoned by imbibing samples of pills, medicines and certain kinds of foods—but it has never been proved in any instance that the illness actually resulted from the use of the article. Where the campaign is part of an interstate movement, distributors assail such ordinances as a tax of restraint on interstate commerce.

The only case decided by the United States Supreme Court in which this question has been involved is popularly known as the Robbins decision. Robbins was a salesman in Tennessee for an Ohio stationery concern. A local ordinance in Tennessee required the payment to the county of a certain sum weekly by persons who offered goods for sale by sample. Robbins was arrested for refusing to pay the tax, and the case was carried to the United States

Supreme Court, which held that this amounted to a tax on interstate commerce and was therefore illegal.

The prohibition of the statutes denies the second-class-rate postage to publications "designed primarily for advertising purposes," or to give them the characteristics of books or other third-class matter.

7. *Protection of trade-marks.*—A brief summary of trade-marks as they relate to the unfair trade law follows:

> Trade-mark law is only a particular phase of unfair trade law. Unfair trade law relates to all matters by which the trade of one person is unfairly obtained by another. Trade-mark law pertains to a special agency used in trade in relation to which certain rules have been established.
>
> It is unfair trade for one dealer under certain circumstances to use the particular shape of a bottle or other container or the same design of label which is owned and used by another, altho there may be no technical trade-mark right in any of these. . . . The question of unfair trade is often raised in those cases in which one trader in his business uses colors, designs or shapes similar to those used by his neighbor. No question of trade-mark infringement is involved in such cases.

It will thus be seen that adequate protection of what the trade-mark stands for embraces more than the mere protection of the mark itself. It is only at the point where the trade-mark itself is actually infringed that the law becomes general. Trade-mark infringement assumes that the trade-mark identifies and protects the rightful owner. Unfair competition may, and often does, exist where no trade-mark is imitated, but *where one attempts to pass off his goods as the goods of another.* The proof of such an attempt is based on the likelihood that the purchaser may be deceived. Imitation of a trade-mark is practical evidence that an attempt is to be made to pass off the goods under the imitative brand for those of the original trade-mark. Unfair competition, on the other hand, commonly must be proved from the evidence of those who know whether or not deception has been practised.

Several years ago an interesting case was decided in the Montreal courts which illustrates what is meant by unfair and fraudulent competition. The Molson's Brewery Company, Limited, entered an action to protect its rights in a trade-mark attached to bottles containing Molson's India Pale Ale. The complaint of the company was that the defendant, a saloon keeper, had infringed its trade-mark by attaching to bottled ale of an inferior quality a label in similar form to Molson's, but bearing the title "Nelson's India Pale Ale"; that bartenders and others had been instructed to place their thumb over the first two letters of the name when serving the ale, so that the customer would see only ". . . . lson's India Pale Ale." This it was alleged was an illegal and fraudulent act and constituted an infringement of the trade-mark of Molson, for which a sum of $5000 damages was asked, together with an injunction to restrain the defendant from such illegal acts. Judgment was rendered condemning the defendant to pay damages of $100 and costs, and restraining him from using the

LEGAL LIMITS AND RESTRICTIONS 315

Nelson label or any label resembling or in any way similar to it upon any goods made, bottled or sold by him.

8. *Registration regulations.*—Section 3 of the United States Statutes concerning the Registration of Trade-Marks gives in detail the restrictions thrown about registration. Distinctiveness is the first essential of a trade-mark. Resemblance between trade-marks so close as to produce confusion is forbidden. The mark must consist of matter neither immoral nor scandalous. Flags, coats of arms or other insignia of any state are non-registrable as trade-marks for goods. The emblem or device of any fraternal society, any institution or corporation must not be adapted or imitated.

The portrait of an individual cannot be registered without the individual's consent.

Section 11 of the Canadian Trade Mark and Designs Act provides that the Minister (the minister of agriculture is in charge of the department) may refuse to register any trade-mark:

(a) If he is not satisfied that the applicant is undoubtedly entitled to the exclusive use of such trademark;

(b) If the trade-mark proposed is identical with or resembles a trade-mark already registered;

(c) If it appears that the trade-mark is calculated to deceive or mislead the public;

(d) If the trade-mark contains any immorality, or a scandalous figure;

(e) If the so-called trade-mark does not contain the essentials necessary to constitute a trade-mark, properly speaking.

9. *Infringements.*—Were trade-marks invariably simple devices, such as some geometrical shape or peculiar figure, the determination of infringement would be a comparatively simple matter. Were all trade-marks, too, as simple and distinctive as the figure used to distinguish Dutch Cleanser, any material imitation would be easily noted and determined. But design alone does not always constitute their distinguishing characteristic. Often there are several elements in the design itself, while the wording may also be made a part of the mark.

As a consequence, infringements may be present under a wide range of conditions. Among the many cases included under unfair competition are:

(a) Imitation of a device used as a trade-mark.

(b) Deception in the use of geographical, personal or descriptive names.

(c) Imitation of the label, container or article itself.

(d) The use of devices of any kind which cause a product to be considered interchangeable in marketing.

(e) Refilling a genuine container with a product other than genuine.

(f) Active or passive substitution.

(g) False representation, as of locality or condi-

LEGAL LIMITS AND RESTRICTIONS

tions under which the product was grown, manufactured or produced.

(h) Deceptive advertising.

It will be noted that some of these cases have to do with imitation of the trade-mark, since the trade-mark of a product distinguishes it from others. As the distinguishing mark may be a device, name, label, design or container, the term "trade-mark infringement" is an element in unfair competition in many cases, or may even constitute unfair competition.

Laws prohibiting the counterfeiting or imitation of labels have been passed in twenty-one states and in the District of Columbia. In Canada the Dominion Parliament has exclusive legislative jurisdiction with respect to trade-marks.

10. *Remedy for infringement.*—The remedy for infringement lies in a court of equity, and in Canada in a superior court. The usual steps are as follows:

A, who is entitled to the use of a trade-mark or other distinctive mark, learns that B is infringing upon the exclusive right held by A. If B's infringement consists of an imitation of the trade-mark, presentation in court of the original and infringing labels is sufficient cause for an injunction. If damage has resulted, the amount must be proved and a money judgment will be entered.

In case B has employed any of the methods of unfair trade, other than the actual copying of the trade-mark, the legal procedure is substantially the same. In order to make his case, however, A must have witnesses to prove his contention, as the trade theft may consist of a large number of acts which can be told only by witnesses.

The name of an individual firm, corporation or association, not written, printed, impressed or woven in some particular or distinctive manner, or in association with a portrait of the individual, or merely in words or devices which are descriptive of the goods with which they are used, or of the character or quality of such goods, or merely a geographical name or term, cannot be registered as a trade-mark.[1]

Such are the restrictions which prevent registration in the United States. Non-observance of these restrictions is a bar to either defense or recovery in court. Property value exists, not because of registration, but because of lawful use. The Canadian Statute provides a penalty of not less than $20 nor more than $200 for any person who knowingly misuses the trade-mark of another or knowingly sells goods marked with a false trade-mark.

11. *Deceptive advertising.*—In a decision handed down by the Supreme Court of the United States, on April 24, 1916, undue exaggeration in advertising is specifically opposed. According to this decision an advertiser has no right to raise false expectations

---

[1] By a statute of the United States the use of the emblem of the Greek Red Cross on a white ground, or the words "Red Cross" or "Geneva Cross," or any simulation thereof for the purpose of trade is prohibited unless use was begun prior to January 5, 1905. A Red Cross mark which is lawfully used is particularly valuable, as it has been impossible to adopt such a mark since 1905. 12 *Modern American Law,* 492–493.

on the part of a customer, or knowingly to invent advantages and virtues that the goods do not possess.

The following paragraph in the decision is significant:

> An article alone is not necessarily the inducement and compensation for its purchase. It is in the use to which it may be put, the purpose it may serve; and there is deception and fraud when the article is not of the character or kind represented and hence does not serve the purpose.

12. *Personal right of privacy.*—There is in law a doctrine which is coming to be widely held, that a person is protected from an unauthorized use of his photograph or likeness.

A well-known New York case centered about the widespread publication of a young woman's face on an advertisement of a brand of flour. The court refused to enjoin such publication. In another case, in New Jersey, the publication of the plaintiff's name and picture on the labels of bottles of a patent medicine supplied the cause for complaint. Here the plaintiff was granted an injunction. In still another case, in Georgia, an unauthorized indorsement of an insurance company was published, accompanied by a likeness of the supposed writer. The court's decision favored the plaintiff.

The courts, which have refused to grant relief in such cases, base their opinion on the fact that no property right is involved and that courts of equity will lend their aid only when such a right exists. A year after the decision by the New York Court of Appeals, the New York legislature enacted a statute which makes the unauthorized use of the name or picture of any person for purposes of trade a misdemeanor. Similar statutes have been enacted in many states. Other states have reached the same result, in the absence of a statute, by recognizing the right of personal privacy as a distinct legal right, irrespective of any question of property.

Of course, where a person has acquired national renown, his name and likeness become, in a measure, public property, and he cannot ordinarily object to the various uses to which his photograph is placed. The above statements are applicable only to individuals who have not acquired this public reputation.

13. *Property right in advertisements.*—Every advertiser has a property right in his advertisement. If these properties are destroyed, the owner has certainly a right of action. Aside from what is afforded by the copyright or trade-mark laws of the Federal government, and the label and trade-mark laws of the several states, the law seems to offer little protection in such cases. Thus it has been held that the mere fact that the plaintiff in an action "has advertised the article extensively and has promoted and increased the demand for the article" does not warrant an injunction. But even this case seems to be simple, for there was no attempt here to confuse the goods of the competitor with those of the earlier advertiser.

LEGAL LIMITS AND RESTRICTIONS

In a case decided in a local court, it was held that a laundry company which had started a campaign by publishing the word "stopurkicken" could not recover from an envelop company which published cards bearing the same word, and under it the name of the envelop company.

Since the courts are thus at sea on the question of property rights in advertising, legislatures, it would seem, should be called on to settle the question.

REVIEW

Give a summary of state laws on the sale of food and drugs.

What are the usual restrictions placed by municipalities upon overhanging signs; upon billboards?

What do you understand by adequate protection of a trademark; by infringement; by unfair competition?

Name some of the restrictions thrown about registration of trade-marks.

What steps would you take if you found some one infringing on your trade-mark?

Discuss the property rights of advertisers in their advertisements.

INDEX

Action, Producing,
Getting decision and action, 83; Process of reasoning, 84; Elements of reasoning act, 84; Creating and maintaining action, 85; Confidence thru testimonials, 86; Confidence thru prestige, 86; Securing action thru argument, 91; Securing action thru suggestion, 92; Suggestion by repetition, 93; Indirect suggestion, 93; Securing action thru "limited time," 95; Securing action thru "free offer," 98; Making it easy to act, 98.

Adjectives, Use of, 131

Advertisement,
Important points in an, 67–82; Forms of an, 72–82

Advertisement, Getting the, Read,
See Interest, Gaining the

Advertisement, Getting the, Seen,
See Attention, Attracting the,

Advertisement, Getting the, Understood,
Simplicity, 67; Sentence structure, 68; Length of sentences, 68; Coherence, 70; Emphasis, 71; Harmony, 71; Copy classified as to form, 72; Argument, 72; Use of incident, 72; Use of monolog, 73; Use of dialog, 74; Use of the story, 76; Educational copy, 79; News copy, 79; Historical contrast, 81

Advertisement, Layout of,
Object of, 229; Objects of display, 232; The optical center, 232; Balance in, 232; Securing emphasis, 233; Value of movement, 234; Display type, 235; Body type, 236; Illustrations, 236; Borders and rules, 237; White space, 237; Of booklets, catalogs and folders, 244.

Advertisement, Preparing the,
Three parts of 210; Heading, 210; Body, 211; Close, 213; Importance of display, 213; The inclosing shape, 215; Size, 217; Margins, 217; Selection and arrangement of materials, 218; Appropriateness of illustration, 219; Importance of headlines, 221; Proper phraseology, 223; The key, 224; The coupon, 225; Grouping the elements, 226; Fitting the advertisement to the medium, 226

Advertisement, Producing action,
See Action, Producing

Advertising,
Meaning of, 1; Economic rôle of, 1; Early development of, 1; Growth of, 3; Influence of war on, 4; Creator of utility, service to the consumer, 6; Assists intelligent selection, 7; Improves quality of goods, 7; Educates the public, 8; Creates new wants, 9; Service to distributor, 10; Reduces price to consumer, 10; Manufacturer's advantage, 11; Purpose of, 13; Appropriation for, 16; Planning, 16; History of, in past, 25

Advertising Campaign, Fundamentals of,
Purpose of advertising, 13; Advertising as insurance, 14; Reduces selling cost, 14; Raising price, 15; Increasing volume of business, 15; Sales by advertising, 16; Determining appropriation, 16; Advantages of correct budgeting method, 17; Detailed methods vary, 18; Need of careful planning, 18; Approaching the plan from proper angle, 19; groundwork of plan, 21; policy of the firm, 21; Product itself in, 22; Present market, 22; Potential market, 23; Competitive products, 23; Mode of distribution, 24; Sales department, 25; History of past advertising, 25; Study of similar problems, 26; Plan of, 26; Survey of the field. 26; Continuity, 27; Consumers' point of view, 27; Stocking the dealer, 28; Selection of, mediums, 28

323

INDEX

Advertising, Human Appeals in,
Meaning of, 101; Appeals to senses, 101; Touch, 102; Taste, 104; Smell, 105; Sound, 109; Emotions, 109; Appeal to instinct, 115; Feminine intuition, 116; Appeal to imagination, 118; Romance of the commonplace, 120; Appeal to reason, 122

Advertising Legal Limits and Restrictions on,
See, Law, and Advertising

Advertising, Services of,
Creator of utility service to the consumer, 6; Improves quality of goods, 7; Educates the public, 8; Creates new wants, 9; Reduces price to consumer, 10; Services to distributor, 10; To the manufacturer, 11; Reduces selling cost, 14; Raising price by, 15; Increases volume of business, 15; Sales by, 16

Advertising Word values in,
See Word Values, in Advertising

Ætna Life Insurance Company Advertisement, 56

Alexander Hamilton Institute Advertisement, 78

American Chain Company Advertisement, 95.

America's Electrical Week Advertisement, 207

Anglo-Saxon Words, Use of, 127

Argument, Use of, 72
Securing action thru, 91

Armour's Trade-Mark, 292

Arrows, Use of, in Advertising, 33

Art in Advertising,
See Drawings and Reproductions

"Ask Your Dealer" Copy, 172
"Ask your dealer or write us" Copy, 174

Atlas Farm Powder Advertisement, 165

Attention, Attracting The,
Necessity for, 30; Elements that secure, 31; Variation, 31; Arrows, darts and designing signs, 33; Contrast, 37; Illustration, 37; Color, 40; Position, 42; Motion, 43; Novelty and uniqueness, 44; Headlines, 45; Teaser copy, 45; Favorable impression, 47; Turning into interest, 48

Bankers Trust Company Advertisement, 122

Bedell Advertisement, 147
Ben Day Process, 265
Big Ben Advertisement, 49
Billboard Restrictions,
Constitutionality of, 310
Booklets, Catalogs and Folders,
See Catalogs, Booklets and Folders
Borden's Milk Advertisement, 194
Buck, Glen, on Trade-Marks, 287
Burnham & Morrill Fish Flakes Advertisement, 35
B. V. D. Advertisement, 299

Catalogs, Booklets and Folders,
Type of advertising, 143; Adaptation of type, 143; Booklets and, 144; Offer, 156; Aim of, 239; Purposes of, 240; Color and typography of, 24; Need for simplicity, 241; Booklets, 242; Catalogs, 243; Layout, 244; Size, 247; Quoting the price, 247; Folders, 248; The dummy, 249

Catch Words and Phrases,
Use of, 304

Circulars and Dodgers,
Distribution of, 311

Clearness, Value of, 126

Clysmic Advertisement, 193

Coca-Cola Advertisement, 193

Coherence, in Advertisements, 70

Colgate's Cashmere Bouquet Advertisement, 108

Colloquialisms, Use of, 132

Color, Use of, in Advertisements, 40

Columbia Batteries Advertisement, 222

Columbia Grafanola Advertisement, 111

Community Plate Advertisement, 88

Confidence.
Creating and maintaining, 85; Confidence thru testimonial, 86; Thru prestige, 86

Conklin's Self-Filling Fountain Pen Advertisement, 290

Consumer, and Advertising, 5
Service to, 6; Point of view of, 27

Contrast, Use of, in Advertisements, 37

Copy, The,
Actual work on, 28; Form of, to secure interest, 59; Classified forms, 72; Educational, 79; News, 79; Difficulties of producing, 226; Layout, 229; Estimating space, 280

INDEX

Copy, Directing the Reader,
Purpose and scope, 171; Methods of directing the reader, 172; "Ask your dealer" copy, 172; "Ask your dealer or write us" copy, 174; "At all good stores," 175; "For sale at Wanamaker's," 175; "Sold nowhere else," 176; Thru display, 178; "Take no other make," 178; Establishing new trade connections, 180; Dealer cooperation, 182; Substitution, 184

Copy, Getting the Inquiry,
Purpose and scope of, 153; Kinds of inquiries and copy, 153; Why inquiries are solicited, 154; Inducement to respond, 155; Catalog offer, 156; Free Sample offer, 156; Booklets and samples at small cost, 159; Limiting replies, 161; The idly curious, 163; Free booklet offer, 164; Follow-up after the sample, 166; Functions of coupon, 166

Copy, Getting the Order,
Purpose and scope, 137; Typical mail-order copy, 137; Mail-order advertising, 141; Catalog type, 143; Adaptations of the catalog type, 143; Booklets and catalogs, 144; Appeals in mail-order copy, 146; Price appeal in, 146; Style appeal in, 146; Free or trial offer, 148

Copy, Molding Public Opinion,
Purpose and scope, 189; Styles of copy, 189; Repetition of name 191; Repetition of name and picture of product, 192; Setting forth a policy, 193; Cooperation copy, 195; "Creating atmosphere" copy, 196; Educational copy, 198; Political purpose, 198; Legislative purpose, 200; Directing public sentiment, 203; Advertising an industry, 204; Change in the public's attitude, 207

Coupon,
Functions of, 166; Examples of, 168; Use of, 225

Coward Shoe Advertisement, 177
Crane, Dr. Frank, 130
Crane's Linen Lawn Advertisement, 60
"Creating Atmosphere" Copy, 196
Crisco Advertisements, 106, 160

Darts, Use of, in advertising, 33
Dealer Cooperation, 182
Dialog, Use of, 74
"Directing the Reader," Copy.
See Copy, Directing the Reader
Display,
Importance of, 213; Objects of, 232
Disston Tools Advertisement, 297
Drawings and Reproductions, 252
Value of illustrations, 252; Tendencies in advertising art, 253; Styles of art, 253; The line, 253; Stipple, tones and masses, 255; Pen drawings, 255; Wash drawings, 256; Oil paintings, 256; Retouched photographs, 256; Sources of art supply, 258; Kinds of engraving, 258; Wood cuts, 259; Zinc etchings, 260; Half tones, 261; Importance of the screen, 262; Lithography, 264; Hand-made engravings, 264; Ben Day process, 265; Electrotyping, 266; stereotypes and matrices, 266; Mechanical processes, 268

Dummy, The, 249
Duofold Health Underwear Advertisement, 38

Educational Copy, 79, 198
Electrotyping, 266
Emotions,
Appeal to, 109; Reaching, 112
Emphasis, in Advertisements, 71
Securing, 233
Engraving, Kinds of, 258
Kinds of, 258; Wood cuts, 259; Zinc etchings, 260; Half tones, 261; Lithograhy, 263; Hand made, 264; Ben Day process 265; Electrotyping, 266
Exactness, Necessity for 126

Fatima Cigarette Advertisement, 257
Feminine Intuition, in Advertising, 116
Figures of Speech, Use of, 131
Flat-Press Bed, 270
Florence Oil Cook Stove Advertisement, 185
Folders, Booklets and Catalogs,
See Catalogs, Booklets and Folders
"Free Offer," Securing Action Thru, 98

INDEX

Free Sample, 156
  Advantage of, 159; Distributing, 164; Follow-up after, 166
French, George, 282

"Getting the Inquiry" Copy, 153
"Getting the Order" Copy,
  See Copy, Getting the order
Gillette Safety Razor Co. Advertisement, 114
Globe-Wernicke Advertisement, 52
Gold Dust Twins Advertisement, 291

Half Tones, 261
Hanes Knitting Company Advertisement, 36
Harland, John W., 253
Harmony, in Advertisements, 71
Hartman Furniture Co. Advertisement, 143
Hazel-Atlas Glass Co. Advertismeent, 132
Headlines, Value of, 44, 221
Historical Contrast, Use of, 81
Hobby, "Playing Up," in Advertising, 57
Human Appeals, in Advertising,
  See Advertising, Human Appeals in
Hupmobile Advertisement, 212

Idioms, Use of, 129
Illustration, Appropriateness of, 219
Images,
  Connected, stimulate interest, 48; Use of proper images, 54; Images should please, 54
Imagination in Advertising, 51
  Appeal to, 118; Romance of the commonplace, 120
Incident, Use of, 72
Infringements, 316
  Remedy for, 317
Instinct, Appeal to, 115
Insurance, Advertising as, 14
Interest, Gaining The,
  Turning attention into interest, 48; Connected images in, 48; Appeal to the imagination, 51; Use of proper images, 54; Images should please, 54; Appeal to self-interest, 55; Offers to, 55; Hobby in, 57; Interest value of copy, 59; Use of type, 61; Emphasis secured by type, 61; Breaking up the reading mass, 63; Use of subheads, 63; Importance of letter spacing, 65

Jeffrey Single Roll Crusher Advertisement, 157

Keen Kutter Advertisements, 301

Law, and Advertising,
  Restriction of the Federal Government, 304; State regulations, 306; Postal regulations, 307; Municipal regulations, 309; Constitutionality of billboard restrictions, 310; Distribution of circulars and dodgers, 311; Protection of trade-marks, 313; Registration regulations, 315; Infringements, 316; Remedy for infringements, 317; Deceptive Advertising, 318; Personal right of privacy, 319; Property right in advertising, 320
"Limited Time," Securing Action Thru, 96
Lithographic Printing, 272
Locomobile Advertisement, 216
Lowney's Cocoa Advertisement, 116

Maher and Grosh Advertisement, 140
Mail-Order Copy,
  Typical mail-order copy, 137; Advertising, 141; Catalog type, 142; Booklets and catalogs, 144; Appeals in copy, 145; Price appeal in, 146; Style appeal, 146; Free or trial offer in, 148
Mary Garden Perfume Advertisement, 94
McCutcheon, James, Trade-Mark, 294
Mead Cycle Company Advertisement, 139
Mennen's Shaving Cream Advertisement, 162
Minute Gelatin Advertisement, 158
Modern Advertising, 1–12
  See Advertising
"Molding Public Opinion" Copy,
  See Copy, Molding Public Opinion
Monolog, Use of, 73
Moon Motor Car Advertisement, 267
"Mortised Copy," 31
Motion, Use of, in Advertising, 43, Value of, 234
Multicolor Process, 27
Munsey, Frank A., Company, Advertisement, 169

INDEX

National Biscuit Company Trade-Mark, 293
National Dairy Council Advertisement, 208
News Copy, 79
New York Telephone Co. Advertisement, 80
Nouns and Verbs, Use of, 130
Novelty and Uniqueness in Advertising, 44

Offer, Use of, in Advertising, 55
Offset Process, 270
Old Dutch Cleanser Advertisement, 289
Oliver Typewriter Company Advertisement, 97
Optical Center, 232
Owl Cigar Advertisement, 133, 134

Palmolive Soap Advertisement, 173
Pantasote Advertisement, 89
Paramount and Artcraft Pictures Advertisement, 119
Parsons, Frank Alvah, 230
Pears' Soap Advertisement, 254
Pen Drawings, 255
Photogravure, 272
Pierce-Arrow Advertisement, 197
Planning an Advertisement, 16
 Need for, 16; Approaching the plan from a proper angle, 19; Groundwork of plan, 21; Product and, 22; Planning campaign, 26–29
Political Purpose, Use of Advertising for, 198
Position, in advertising, 42
Postal Regulations, on advertising, 307
Premium Bacon Advertisement, 214
Prestige,
 Gaining confidence thru, 86
Printing Art, in Advertising, 270
 Relation to advertising, 270; Standard flat-press bed, 270; Offset process, 270; Multicolor process, 271; Lithographic printing, 272; Photogravure, 272; Copperplate printing, 273; The make-ready, 273; Correcting the proof, 273; Styles of type, 275; Families of, 276; The point system, 277; Type bodies, 278; Practical type arrangement, 279; Estimating space for copy, 280; Figuring stock, 281; Selection of material, 282

Product, The,
 Analysis of, 22; Competitive, 23; Retailers and jobbers and, 24; Trade and, 24
Proofreading, 273
Prophylactic Advertisement, 50
Public, Educating, by advertising, 8, 203

Reader, The,
 Attracting attention of, 30; Mental phenomena of, 30–31; Economizing time of, 125; Directing the reader, 171–188
Reasoning,
 Elements of, 84; Appeal to, 122
Redfern Corsets Advertisement, 179
Repetition, Value of, 191
Reproductions and Drawings,
 See Drawings and Reproductions
Revillon Frères Advertisement, 121
Reznor Gas Heater Advertisement, 117
Rinnell System Advertisement, 77
Royal Baking Powder Advertisement, 107

Sales,
 Increase thru advertising, 16; Department, and advertising, 25
Sears, Roebuck Advertisement, 148
Self-Interest, Appeal to, 55
Senses, Appeal to, 101,
 Touch, 102; Taste, 104; Smell, 105; Sound, 109
Sentences,
 Clear structure of, 68; Length of, 68
Sherbow, Benjamin, 62
Simplicity, in Advertising, 67
Size, of Advertisements,
 See Advertisement, Preparing the,
Slang, Use of, 133
Slogan,
 Use of, 298; Catch word or phrase and, 301
Smell, Appeal to sense of, 105
Sound, Appeal to sense of, 109
Spencer, Herbert, 125
Spies and Lies Advertisement, 203
Stereotyping, 266
Stipple, Tones and masses, Use of, 255
Story, Use of, 76
Subheads, Use of, in advertising, 63
Substitution,
 Use of, 184
Suggestion,
 Securing action thru, 92; Methods

INDEX

of making persons susceptible to, 93; By repetition, 93; Indirect, 93
Systems Bond Advertisement, 64

Taste, Appeal to, 104
Teaser Copy, in advertising, 45
Tecla Pearl Advertisement, 220
Testimonials, Confidence thru, 86
Touch, Appeal to, 102
Trade Connections, establishing new, 180
Trade-Marks,
Origin of, 285; Purpose of, 286; Early restrictions, 286; Creating, 287; Individuality in, 289; Appropriate, 294; Use of, for perishable eatables, 295; Use of, as a reminder, 295; Preventing substitution, 296; Registration of, 298; Slogan and, 298; Catch words and phrases, 301; Tendencies in, 303; Protection of, 313; Registration regulations of, 315
Trade-Marks, Slogans and Catch Phrases, 285–303
Tuxedo Tobacco Advertisement, 110
Type,
Proper use of, 61; Emphasis secured by, 61; Breaking up reading matter, 63; Use of subheads, 63; Importance of letter spacing, 65; Construction and diction, 65; Display, 235; Body, 236; Borders and rules, 237; White space, 237; Styles of, 275; Families of, 276; Point system, 277; Bodies of, 278; Practical arrangement of, 279; Estimating space for copy, 280; Figuring stock, 281

Typewriter Emporium Advertisement, 150

Union Pacific Salt Lake Route Advertisement, 58

Vul-Cot Advertisement, 90

War, and Advertising, 4
Warner-Lenz Advertisement, 39
"Wear-Ever" Aluminum Advertisement, 183
Weed Chains Advertisement, 95
Western Electric Advertisement, 34
Western Union Telegraph Company Advertisement, 113
Whitman's Sampler Advertisement, 40
Woodbury's Soap Advertisement, 100
Wood Cuts, 259
Word Atmosphere, 136
Word Values, in Advertising,
Words are tools of advertising, 124; Economizing the reader's time, 125; Clearness, 126; Exactness, 126; Emotional and intellectual, 128; Short words, 128; Long words, 129; Idioms, 129; Nouns and verbs, 130; Adjectives, 131; Figures of speech, 131, Colloquialisms, 132; Slang, 133; Word atmosphere or setting, 133

Yale Lock Trade-Mark, 290
Youngstown Sheet and Tube Co. Advertisement, 201

Zinc Etchings, 260